The Couple and Fami
Framework

Couples and families worldwide have a constant electronic connection to others, a fact that is influencing the concerns and issues they bring to therapy. The authors of this resource help mental health practitioners to better deal with concerns such as online infidelity, online dating, Internet addictions, cyberbullying, and many more by introducing the **Couple and Family Technology (CFT) framework**, a multitheoretical approach that doesn't require clinicians to change their preferred clinical approaches.

The CFT framework acknowledges the ways in which couples navigate their relationships with technology and a partner simultaneously, and it attends to, and in some cases incorporates, the role of technology in therapeutic ways. Included in the authors' discussion of how different technologies affect relationships is

- a survey of what individuals' motivations of usage are;
- an examination of the specific issues that emerge in treatment;
- a study of the risks particularly relevant to intimate relationships;
- an introduction of the first-ever technology-based genogram.

They also examine technological usage across different developmental points in a couple's life span, with attention given throughout to people from various cultural backgrounds. Along with the CFT framework, the authors also introduce a new discipline of family research: Couple and Family Technology. This discipline integrates three broad perspectives in family science and helps therapists maintain a systemic focus in assessing and treating couples where issues of the Internet and new media are problematic. Online resources can be accessed by purchasers of the book and include videos, additional case studies, a glossary, and forms.

Katherine M. Hertlein, PhD, is an associate professor and program director of the Marriage and Family Therapy program at the University of Nevada, Las Vegas.

Markie L. C. Blumer, PhD, is an assistant professor and the Delta Kappa (International Marriage and Family Therapy Honor Society) Zeta chapter faculty advisor in the Marriage and Family Therapy program at the University of Nevada, Las Vegas.

The Couple and Family Technology Framework

Intimate Relationships in a Digital Age

Katherine M. Hertlein and
Markie L. C. Blumer

NEW YORK AND LONDON

Please visit the eResources site at www.routledgementalhealth.com/9780415641548

First published 2014
by Routledge
711 Third Avenue, New York, NY 10017

Simultaneously published in the UK
by Routledge
27 Church Road, Hove, East Sussex BN3 2FA

Routledge is an imprint of the Taylor & Francis Group, an informa business

Library of Congress Cataloging in Publication Data

Hertlein, Katherine M.
The couple and family technology framework: intimate relationships in a digital age / authored by Katherine M. Hertlein & Markie L. C. Blumer. — 1 Edition.
pages cm
Includes bibliographical references and index.
1. Couples therapy. 2. Couples—Psychology. 3. Marital psychotherapy. I. Blumer, Markie L. C. II. Title.
RC488.5.H478 2013
616.89'1562—dc23
2013001411

ISBN: 978-0-415-64153-1 (hbk)
ISBN: 978-0-415-64154-8 (pbk)
ISBN: 978-0-203-08181-5 (ebk)

Typeset in Sabon
by Apex CoVantage, LLC

Printed and bound in the United States of America
by Edwards Brothers, Inc.

To my son Adam Joseph—you are my inspiration

—Katherine M. Hertlein

To all my relations, now and forever, I love and thank you

—Markie L. C. Blumer

Contents

About the Authors

Katherine M. Hertlein, PhD, is an associate professor and program director of the Marriage and Family Therapy program at the University of Nevada, Las Vegas. She received her master's degree in marriage and family therapy from Purdue University Calumet and her doctorate in human development, with a specialization in marriage and family therapy, from Virginia Tech. Across her academic career, she has published more than 40 articles, 5 books, and more than 25 book chapters. She has coedited a book on interventions in couples treatment, on interventions for clients with health concerns, and on infidelity treatment. She also serves on the editorial boards of several journals, including *Contemporary Family Therapy, Journal of Couple and Relationship Therapy,* and *Journal of Communication Technology and Human Behavior.* Recently, Dr. Hertlein published *Systemic Sex Therapy* and *A Clinician's Guide to Systemic Sex Therapy.* These two books are used in over 20 couple and family therapy training programs around the United States. In 2009, *Systemic Sex Therapy* was nominated for a Professional Health Book Award through the Society for Sex Therapy and Research (SSTAR). Dr. Hertlein has also produced the first multitheoretical model detailing the role of technology in couple and family life. She presents nationally and internationally on sex, technology, and couples. Dr. Hertlein has won numerous awards for her teaching and research. She is featured weekly as a guest on "Davenport After Dark," a radio program broadcast out of Dublin, Ireland, and currently maintains a private practice in Las Vegas.

Markie Louise Christianson (L. C.) Blumer, PhD, is an assistant professor and the Delta Kappa (International Marriage and Family Therapy Honor Society) Zeta chapter faculty advisor in the Marriage and Family Therapy program at the University of Nevada, Las Vegas. She received her master's in education from Northern Arizona University, a master of arts in marriage and family therapy with emphasis in sex therapy from the University of Louisiana at Monroe, and her doctorate in human development and family studies, with a specialization in marriage and family therapy, at Iowa State University. She has published more than

25 articles and 5 book chapters and has presented 75 times at various local, regional, national, and international conferences. She also serves on the editorial boards of *Journal of Feminist Family Therapy: An International Forum* and *Journal of Couple and Relationship Therapy*. Across her academic career, Dr. Blumer has won numerous awards for her teaching and research. Most recently, she was a corecipient of a 2012 National Council on Family Relations (NCFR) Education and Enrichment Section Outstanding Paper Award for her coauthored work "Are We Queer Yet? Training Away the Anti-gay." She was also the lead recipient of a 2011 NCFR Family Therapy Section Best Research Paper Award for her first-authored work "Reflections on Becoming Feminist Therapists: A Model of Intergenerational Feminist Mentoring."

Preface

Purpose of the Book

The field of Couple and Family Technology (CFT), as identified by Katherine M. Hertlein, encompasses both family and couple relationships in a broad sense. The primary purpose of this book is to focus on two specific aspects of CFT. First, we articulate the ways in which couples navigate their relationships with technology and their relationships with a partner simultaneously. This includes a discussion of the motivations of usage of specific technologies and social media, an exploration of specific issues that emerge in these treatments, and a presentation of particular risks relevant to intimate relationships. Second, we present a treatment approach informed by CFT that attends to and, in some cases, incorporates the role of technology in therapeutic ways. This is accomplished through discussion of technological usage across different developmental points in a couple's life span, with attention given throughout to people from various cultural backgrounds, and via a discussion of the CFT framework.

A portion of this book is also devoted to the application of the CFT framework. Because it is multitheoretical, the introduction of the CFT framework does not imply that clinicians need to change their preferred clinical approaches; instead, it serves as an invitation to find ways to incorporate such a framework into current practice. We believe this is a more inclusive approach to working with couples and families, particularly around technology-related issues. Clinicians will find information that will help them address the following kinds of common concerns:

- Internet or online infidelity
- online pornography–related issues
- online dating
- Internet-related dissolutions
- everyday usage of technology and new media
- online video gaming
- cybersex
- Internet addictions

- cyberbullying
- cyberstalking
- electronic intimate partner violence.

Put simply, our book is about the way that different technologies affect relationships in different ways and the way that relationships affect the use of different technologies. It presents the state of the interdisciplinary research and scholarly thoughts on how new media is integrated into couples' lives and introduces a new discipline of family research called Couple and Family Technology. It also walks readers though how to apply the CFT framework to couples in treatment and assists readers in recognizing risks and concerns related to technology and new media.

It is important to note that this book, while it contains some information regarding online dating, dating in and of itself is not the focus. In part, this is because there are a number of high-quality texts already on the market with this dedicated focus. There are actually quite a few books with a focus on online dating. Diane M. Berry's *Romancing the Web: A Therapist's Guide to the Finer Points of Online Dating* focuses on online dating with the primary reading audience being clinicians, and Tamsen Butler's *Meeting Your Match Online: The Complete Guide to Internet Dating and Dating Services—Including True Life Date Stories* focuses on individuals seeking partners online. In Regina Lynn's *The Sexual Revolution 2.0: Getting Connected, Upgrading Your Sex Life, and Finding True Love—or at Least a Dinner Date—in the Internet Age*, sex and technology are the focus. Instead of focusing on more of the how-to of online dating, this book attends to how couples communicate with one another, including their initiations, but within the context of technology and new media.

As younger-age cohorts' involvement with technology has certainly received more media attention over the years, the primary goals of such texts is to assist parents in protecting their children and teaching them to interact with new media responsibly, such as Larry Rosen does in *Me, MySpace, and I: Parenting the Net Generation* and Candice Kelsey does in *Generation MySpace: Helping Your Teen Survive Online Adolescence*. Another related book, *Life and Death on the Internet: How to Protect Your Family on the World Wide Web*, edited by Keith Schroeder and Julie Ledger, attends to some of the more serious online threats toward children and toward families in general. Our text is different in that we discuss the topics related to parents and children within the context of couple development.

This book is also not focused on Internet or online infidelity or on cyberaddictions, although both are given some attention to varying degrees. Several recent books have been released that focus on Internet addictions, such as Kimberly Young and Cristiano Nabuco de Abreu's edited volume *Internet Addiction: A Handbook and Guide to Evaluation and Treatment*, whose primary audience is clinicians. Two other popular texts include one focused on online gaming–related addiction, *Cyber Junkie: Escape the Gaming and Internet Trap*, by Kevin Roberts, and *Infidelity and the Internet: Virtual Relationships and Real Betrayal*, by Marlene Maheu and Rona Subotnik. We instead focus on how to understand these issues through the lens of the field of CFT.

Outline of Chapters

The first few chapters of the book provide general information with regard to technology and practices. In Chapter 1, "Couple and Family Technology: The Emergence of a New Discipline," we review the presence technology and new media have in our lives. In so doing, we provide a context for understanding the experiences of couples in today's society with regard to technology and new media. In Chapter 2, "The Basics of Online Coupling," we provide information about the characteristics of online communication as compared to face-to-face communication. We also review personality characteristics and motivations of those engaging in electronically based communication as well as different types of online relationships. The next chapter, titled "Issues E-merging in Couple Life," highlights the key issues related to technology that may emerge in couple and family treatment, namely, online infidelity, sex addiction, and online video gaming. We also address some of the larger areas that may be secondary issues related to these specific issues in new media, such as accountability, shared time and interests, gender and power, and suspicion and jealousy.

Following chapters, more specifically, focus on describing the CFT framework. Chapter 4, "The Couple and Family Technology Framework," outlines the main components of the framework and how they reciprocally influence one another. A case example is provided as a way to assist the reader in applying the framework. The next chapter, "Ecological Influences on the Couple System," provides a detailed description of the manner in which each of the qualities germane to the Internet affects a couple's satisfaction, structure, and processes. This discussion leads into Chapter 6, "The Interactional Nature of Structure and Function." The purpose of this chapter is to review how the structure of relationships as well as technology affect relational functioning. This chapter is followed by Chapter 7, "Assessment in the CFT Framework." This chapter provides a summary of popular assessments used to evaluate and/or diagnose Internet-related problems. It also presents the first-ever technology-based genogram as developed by Markie L. C. Blumer, complete with a supplemental series of questions contained within the appendices. "Treatment of Internet-Based Problems Through the CFT Framework" (Chapter 8) outlines ways in which the CFT framework can be used as a guide to treating problems in couples related to technology, with specific attention to the ecological elements, structure, and process.

The final set of chapters attend to the broader context in which couples are embedded. Chapter 9, "Electronically-Mediated Communication Across a Couple's Developmental Lifespan," focuses on how couples and technology evolve together over the life span. Some of these specific areas include couple initiation facilitated by electronic means, the use of technology in a couple's life as they raise children, and discussion of relationship termination in a digital age. In addition, technology usage in relationships does not come without risk. Therefore, we devote Chapter 10 to exploring the impact of cyberbullying, cyberstalking, and technology-facilitated violence in couple relationships. We close with Chapter 11, which focuses on the state of the field of CFT now and in the future, with implications for research, training, and practice.

Key Terms

Throughout the course of this text, we will be using the terms *technology* and *new media*. For our purposes, *technology* is defined as the application of innovations specifically within the fields of communication and electronics. *New media* is a term encompassing a broad range of technologies that enable electronic communication. These include objects such as smartphones and tablets, websites such as Facebook and other social networking sites, and forms of art and entertainment such as video games and electronic art.

Literature in the fields of information systems as well as the social sciences use the acronym CMC to stand for "computer-mediated communication." While this originated at a time when cellular technologies were not advanced enough to communicate via text or similar messaging, it is clear people are using the Internet to communicate on more mechanisms than a computer. In the field of CFT, we introduce the term *electronic-based communications* (EBC) to refer to the wide variety of communications that occur as web-based (including text messaging), in addition to the types of communication facilitated by personal computers.

A Note on Timeliness

We also acknowledge that this book, as timely as it may be to the field at its publication, may contain statistics and figures regarding computer usage that will be quickly outdated. Therefore, we want to assert that while the statistics may be flexible, the concepts related to the CFT framework and information about family and couple dynamics affected by technology will remain quite stable. We provide examples describing how common experiences (e.g., online dating, online endings, cyberthreats and risks, cybersex, Internet infidelity, parental concerns related to technology) operate in couple relationships in the context of technology. Also explored in this book are the unique challenges that technology introduces into couple's lives as well as strategies for managing such issues. Our book is primarily aimed at assisting mental health care professionals working with couples, though we believe people interested in enhancing their relationships in an ever-growing digital age will find benefit in its pages.

We sincerely hope that clinicians, academics, and students alike will find this book descriptive enough to be useful but flexible enough to be adapted to various couple types and, eventually, to families. As technology and new media continue to evolve, we anticipate and embrace further exchanges of ideas about this book and these topics for years to come.

Katherine M. Hertlein
Markie L. C. Blumer

Acknowledgments

No book is written without the invaluable assistance, support, and feedback of many, many others. Likewise, this book would not be complete without the dedication of many hardworking and intelligent people. We would like to start by thanking one of our amazing mentors, Gerald R. Weeks. Dr. Weeks was instrumental in advising how to package these ideas and provided encouragement toward the development of the framework. He also was the first to suggest that we had enough information for a text and was pivotal in shaping this book and our careers. We thank him for his mentorship, advice, insight, and friendship.

Our gratitude and thanks also go to Ms. Anna Moore and Ms. Marta Moldvai at Routledge. This book would have remained just an idea had it not been for Anna's invitation and work with us on the outline and proposal. Furthermore, Marta has been wonderful in providing feedback, structure, and ideas regarding the manuscript, and we would not have as high a quality of project without her involvement, her encouragement, and her excitement about this topic. We are thankful to all at Routledge who worked on this book to make our vision become a reality.

We also could not have done it without the research support of our graduate students at the Marriage and Family Therapy (MFT) program at the University of Nevada, Las Vegas (UNLV). These students worked tirelessly on reference checks, editing, designing genograms, and developing the assessment tools. These students include Katrina Ancheta, Mackenzie Clark, Joe Dentice, Kathy Disney-Fairchild, Jennalyn Eigner, Amna Haider, Alicia Hite, Quintin Hunt, Clai Joiner-Ransom, Tamara Marsar, Lauren McCoy, Christine Morehead, Matt Nelson, Caitlin Olsen, Gianna Russo-Mitma, Sarah Schonian, Sarah Steelman, Michael Thomas, Nicole Thomte, Sam Tielemans, Linda Tran Walker, and Tod Young. Appreciation is also extended to a few UNLV students outside of the MFT program, specifically, Jamie Bichelman, for his assistance with the literature review, and Nikolos Hulet, for his feedback regarding helpful resources around adoption. We also would like to thank Ashley M. Barrera for her contributions to the risk resource list as well as her contributions to the reference page.

More acknowledgments go to my (K. H.) husband, Eric, who, after 15 years, seems to know when to tell me to set something aside for a night and rest, but also knows when I need to work and has assisted me in making one last push to get the book done through carving out time to do so. I appreciate his enduring support for my passion and my work. Also, his occupation as a senior software developer has added much to the project, and I will forever be grateful for his insight and feedback on the material. I would also like to thank my clients for their honesty and their appreciation of our work together. I am humbled to think that I may have been of some assistance on their journey with technology and one another. I would like to extend a thank-you to my coauthor, Markie, for her attention to the greater context in which couples are embedded. For the many things you taught me that I was not aware I needed to learn, I will be forever thankful.

And finally, to my immediate and extended family: every one of you has demonstrated nothing but support and love toward my career, and I appreciate that you listened to me talk about this book for the better part of a year intently and with interest. To my mom—thank you for reading everything I've ever written and listening to every radio show and interview I have done. I so much appreciate it. To my dad—I'm sorry there aren't any pictures. Maybe you could draw some in the margins or wait for the movie. Thank you for all of the intellectual exchanges, for use of your computer, for letting me follow you to the library, and for the support of my work. To all my sisters—I remember our first bit of technology, the Atari game console and a Prodigy computer! I'll take on any one of you in a game of Kaboom! or Circus Atari anytime. To my sister Denise—I am grateful for the way you help me open my eyes in helpful and adaptive ways through presenting different, broader, and more useful perspectives, both about work and life. I am also hoping some of your intelligence, wit, and humor has rubbed off on me. To my sister Anne—you inspire me more than you can even know with your ability to take on the hardest of challenges with ease. To my sister Lynn—I appreciate your giving me a dose of perspective and showing me there is more to the world than work. And, of course, to my dear son Adam: I hope you know how many lessons are in this book for you—both for your future relationships but also to see you can do anything you want if you set your mind to it. I hope you learn from my example to be strong, driven, and compassionate to others. This book contains just over 96,000 words, and they are nowhere near enough to tell you how much you mean to me, how grateful I am to be a part of your life, and the amount of love I feel for you.

I (M.L.C.B.) want to thank my coauthor and best colleague friend Kat for the invitation to work on this exciting and innovative project. I want to thank my colleague Jacqueline M. Cravens for her assistance in developing a few of the clinical examples. I also want to thank my family and friends for their continual encouragement throughout the writing of this manuscript (and my academic career). On more than one occasion, I felt exhausted, and it was in these moments that the support from each of you made it possible for me to continue. Specifically, I want to express my appreciation for my brother Brennan D. Christianson, for his impeccable use of the English language, including his excellence in writing, which, over the years, served to better my literary competency. I also want to thank my brother for helping me to better understand the role of technology in the context of family relationships, as many an hour was spent in our youth and young adult lives engaging in (and sometimes fighting over) technology-related activities together. What I wouldn't give for another game of Super Contra bro. or a text message from you reading, "Do you like dogs?" My sincere love and appreciation go to my partner, Timothy Michael Christianson Blumer, for his love and support from the start of this project to its end. Your actions, thoughts, words, and expressed emotions have all been ones aimed at improving our life together, and I want you to know you are appreciated, loved, and, most importantly, heard. Finally, I thank my son Leif Brenmark Christianson Blumer for the joy that he brings to life, including his abundant curiosity with all things technology related. Sonshine, when I see technology through your eyes, I see the magic that it truly is and the ways in which it can be used for good.

1 Couple and Family Technology
The Emergence of a New Discipline

When I took office, only high energy physicists had ever heard of what is called the Worldwide Web. . . . Now even my cat has its own page.
—*Bill Clinton*

The Prevalence of Technology in Daily Life

A short time ago, I (K.H.) was having dinner at a local restaurant with a colleague. As we sat and talked, I could not help but notice a couple sitting together at a table just behind my companion. They appeared very much in love: They spent some time holding hands, facing each other, gazing in each other's eyes, and smiling at one another a good proportion of the time. Then, as the dinner continued, I noticed the emergence of their mobile phones. At first, the involvement of the phones seemed rather innocuous: one person brought out a phone to show his partner something, and the phone was quickly put away. As I continued to observe them, new media made an increasing presence in the date. After taking photos of the meal and making it most of the way through dinner, one of the phones made another appearance at the dinner table. One partner offered the phone to the other to view something on the screen. This continued for several minutes. By the end of the meal, their phones had made another appearance, but in a different way. The couple stopped talking to one another; one partner was sitting at the table, and the other was positioned with her body away from the table and, consequently, her partner. Each had a cell phone in hand, and they were seemingly not engaged with one another. They both appeared to be scrolling through options and reading things on their independent screens. This continued for several minutes, and they appeared so disconnected to me that I wondered if I had missed an argument and they were no longer speaking. After the check was paid, however, they put away their phones, smiled at one another, and left the restaurant quietly, hand in hand.

As interesting as this couple's behavior was to me, my observations about couples and technology at this one restaurant are not unique. Airports, universities, grocery stores, and even driving down the street provide us with ample opportunities to observe the extent to which new media and technology are integrated into our personal lives. Whether we are eating, socializing, or working, couples and families worldwide have a constant electronic connection to others and often exercise that connection in a variety of contexts, even on a dinner date.

The ways in which technology and new media have become a fabric of our everyday lives in general are undeniable when the numbers tell the story. The world population is increasing dramatically. Of the nearly 7 billion people in the world, just over 2 billion people are online (Internet World Stats, 2011), a 484% increase over the last decade. In North America, an estimated 78% of the 3 million citizens (approximately 245 million) are regular users of the Internet, making up only 13% of the Internet users worldwide. North America also boasts a higher percentage of penetration than any other region in the world. Some countries, such as China, have a fewer proportion of their population using the Internet (36%), however, this is a percentage that actually represents a higher number of actual users at 485 million. The majority of Internet users actually (44%) reside in Asia, followed by Europe (22.7%), North America (13%), Latin America/Caribbean (10.3%), Africa (5.7%), the Middle East (3.3%), and Oceania/Australia (1%) (Internet World Stats, 2011).

The predominant presence of technology is also apparent in the development of a new lexicon integrated into contemporary society. Terms such as *www, http, LOL, blog*, and *webcast* have become woven into our vernacular. In late 2011, the Global Language Monitor reported that *Web 2.0* was officially accepted as the 1 millionth English word, following the addition of *sexting, noob, cloud computing,* and *defriend.* Furthermore, a number of in-print and online dictionaries have emerged to assist with translating words related to technology and social media. Webopedia,[1] for example, is a website dedicated to defining terms for the business professional who has to interact with computers regularly. Some functions of this site include a term of the day, a search engine for particular terms, a quick reference page, and a blog. In fact, the benefit of online dictionaries over in-print versions may be that the online versions can more readily keep up with the new terms in an ever-changing field, with the English language creating one new word every 98 minutes (Global Language Monitor, 2011).

Advances in information communication that have also contributed to language are conceptualized as a new form of literacy (Leu, Kinzer, Coiro, & Cammack, 2005). Imagine a situation in which, for example, you travel to a different country and are not familiar with the language: While you may be able to get around, it will take you more time, and it is likely you will miss out on some important resources that could guide you along the way. Literacy with regard to the growing digital world is similar. The less literate one is in the world, the more time it will take one to navigate through that world efficiently. This literacy is generally classified as two different types: electronic literacy (i.e., knowledge about how to access resources and participate in online activities) and technological/computer literacy (i.e., knowledge about how to navigate an actual computer and other new hardware; Cohen & Cowan, 2007; Topping, 1997). This development is important when one considers that its adoption is a critical mechanism to acquiring knowledge and using resources (Leu et al., 2005): The less literate one is, the more challenging it will be to acquire new skills and move about in the digital world efficiently. In short, the emergence of technology and new media has shaped our communications with one another on multiple levels.

A Technological Revolution

Hoffman, Novak, and Venkatesh (2004) wrote that

> we seem to be in the midst of an Internet Revolution and entering an era of enhanced digital connectivity. The pace of social change resulting from the diffusion of this technology, both in the United States and globally is by many accounts dramatic. In less than ten years, the Internet has become indispensable to many people in their daily lives. (p. 2)

Technology is clearly a phenomenon that is well integrated into society and whose impact on society has previously been characterized as revolutionary (Hughes & Hans, 2001).

A communications revolution, as described by Robert G. Albion, focuses on the extent to which a society can grow through changes in communication technologies. Part of this claim dealt with the assumption that the growth of America was going to be largely dependent on the communication technology and the infrastructure to support it (Behringer, 2006), thus underscoring a communications revolution. Albion (as cited in Behringer, 2006) argued,

> The change in communications has knit the world closer together. It has widened the horizons of every community, partly through the rapid dissemination of news and partly through the breaking down of provincialism with new facilities for travel. It has been of vital importance in opening up the wilderness and in linking together the far flung possessions of the world empires. (p. 335)

This quote could also be applied 80 years later to describe the profound impact technology has on daily life. Advances in cellular technology, accessibility and affordability of Internet services, and the ability to reach out to international venues have mimicked the general increases and changes outlined by earlier communication revolutions.

Like the Industrial Revolution, the technological revolution is characterized by specific and obvious changes that occurred within daily and family life. One change was the development of new ways to accomplish tasks and receive information more quickly (Appleby, 2010; Bargh & McKenna, 2004). For example, researching and gathering information on particular topics is accomplished now primarily from the comfort of one's own home rather than by physically commuting to a local library. Writing letters or placing phone calls to communicate with one another can be accomplished with a quick e-mail or text message rather than requiring the time investment of a phone call or a letter sent through the U.S. Postal Service. We can also receive information merely by entering search words or checking electronic mailboxes more quickly than we can by waiting to connect with someone in person.

The Industrial Revolution and technological revolution also found ways to transmit messages to loved ones at a significantly reduced cost and more quickly. One of the key factors by which Albion characterized the communication revolution was the speed with which information was received (Behringer, 2006). While Albion was referring to changes in the U.S. Postal Service in the late 1700s, in today's society, information is transmitted nearly instantly. E-mail, instant messaging programs, and communication through social networking sites can be accomplished at a monthly cost with an Internet service provider. Communication can be accomplished through shared sites and lists, such as calendars, shopping lists, and other applications that allow information to be shared with a certain group of people. Messages can also be transmitted through video channels in a way that was not experienced previously for little to no cost. Prior to the development of free video conferencing, the ability to see friends and family who lived distantly from each other was only accomplished through expensive programs or through making travel arrangements. In today's world, however, the ability to see loved ones through web and video camera services is now open to people from a wide variety of financial and social backgrounds.

Both revolutions have also had some effect on family structure and process. After the Industrial Revolution, family structures changed from predominately extended families to a nuclear version of the family (Bengston, 2001). The technological revolution, however, has reintroduced the value of extended families into daily life with the ease and accessibility of maintaining communication over broad geographical distances (Bacigalupe & Lambe, 2011). Process changes occurred in both revolutions in that there was a period of difficulty differentiating between work and family time (Kennedy, Smith, Wells, & Wellman, 2008; Rapoport & Rapoport, 1965). In the Industrial Revolution, the primary time for work was during the week, and weekends began to move toward family time. In the technological revolution, this concept is known as negative work spillover (Chelsey, 2005) or a crossing of the work–family boundary. The specific intrusion of technology and employment responsibilities into one's personal life (for example, moving from a clear 40-hour Monday through Friday work week to responding and working at various times throughout the entire week) has been termed *technoinvasion*, which subsequently increases anxiety and decreases productivity (Tu, Wang, & Shu, 2005). Specifically, the more pressure one feels with regard to technology at work, the more likely one will be to experience interference at home and experience work–family conflict (Harris, Marett, & Harris, 2011).

There is, however, one key difference between the revolutions: The Industrial Revolution was highly visible, whereas the technological revolution seems to be somewhat insidious. In the Industrial Revolution, obvious changes to society included the development of larger and taller buildings, the presence of women in the workforce, and the development of new machines. The actual physical landscape changed rapidly and in very obvious ways. The technological revolution, is less conspicuous. The outside landscape has not changed as much as the landscape within the home. Activities have shifted from taking place outside of the home to inside the home with monitors, screens, and keyboards. Our lives and jobs may require the same skill set to accomplish, but the ways in which we accomplish them have drastically changed.

The Rise of the Machines

Computers and the Internet

A proportion of the impact of the Internet in our lives has in part to do with the integration of the personal computer into our lives. The projected 170 million personal computers to be purchased in 2010 was only half of the actual total purchased—an estimated 340 to 350 million worldwide (Thompson, 2011). Approximately 58% of married couples with children live in households with two or more computers. The U.S. Census reported that nearly 70% of the population surveyed had computers with Internet access at home in 2009, compared to 18% in 1997.[2] In fact, in my own home (K.H.), at one time, we had more computers than we had living beings—four computers (three of them laptops) for two adults and a sleepy cat. The age of personal computing has unapologetically moved in and had, at least in my household, its very own room.

Yet the use and experiencing of technology and the Internet is not evenly distributed around the world. There are several reasons for these apparent barriers. For instance, Shetzer and Warshauer (2000) estimated that 85% of the language stored online is in English, which means that those more comfortable with this language may be better able to access the Internet. In addition, there are likely economic barriers. For instance, 70% of people who use the Internet live in wealthier and industrialized countries, whereas only 24% of those living in poorer, developing nations are using such technologies (Goldberg, 2012). Technology use in the United States tends to be quite high, with 88% of adults having a cell phone, 57% a laptop, 19% an e-book reader, and 19% a tablet computer (Zickuhr & Smith, 2012). In addition, technological ownership in the United States is generally correlated with younger adulthood (18–29 years), higher education, and greater amounts of household income (Zickuhr & Smith, 2012). Internet use in the United States does vary slightly by ethnic background. White American use is slightly higher at 78%, followed by Latino/a American use at 75%, and then African American use at a rate of 68% (Smith, Rainie, & Zickuhr, 2011). It is important to note that there are adults in the United States who do not use the Internet: about 1 in 5 (Zickuhr & Smith, 2012). Part of the reason for non-Internet usage may be related to living with a disability. After controlling for demographic variables related to age, level of education, and income, researchers found that 54% of adults living with a disability use the Internet, as compared with 81% of adults without a disability who use the Internet. In roughly 2% of these cases, American adults are experiencing disabilities that make it virtually impossible to utilize the Internet at all (Zickuhr & Smith, 2012).

There also seem to be some differences with regard to computer use and gender. A study using a sample of college students in Germany found that, while female students spend approximately the same amount of time on the computer as their male counterparts when it comes to classroom activities, men are the predominant users of the computer for personal activities. Male students "play more online games . . . shop more often . . . share more files . . . do more Internet research . . . and read the daily news on the net more often [than women]" (Imhof, Vollmeyer, & Beierlein, 2007, p. 2380). This difference is also reflected in the amount of time spent on personal activities while computing—6 hours for women and 8 hours for men. Conversely, the gap in age and gender with regard to computer use in the workplace seems to be closing, except in cases where one is anxious about one's computer abilities (Knight & Pearson, 2005).

Adoption of computers and Internet services is also driven to some degree by the socioeconomic nature of technological adoption. As mentioned earlier, some of the studies describing the participants indicated that there were specific groups that had access to and benefited from advances in technology and new media, namely, those with college degrees and who may be of a higher economic status. The U.S. Bureau of the Census reported that of the 68.7% of households reporting access to the Internet, 69% of those households of people aged 25 or older reported they held either a bachelor's or associate's degree, as compared to 24% whose highest degree was a high school diploma (U.S. Census Bureau, 2009).

In a study conducted to understand the integration of technology into the educational system in Brunei (a sovereign state located on the north side of the island of Borneo, in Southeast Asia), 100% of the respondents indicated that they had at least one computer in their home, with 75% of these indicating they had a computer with a high-speed connection (Ganzske & Hamidon, 2006). A similar investigation conducted in the United States regarding parents' perceptions of Internet use in their children's educational lives revealed that 98% of those parents had home computers. In this case, however, the authors acknowledged, "This finding was not surprising given that the parents in the study resided in middle to upper socioeconomic neighborhoods, with most having attended college and earning substantial, annual incomes" (Ortiz, Green, & Lim, 2009, p. 209). Some of these differences might also be based on language and ethnicity of the user, most notably, those who speak English have the highest rates of Internet usage. Whites and Asian Americans also use the Internet more than other ethnic groups.

Cellular Phones

Homes are not the only place into which computers have moved. In the case of cell phones and mobile technology, computers have nearly become an extension of our physical beings. According to a 2012 report released by the United Nations Telecom Agency there are now approximately 6 billion cell phone or smartphone subscriptions worldwide, which averages out to about one in three in the population having this kind of technology. The development and integration of smartphones in our lives is commonplace and has profound implications for personal relationships. Just over 80% of American adults have a cell phone (Smith, 2011) and 95% of people in Korea own a cell phone (Kim, Kim, & Kim, 2011). Kids are also getting into the action, with more than half owning a personal cell phone in both the United States and Japan (Ito, Okabe, & Matsuda, 2005; Kennedy et al., 2008). The number of homes without a landline phone and sole reliance for telephone services on one or more cell phones is estimated at 25% (Blumberg & Luke, 2009). With the prevalence of smartphones comes a certain degree of acceptance around cell phone ownership. In many cases, people prefer mobile communication as the method by which they connect with their friends and acquaintances (Hampton, Sessions, Her, & Rainie, 2009). In many ways, it is expected that people be able to be contacted at any time of day because of the assumption of pervasive cell phone ownership. In addition, the majority of adults (53%) report that they would prefer someone contact them via voice call rather than via texting, with 31% of this later group reporting that they would prefer texting to voice calls, and the remaining 14% reporting that their preferred contact method is dependent upon the situation (Smith, 2011). Young adults (ages 18–24) have higher than average levels of smartphone ownership at 95%, regardless of income or education levels (Zickuhr & Smith, 2012). Adults in this age range also text more than those in any other age category, with 97% texting daily.

The average number of daily texts in this age group is 109.5, versus 87.7 for those in the age range of 18–29 years (Smith, 2011). Rates, amounts, and frequency of texting decreases with age (Smith, 2011). In addition, non-White individuals, particularly those identifying as African American, text more often than White Americans, and those with relatively lower levels of education and income tend to text more often than those with higher levels (Smith, 2011).

Mobile phones are also used most frequently in the home. When looking at mobile phone usage over the course of an entire week, approximately 50% of the minutes used are used at home. When evaluating the context of when cell phone minutes are used in an hourly basis throughout the day, however, close to 80% of the minutes in a given hour are associated with home usage (Verkasalo, 2009), with the exception of hours 9 through 14 in the day, where usage of the mobile phone in the home drops to no more than 20%.

There is a wide variety of reasons for the usage of cell phones. Cell phones are commonly used for sending text messages and using other forms of instant messaging, checking e-mail, and searching the web for news items and updates, checking weather, and using mapping functions (Barkhuus & Polichar, 2011; M. Metrics, as cited by Rice & Katz, 2008). Close to 30% of the total time spent using a smartphone is dedicated to text messaging (Verkasalo, 2009). According to a recent survey the United States, at least half of the respondents who had a cell phone noted that they employ it to retrieve information immediately. Just over one-quarter of Americans indicated experiencing at least one time where they needed information and were not able to access it in the moment, creating an uncomfortable circumstance. Other uses of the texting function of smartphones to keep partners or spouses apprised of a daily schedule, to send reminders to people, to have gain access to others who would otherwise not be sitting in front of a computer, and "convenience, pragmatics, and urgency" (Barkhuus & Polichar, 2011, p. 632). In cases where parents need to contact children immediately, they "are best appreciated in the relations between parent and child" (Rizzo, 2008, p. 141). Having a cell phone prevents "unwanted personal interactions" as well as a mechanism through which to stave off boredom (Smith, 2011, p. 2). Many applications on cell phones are also designed for participation in portable entertainment, either playing games with others or independently (Rice & Katz, 2008). In fact, 55% of people who identify as gamers indicated they play games on their phone (Entertainment Software Association [ESA], 2011).

Just as there are particular patterns regarding computer usage among different demographic groups, there are also some demographic differences in cell phone adoption (Rice & Katz, 2008). Those who are more quickly adopting sell phone services are African Americans and those of Hispanic/Latino(a) background. Still, those from low income background and senior citizens are the groups slower to adopt such technologies.

The Rise of the Applications

Online Video Games

Not limited to the phone, participation in online and video-based gaming has increased most notably over the last few years (Anderson, 2007; ESA, 2011). The introduction of electronic video games entering the household has increased dramatically since its introduction in the late 1950s. As gaming systems became more sophisticated, the gaming environment has moved from the living room to the office and laptops. The introduction of massively multiplayer online games into home life can be traced back to 1979, but really gained its footing in 1997 when a company released an online game for home computers ("History of Video Games," as cited in Freddolino & Blaschke, 2008). According to Freddolino and Blaschke (2008): "In less than 40 years, online gaming has evolved from a two-person game played on one university campus to millions of people interacting in three-dimensional virtual worlds, becoming a significant part of future socialization, business, and education for millions of people" (p. 426). Estimates by Screendigest.com (as cited in Zhong, 2011) found that in 2008, the market for massively multiplayer online role-playing games (MMOPRGs) grew 22% in that year alone. While MMORPGs have had a pronounced impact on the North American market, there is also a significant impact in international markets. "According to China Internet Network Information Centre (CNNIC), there are 147 million Chinese people playing online games, and 53% of them are playing MMORPGs" (Zhong, 2011, p. 2352). In 2010, gaming revenues were over $25 billion and that number is expected to increase (NPD Group, 2011). The ESA (2011) reported that 72% of American homes have a resident who plays computer or video games.

While a predominant belief that the typical gamer is in their adolescence or early adulthood, the prevalence of gaming in the adult population is the most striking: the average age of computer gamers is well into their adulthood (Wood, Griffiths, Chappell, & Davies, 2004), averaging 37 years old and those purchasing games averaging 41 years. In fact, 29% of the gamers indicate they are age 50 or older (ESA, 2011). As of 2008, there were an estimated 8 million people playing World of Warcraft,[3] a popular massively multiplayer online game and 6 million accounts active to play in Second Life,[4] another virtual world (Freddolino & Blaschke, 2008).

Social Networking

In addition to the enjoyment and social interaction in video gaming, millions of people also participate in social networking sites (Volpe, 2009). According to research conducted by Facebook, there is now on average only 3.7 degrees of separation between any one user and another on their popular social networking sites (BBC, 2011). Some indicate that access to social networking sites occurs approximately one in every four minutes (Nielsen, 2010). According to Alexa Global Traffic Rank (2012), Facebook[5] boasts over one billion users, coming second in terms of Internet traffic only to Google[6] (Alexa, 2012). Other very popular social networking sites are Twitter[7] at rank 9 (200,000,000 users) and LinkedIn[8] at rank 11 (150,000,000 users). Approximately 73% of a sample of postgraduate students have an account on a social networking site (Facebook or LinkedIn; Horvat, Oreski, & Markic, 2011).

Social networking is now being engaged in by about two-thirds (65%) of all U.S. adult Internet users (Madden & Zickuhr, 2011). African Americans tend to use Twitter at higher rates than their White American or Latino/a American peers (Smith, 2011). One in 10 African American Internet users Tweet at a rate that is almost double that of Latino/a Americans, and four times that of White American users (Smith, 2011). In terms of differences in usage by sexual orientation—lesbian, gay, and bisexual (LGB) individuals make use of the Internet and social networking sites in greater numbers than those identifying as heterosexual males or females (HarrisInteractive, 2007). Women, particularly young adult women ages 18–29, tend to be the power users of social networking sites (Madden & Zickuhr, 2011). As with other forms of communication that one might have with others, these sites also provide a place to post electronic photos, maintain records such as address books, and play interactive games with other users. Given the varied types of new media and the multiple applications available, it is clear that we are a wired society.

Implications of Increased Technology Use on Relationships

Because the technological revolution has inserted itself into couple life in inconspicuous ways, couples may not always be overtly aware of the changes that have emerged in their relationship with the introduction of these technologies. Couples may operate the same as we did in previous generations, the ways we accomplish the tasks are different. For example, communication with individuals outside of their home quarters may now be accomplished through e-mails to one member of the couple rather than the couple as a unit, thus creating opportunities for individual development more relationships excluding to the primary partner. In addition, while the computer and Internet certainly occupy time previously spent on other activities such as reading the newspaper (Woodard & Gridina, 2000), some research has demonstrated that some protect their family time when other activities are compromised (Ganske & Hamidon, 2006).

Another implication is in the case of technological literacy. The term common couple literacy means the extent to which couples overlap in terms of their electronic and technological literacy. Specifically it is comprised of the common ways members of a couple are able to access resources online and navigate the actual hardware and software of computer systems. Some couples today have an adequate level of common couple literacy. While they may not have the same position or work in the same field, both may have the same types of new media available to them and, therefore, have developed a common literacy level. There are also cases, however, where couples do not experience a common literacy. One partner may, for example, be more technologically or electronically literate than their partner, thus resulting in power issues between the members because the partner who is more literate has more access to resources and, consequently, more power. One only needs to consider the generation gap in computer usage as an example. Youth, for example, may be more computer literate than their parents. One study conducted by Aarsand (2007) highlights the notion that information parents receive about computer usage is actually provided to them by their children.

Recent developments in technology have also contributed to health issues that can potentially shape the way that we view our interactions with our partner. In a study on the impacts of psychophysiological patterns produced during usage of text message, a small sample of college students was measured in terms of physical comfort, heart rate, respiration, and related variables during texting. Researchers observed a number of physiological reactions when texting, including tension in one's shoulders, tightening of the neck, and shallow breathing (Lin & Peper, 2009). This study's findings corroborated those in previous research citing the development of physical issues among users of technology. Hupert et al. (2004) found that a rather large sample of college students experienced neck, shoulder and other pain in the upper body. While there was no relationship to the type of work/major in which the students were enrolled with the symptoms, nor was there a significant difference with regard to symptoms between men and women. There were differences, however, between students of minority background with regard to symptomology as compared to students not from a minority background. Specifically, minority students reported experiencing more pain symptoms in the upper body and were more likely to note these symptoms occurring within an hour of sitting down at a computer (Hupert et al., 2004). Sitting at a computer for 3 hours or more was related to increase chance of individuals reporting musculoskeletal symptoms (Chang et al., 2007).

In addition to the physical symptoms experienced by computer users, there may also be an experience of psychological symptoms. Hupert et al. (2004) found that students who indicated that they had limited functionality or a negative impact of pain in their upper extremity scored lower (worse) on a 5-item Mental Health Inventory than students who did not. Just below three-quarters of the sample scored below a cutoff, which would indicate that these people may be evaluated for mood disorders.

These findings, however, are from a small sample and need to be evaluated more rigorously through a larger sample and multiple measures.

In addition to the individual physical consequences that these symptoms might foster, the physiological symptoms might also have relational consequences. For example, some indicate that they feel stress upon receiving a text message (Lin & Peper, 2009). This experience of stress and the attempt to interpret and respond to a message might affect message construction or interpretation of how a message comes across. The next steps are that the message has to then be decoded. One of the other issues around the text message is the limited opportunity to see face-to-face interactions.

Scholarly Attention to Technology in Relationships

The increase in computers in the home, tablets, predominance and performance of cellular phones, the emergence of social networking, and increased entertainment opportunities affect the tempo, rhythm, and content of individual, couple, and family relationships. The changes to couple and family life from new media and technology have inspired both obvious and subtle changes in couple and family life that have been understudied for two main reasons. First, technologies are ever changing. We acknowledge some of the information included about prevalence of technologies and specific usage patterns provided in this text, for example, may be outdated before it is printed and distributed. This means that by the time a study on these technologies is conceived, executed, and disseminated in an academic journal, the topic under investigation may have changed in substantial ways.

Second, technology in relationships may be understudied due to the decentralization in the dissemination of scholarly literature. Literature in the field of couple and family technology (CFT) is spread across a number of varied disciplines and journals, including information technology, sociology, psychology, media studies, and others. In this way, it is difficult to compile a comprehensive data base of articles which allows researchers to build upon previous literature. The organization of this body of knowledge into a distinct discipline will enable researchers to move toward programmatic research and be able to develop more comprehensive theories and applications.

Finally, aspects of a client's life related to technology are not routinely assessed by therapists in couple and family cases, with the notable exception of when they work with children (Hertlein, Blumer, & Smith, 2012). When therapists do inquire as to the use of the Internet in couple and family treatment, the most frequent topic assessed is Internet infidelity, followed by safety, online networking, and addiction (Hertlein et al., 2012). With few therapists inquiring as to the impact of technology in a client's life, there is little information on which to continue to build a more comprehensive body of literature.

The Couple–Family–Technology Interface: Reconceptualizing Relationships in a Digital Age

Technology and new media have transformative effects on our relationships with work and family, can alter a couple/family lifecycle, and likely have implications for daily, monthly, and even yearly communication patterns. Despite the evidence of technology's predominant presence, family scholars and practitioners have not addressed these strategies consistently in their conceptualization of relationships or treatment of couples and families. Any attention given in articles or at workshops about technology's impact on relationships is surprisingly scarce (Blumer, Hertlein, Smith, & Allen, in press), even in the literature specifically dedicated to computers and human behavior. Yet the sheer immersion of technology in our lives suggests we now have a responsibility to be sensitive to influences of technology on our individual and relational selves.

The branch of study described in this text, Couple and Family Technology (CFT), is a broad area of study exploring the effect of technology on relationships of individuals, couples, and families. It attends to both the challenges that interfere with couple and family processes and builds on the advantages that technology introduces into relationships. This branch of study also includes the following:

- a valuation of the benefits and drawbacks of one's technology use for individuals, couples and families within their lives and relationships;
- research into the topics related to technology that are the most relevant for couples and families;
- development and implementation of testing of assessment tools for identifying the presence of problematic Internet or technology usage;
- development and application of treatment models, frameworks, and strategies sensitive to individuals, couples, and families with a digital presence;
- incorporation of technology-based strategies to augment therapeutic goals and practices.

Theoretical Origins of CFT

CFT is a branch of study which draws off the work of other disciplines, namely computer technology, information systems, media studies, psychology, and communication studies. Much of the literature borrowed from these other disciplines does not discuss direct application to couples and families but provides a way for CFT researchers to extrapolate implications for couple and family relationship from the basic research questions and studies with individual usage.

To date, most of the theories around how to explain online behavior, intimacy patterns, and changes to the way people communicate focus on basic interactional patterns. Each perspective attends to different but relevant areas of relationships and can generally be considered as falling into one of three main classes: (a) theories that attend to the communication aspect of technology and new media, (b) theories that attend to the developmental aspect of technology and new media, and (c) theories that attend to the social aspects of technology and new media. Each of these theories' main tenets, limitations, and potential applications are shown in Table 1.1.

Media richness theory (Daft & Lengel, 1984; Dennis & Kinney, 1998) and hyperpersonal computer-mediated communication theory (Rabby & Walther, 2002) are two perspectives that attend to the communicative aspect of new technologies. Media richness theory suggests that communication occurs more quickly, with greater clarity, and results in better performance on certain tasks when the electronic media used provides immediate feedback, personalized messages, and can better estimate social cues (Balaji & Chakrabarti, 2010). In other words, the more technology mimics daily life, the more successful people will be in their interactions with one another because they are able to accurately interpret the messages. Hyperpersonal computer-mediated communication theory (Rabby & Walther, 2002) is a multitheoretical model describing how computer-mediated communication contributes to greater levels of intimacy in relationships because of the nature of disclosure in a text-based medium: Users can select which characteristics they wish to present, both in content of messages and the process in which the messages are constructed (Walther, 2007). Both of these theories allude to applications in message construction and importance of clarity, and are highly valuable for considering the initiation of contact in relationships. On the other hand, the limitations for the communicative models are potentially little consideration of other contextual factors which might be operating (see Table 1.1).

Two theories attend to the socially focused theories of computer usage and interactions. Social penetration theory, a framework introduced by Altman and Taylor (1973), was applied by Yum and Hara (2005) to explain how self-disclosure manifests in computer-mediated communication across different cultures. Social penetration theory means that people share information characterized by both depth and breadth in an effort to grow more closely to people. They also expect that a similar process will be followed by those to whom they are sharing information. Similarities were found with regard to the extent of self-disclosure in relationships facilitated by computer-mediated communication as is in face-to-face relationships. Similarly, social presence theory (Short, Williams, & Christie, 1993) proposes that the extent one feels another's social presence is shaped by the intimacy and immediacy of their interactions with others through various mediums. As applied to the digital world, interactions over immediate communication methods such as texting or other forms in instant messaging would theoretically be linked to a higher level of

Table 1.1 Theoretical Origins of CFT

Class	*Theory and authors*	*Main tenet*	*Limitations*	*Potential applications for relationships*
Communication aspects	**Media Richness** Daft & Lengel (1984)	Different types of media have varying implications for task completion, speed, and clarity	Scope is limited to individual user characteristics and some application with intimacy, but not many studies on other applications; little consideration of other contextual factors which may be operating	Couples who use Skype of other video-conferences technologies to communicate would have an advantage over couples and families that use text-based communication methods; mediums that are rich in presentation may be augmented quite well in text-based mediums in the initial relationship development phase
	Hyperpersonal CMC Rabby & Walther (2002)	Users can construct what they want to represent through text based-mediums, thereby increasing perceived intimacy		
Social aspects	**Social Penetration** Altman and Taylor (1973)	Sharing both depth and breadth of experiences with another facilitates intimacy	Discussion of social presence and its contribution to other processes in relationships (i.e., more than intimacy) are not considered	Couples may have different perceptions of the circumstances in which depth would be more important co couple development than breadth; social presence may be a useful concept to discuss with couples who are concerned about their partner's online presence.
	Social Presence Short, Christie, & Williams (1993)	Social presence is experienced through speed and interactions characterized by intimacy		

(*continued*)

Table 1.1 (continued)

Class	*Theory and authors*	*Main tenet*	*Limitations*	*Potential applications for relationships*
Developmental aspects	**Developmental model** Watt & White (1999)	Computers introduced changes in the way that we work, play, and interact with one another. The manifestation of the changes depends on stage in the lifecycle and other demographic information.	Limited attention to specific couple dynamics; do not include some of the information related to intimacy development in CMC relationships; heavy focus on computers and more focus needed on other forms of new media	The integration of computers and new media in relationships is, at best, a complex interaction. This perspective enables more opportunities for couples to experience challenges or opportunities for relationship enhancement.
	Domestication theory Silverstone, Hirsch, & Morley (1992)	Computers and other forms of new media influence family operations and, in so doing, change the way a family interacts with technology		

social presence. The power in these theories is their attention to interaction between two others across an electronic medium. Both theories in this class posit that one's behavior, in some way, is based on the initiation and reaction to another, thus promoting a circular causality and emphasizing the reciprocal nature of relationships—a more accurate (if not more complicated) view.

Two models of development are also discussed in the literature. The first is a framework sensitive to the introduction of computers into family life proposed by Watt and White (1999). This model attends to both the introduction and use of technologies at various stages of family development and specifically attends to the roles played by both technology and family members. It acknowledges the role that computers play in shaping interactions, education, recreation, work habits, and across the life span and how the impact on family life varies based on demographic variables. Likewise, domestication theory (Haddon, 2006; Silverstone, Hirsch, & Morley, 1992) describes a process by which computers are integrated into family life. In this model, less attention is paid to stages of development; instead, focused attention is placed how technology recursively influences and becomes integrated into the family. The strength of these two theories is that they complement each other well and attend to the complexity inherent in individual, couple, and family relationships. Developmental theories have to consider, by nature, the differences at each stage in one's life. This entails ascribing different meaning and articulating different decisions making patterns for usage of technology that allows for a contextual interpretation of participating in a variety of Internet-based applications and products.

While these theories form the foundation of CFT, none of the theories incorporates the specific structure of technology and the characteristics germane to new media into a model that highlights how technology interfaces with roles, rules boundaries, and couple/family dynamics. Therefore, we will also present a multitheoretical framework though which couple and family interactions around technology can be viewed. This framework introduced by Hertlein (2012) is the most inclusive approach to understanding the impact of technology in couples and families. It is informed by research and includes the research on development, characteristics about the mechanics of electronically-based communications (EBC), and the social aspects of EBC. It also considers the role of process and content in relationships alongside the specific information related to communicative technologies.

Notes

1. http://www.webopedia.com/. Other examples include Techdictionary (http://techdictionary.com/), Techterms (http://www.techterms.com/), NullModem (http://www.nullmodem.com), and the Social Media Glossary (http://www.socialbrite.org/sharing-center/glossary/).

2. It is difficult to separate out the presence of computers in the home without Internet access, as after 2007, survey responders were not requested to provide information about this (U.S. Census, 2009).
3. http://us.battle.net/wow/en/?-.
4. http://secondlife.com/.
5. http://www.facebook.com/.
6. http://www.google.com/.
7. https://twitter.com/.
8. http://www.linkedin.com/.

References

Aarsand, P. (2007). Computer and video games in family life: The digital divide as a resource in intergenerational interactions. *Childhood: A Global Journal of Child Research, 14*, 235–256. doi:10.1177/0907568207078330

Alexa Global Traffic Rank. (2012). *Facebook.com*. Retrieved from http://www.alexa.com/siteinfo/facebook.com

Altman, I., & Taylor, D. A. (1973). *Social penetration: The development of interpersonal relationships*. Oxford, England: Holt, Rinehart & Winston.

Anderson, N. (2007). *Video gaming to be twice as big as music by 2011*. Retrieved from http://arstechnica.com/gaming/news/2007/08/gaming-to-surge-50-percent-in-four-years-possibly.ars

Appleby, J. (2010). *The relentless revolution: A history of capitalism*. New York: W. W. Norton.

Bacigalupe, G., & Lambe, S. (2011). Virtualizing intimacy: Information communication technologies and transnational families in therapy. *Family Process, 50*(1), 12–26. doi:10.1111/j.1545-5300.2010.01343.x

Balaji, M. S., & Chakrabarti, D. (2010). Student interactions in online discussion forum: Empirical research from "media richness theory" perspective. *Journal of Interactive Online Learning, 9*(1), 1–22.

Bargh, J. A., & McKenna, K. A. (2004). The Internet and social life. *Annual Review of Psychology, 55*, 573–590. doi:10.1146/annurev.psych.55.090902.141922

Barkhuus, L., & Polichar, V. E. (2011). Empowerment through seamfulness: Smart phones in everyday life. *Personal and Ubiquitous Computing, 15*, 629–639. doi:10.1007/s00779-010-0342-4

BBC. (2011). *Facebook users average 3.74 degrees of separation*. Retrieved from http://www.bbc.co.uk/news/technology-15844230

Behringer, W. (2006). Communications revolution: A historical concept. *German History, 24*, 333–374. doi:10.1093/0266355406gh378oa

Bengston, V. L. (2001). Beyond the nuclear family: The increasing importance of multigenerational bonds. *Journal of Marriage and the Family, 63*(1), 1–16.

Blumberg, S. J., & Luke, J. V. (2009). Reevaluating the need for concern regarding noncoverage bias in landline surveys. *American Journal of Public Health, 99*(10), 1806–1810. doi:10.2105/AJPH.2008.152835

Blumer, M., Hertlein, K. M., Smith, J., & Allen, H. (2013). How many bytes does it take? A content analysis of cyber issues in couple and family therapy journals. *Journal of Marital and Family Therapy.*

Chang, C. J., Amick, E., Benjamin, C., Menendez, C. C., Katz, J. N., Johnson, P. W., . . . Dennerlein, J. T. (2007). Daily computer usage correlated with undergraduate students' musculoskeletal symptoms. *American Journal of Industrial Medicine, 50*(6), 481–488. doi:10.1002/ajim.20461

Chelsey, N. (2005). Blurring boundaries: Linking technology use, spillover, individual distress, and family satisfaction. *Journal of Marriage and the Family, 67*, 1237–1248.

Cohen, V. L., & Cowan, J. E. (2007). *Literacy for children in an information age: Teaching reading, writing, and thinking*. Belmont, CA: Wadsworth.

Daft, R. L., & Lengel, R. H. (1984). Information richness: A new approach to managerial behavior and organizational design. In L. L. Cummings & B. M. Staw (Eds.), *Research in organizational behavior* (pp. 191–233). Homewood, IL: JAI Press.

Dennis, A. R., & Kinney, S. T. (1998). Testing media richness theory in the new media: The effects of cues, feedback, and task equivocality. *Information Systems Research, 9*, 256–274.

Entertainment Software Association. (2011). *Essential facts about the computer and video game industry*. Retrieved from http://www.theesa.com/facts/pdfs/ESA_EF_2011.pdf

Freddolino, P., & Blaschke, C. (2008). Therapeutic applications of online gaming. *Journal of Technology in Human Services, 26*, 423–446. doi:10.1080/15228830802099998

Ganske, L., & Hamidon, Z. (2006). Technological immersion in Brunei. *International Journal of Instruction Media, 33*, 55–73.

Global Language Monitor. (2011). Web 2.0 beats Jai Ho & N00b as 1,000,000th English Word. Retrieved March 15, 2013 from http://www.languagemonitor.com/no-of-words/

Goldberg, A. (2012). *World has about 6 billion cell phone subscribers, according to U.N. telecom agency report*. Retrieved from http://www.huffingtonpost.com/2012/10/11/cell-phones-world-subscribers-six-billion_n_1957173.html

Haddon, L. (2006). The contribution of domestication research to in-home computing and media consumption. *The Information Society, 22*, 195–203.

Hampton, K., Sessions, L., Her, E. J., & Rainie, L. (2009). *Social isolation and new technology: How the Internet and mobile phones impact Americans' social networks*. Retrieved from http://pewresearch.org/pubs/1398/internet-mobile-phones-impact-american-social-networks

Harris, K., Marett, K., & Harris, R. (2011). Technology-related pressure and work–family conflict: Main effects and an examination of moderating variables. *Journal of Applied Social Psychology, 41*, 2077–2103. doi:10.1111/j.1559–1816.2011.00805.x

HarrisInteractive. (2007). *Gays, lesbians, and bisexuals lead in usage of online social networks*. Retrieved from http://www.witeckcombs.com/news/releases/20070102_socialnetworks.pdf

Hertlein, K. M., Blumer, M. L. C., & Smith, J. (2012). *Couple and family therapists' use of web-based technologies in clinical practice* (Unpublished manuscript).

Hoffman, D. L., Novak, T. P., & Venkatesh, A. (2004). Has the Internet become indispensable? *Communications of the ACM, 47*(7), 37–42.

Horvat, J., Oreski, D., & Markic, D. (2011). *Gender differences in the Internet usage among postgraduate students*. Retrieved from http://ieeexplore.ieee.org/stamp/stamp.jsp?arnumber=05974036

Hughes, R., Jr., & Hans, J. D. (2001). Computers, the Internet, and families: A review of the role new technology plays in family life. *Journal of Family Issues, 22*, 776–790.

Hupert, N., Amick, B. C., Fossel, A. H., Coley, C. M., Robertson, M. M., & Katz, J. N. (2004). Upper extremity musculoskeletal symptoms and functional impairment associated with computer use among college students. *Work: Journal of Prevention Assessment & Rehabilitation, 23*(2), 85–93.

Imhof, M., Vollmeyer, R., & Beierlein, C. (2007). Computer use and the gender gap: The issue of access, use, motivation, and performance. *Computers in Human Behavior, 23*, 2823–2837.

Internet World Stats. (2011). *Internet world stats*. Retrieved from http://www.internetworldstats.com/stats.htm

Ito, M., Okabe, D., & Matsuda, M. (2005). *Personal, portable, pedestrian: Mobile phones in Japanese life*. Cambridge, MA: MIT Press.

Kennedy, T. L. M., Smith, A., Wells, A. T., & Wellman, B. (2008). *Networked families*. Retrieved from http://www.pewinternet.org/Reports/2008/Networked-Families.aspx

Kim, M. S., Kim, Y. C., & Kim, J. (2011). Divergent meaning of convergent mobile phone from generic mobile phone. *Academy of Marketing Studies Journal, 15*(2), 45–68.

Knight, M. B., & Pearson, J. M. (2005). The changing demographics: The diminishing role of age and gender in computer usage. *Journal of Organizational and End User Computing, 17*(4), 49–65.

Leu, D. L., Kinzer, C. K., Coiro, J. L, & Cammack, D. W. (2005). *Toward a theory of new literacies emerging from the Internet and other information and communication* (Unpublished manuscript).

Lin, I., & Peper, E. (2009). Psychophysiological patterns during cell phone text messaging: A preliminary study. *Applied Psychophysiol Biofeedback, 34*, 53–57. doi 10.1007/s10484-009-9078-1

Madden, M., & Zickuhr, Z. (2011). *65% of online adults use social networking sites: Women maintain their foothold on SNS use and older Americans are still coming aboard*. Retrieved from http://pewinternet.org/~/media//Files/Reports/2011/PIP-SNS-Update-2011.pdf

Nielsen. (2010, June 15). Social networks blogs now account for one in every four and a half minutes online. Retrieved from http://www.nielsen.com/us/en/newswire/2010/social-media-accounts-for-22-percent-of-time-online.html

NPD Group. (2011). *The NPD Group, Inc*. Retrieved from https://www.npd.com

Ortiz, T., Green, R., & Lim, H. (2009). Korean parents' perceptions on the importance of computer usage for themselves and their children: An exploratory study. *International Electronic Journal of Elementary Education, 1*(2), 55–66.

Rabby, M., & Walther, J. B. (2002). Computer-mediated communication impacts on relationship formation and maintenance. In D. Canary & M. Dainton (Eds.), *Maintaining relationships through communication: Relational, contextual, and cultural variations* (pp. 141–162). Mahwah, NJ: Lawrence Erlbaum Associates.

Rapoport, R., & Rapoport, R. (1965). Work and family in contemporary society. *American Sociological Review, 30*, 381–394.

Rice, R. E., & Katz, J. E. (2008). Assessing new cell phone text and video services. *Telecommunications Policy, 32*, 455–467. doi:10.1016/j.telpol.2008.05.005

Rizzo, S. (2008). The promise of cell phones from people power to technological nanny *Convergence: The International Journal of Research into New Media Technologies, 14*(2), 135–143. doi:10.1177/1354856507087940

Short, J., Williams, E., & Christie, B. (1993). Visual communication and social interaction. In *Readings in groupware and computer-supported cooperative work: Assisting human–human collaboration* (pp. 153–164). Palo Alto, CA: Morgan Kaufmann.

Silverstone, R., Hirsch, E., & Morley, D. (1992). Information and communication technologies and the moral economy of the household. In R. Silverstone & E. Hirsch (Eds.), *Consuming technologies* (pp. 15–31). London: Routledge.

Smith, A. (2011). *Americans and their cell phones*. Retrieved from http://pewinternet.org/~/media//Files/Reports/2011/Cell%20Phones%202011.pdf

Smith, A., Rainie, L., & Zickuhr, K. (2011). *College students and technology*. Retrieved from http://pewinternet.org/Reports/2011/College-students-and-technology.aspx

Thompson, B. (2011). *Global PC Sales top 350 million in 2010*. Retrieved from http://www.digitalhome.ca/2011/01/global-pc-sales-top-350-million-in-2010/

Topping, K. (1997). Electronic literacy in school and home: A look into the future. *Reading Online*. International Reading Association http://www.eric.ed.gov/PDFS/ED416437.pdf.

Tu, Q., Wang, K., & Shu, Q. (2005). Computer-related technostress in China. *Communications of the ACM, 48*(4), 77–81.

U.S. Census Bureau. (2009). *Internet use in the United States*. Retrieved from http://www.census.gov/hhes/computer/publications/2009.html

Verkasalo, H. (2009). Contextual patterns in mobile service usage. *Personal and Ubiquitous Computing, 13*, 331–342. doi:10.1007/s00779-008-0197-0

Volpe, J. J. (2009). Brain injury in premature infants: A complex amalgam of destructive and developmental disturbances. *Lancet Neurology, 8*(1), 110–124.

Walther, J. B. (2007). Selective self-presentation in computer-mediated communication: Hyperpersonal dimensions of technology, language, and cognition. *Computers in Human Behavior, 23*, 2538–2557. doi:10.1016/j.chb.2006.05.002

Watt, D., & White, J. M. (1999). Computers and the family life: A family development perspective. *Journal of Comparative Family Studies, 30*(1), 1–15.

Wood, R. T. A., Griffiths, M. D., Chappell, D., & Davies, M. N. O. (2004). The structural characteristics of video games: A psycho-structural analysis. *Cyberpsychology & Behavior: The Impact of the Internet, Multimedia and Virtual Reality on Behavior and Society, 7*(1), 1–10. doi:10.1089/109493104322820057

Woodard, E. H., & Gridina, N. (2000). *Media in the home*. Philadelphia, PA: Annenburg Public Policy Center for the University of Pennsylvania.

Yum, Y., & Hara, K. (2005). Computer-mediated relationship development: A cross-cultural comparison. *Journal of Computer-Mediated Communication, 11*, 133–152.

Zhong, Z. (2011). The effects of collective MMORPG (massively multiplayer online role-playing games) play on gamers' online and offline social capital. *Computers in Human Behavior, 27*, 2352–2363. doi:10.1016/j.chb.2011.07.014

Zickuhr, K., & Smith, A. (2012). *Digital differences*. Retrieved from http://pewinternet.org/Reports/2012/Digital-differences.aspx

2 The Basics of Online Coupling

On the Internet, nobody knows you're a dog.

—Peter Steiner

As the field of couple and family technology has emerged from multidisciplinary theoretical origins, its scope is to understand a variety of concepts related to technology and new media including motivations, mechanics, and consequences of interactive communication technologies on relationships. The purpose of this chapter is to provide an overview of the building blocks of online interacting in close relationships.

Comparing and Contrasting Face-to-Face and Computer-Mediated Communication

There are several key areas in which face-to-face (FTF) interactions are alike and differ from computer-mediated and electronically-based communication (EBC). In general, Internet communicative technologies allow us to be able to communicate with others in much of the same way as we did prior to the innovations of technology, if not more frequently (see Table 2.1). For example, people can still talk to each other, be emotional, share parts of their day; in other words, they can build relationships steadily and progressively. Differences include in self-presentation, nonverbal relationship signals, and the development of rituals and sense of "everydayness" (Hertlein & Nelson, 2005).

Self-Presentation

One of the key points of both similarity and difference is the point of self-presentation. In both FTF and EBC relationships, people have a greater degree of control over what they present to other people. In any dating scenario, the individuals involved may opt to attend to their presentation in a way that would make them more attractive to the other partner. When relationships are initiated offline, the ability to manage one's self-presentation

Table 2.1 Comparing and Contrasting Face-to-Face and Computer-Mediated Communication

Similarities	*Differences*
Self-presentation	Self-presentation can be heavily edited
Shared data	Manner in which data is shared is different
Shared nonverbals	Nonverbals communicated through emoticons
Development of rituals	Internet is the medium to conduct the rituals
Sense of everydayness	Everydayness is structured
Emotional intimacy	Emotional intimacy is heavily dependent on text
Shared time/interests	Shared time may be difficult to accomplish when distant from one's partner

may be evident in one's physical presentation—their clothing, the manner in which they care for their home, how they style their hair, and so on. Relationships that initiate online, however, may be characterized by self-presentation management earlier in the relationship and in two primary, structured ways: (a) withholding information regarding mood states, emotional states, and activities, and (b) actively presenting false information. Individuals in online relationships withhold they are communicating with more than one love interest at the same time or present false information regarding physical attributes.

The main difference between FTF and computer-mediated relationships is the extent to which one can edit one's presentation. The greater the ability to edit oneself, the less likely another will be able to trust the information presented. As a result, these relationships lose credibility and result in a negative attitude toward those who find love online (Anderson, 2007; Donn & Sherman, 2002; Wildermuth, 2004). Specific characteristics that are attributed to people who prefer to participate in online dating are

- shyness
- social awkwardness
- lonely
- experience general difficulty with interpersonal interaction
- primarily interested in sex rather than an emotional relationship
- potentially deceitful (Donn & Sherman, 2002; Peris, et. al, 2002).

In FTF interactions, one may observe certain things about one's partner that are not consistent with the image that the other individual wants to project, such as bad mood, bad breath or an unkempt appearance. Women, for example, are more likely to misrepresent their hobbies, activities, and age in online personal profiles where men are more likely to misrepresent their physical attributes (Ben-Ze'ev, 2004). These same characteristics, however, are unobservable in the context of EBC. This dilemma of self-editorializing leading to mistrust of others is not an uncommon one in online relating. Literature focusing on online dating discusses the difficulty in assessing whether someone's online presentation is genuine. At times, the potential to be deceived by someone's online presentation may prohibit participation in particular online activities and may activate the implementation of a "warranting" process (Gibbs, Ellison, & Lai, 2011; Walther, Van der Heide, Hamel, & Shulman, 2009). In the context of online interacting, warranting refers to how people check to ensure that the personal identification information provided to them from other Internet users is verifiable. In part, warranting is accomplished through valuing information provided by a third party instead of the person with whom one is interacting because the information from the third party cannot be manipulated (Gibbs et al., 2011).

This may be one of the first blocks a new couple has to navigate within their relationship and may manifest several ways. First, after the initial interaction, each individual has to determine the extent to which one will assess the accuracy of his or her partner's self-presentation. In other words, does the individual test the accuracy of the information prior to a relationship developing further, or does one make a decision about whether to pursue another after a series of interactions? There are pros and cons to each of those arrangements. Individuals who make a decision to continue the warranting process may experience a trade-off around trust (i.e., the partner that is the recipient of the warranting process may experience anger about not being trusted). Individuals who make a decision to not implement the warranting procedure may have some difficulty in resolving any inconsistencies once the relationship becomes more serious. For example, women under the age of 50 are more likely to be deceitful about their age in online dating profiles than older women (Hall, Park, Song, & Cody, 2010). Despite both the anecdotal and empirical evidence that people use some creative license in their profile information as well as other interactions, there is little information as to how people resolve the inconsistencies. One way it is described in the literature as a consequence of inconsistency between the online profile and the person is the discontinuation of the relationship upon the recognition of inconsistencies (Heino, Ellison, & Gibbs, 2010). Further, relationships may end when the physical characteristics of the potential partner offline do not match with the expectations of others (Houran & Lange, 2004; Whitty & Carr, 2006), which may be the result of (a) inaccurate message sent about one's physical appearance to the other, (b) the imagination of the individual, regardless of what is communicated, or (c) both (a) and (b). Houran and Lange (2004) note, "It might be expected that individuals actively pursuing a soul mate with online dating assign an artificially high likelihood to finding someone who is perfectly compatible" (p. 299), though the findings of their research actually show that these high expectations coexist with a dose of realism about what they might find.

In essence, the Internet allows people to present whatever they want about themselves. In a study conducted on online dating, one individual reported that he would no longer trust anyone's online profile because he had one bad interaction with someone who was at least 10 years older than their posted photo (Heino et al., 2010). In another example, Claire met Marty through an online dating profile. In his profile, Marty listed himself as 25 years old and a DJ at a local establishment. In truth, he was a 28-year-old officer in a branch of the U.S. Armed Forces. As their relationship grew more serious, Claire discovered that he was in the same branch—and, incidentally, outranked him. In addition, approximately 1 year into their relationship, she learned Marty's true age from his father. This inauspicious beginning of the relationship created problems a short time later when Claire accused Marty of being unfaithful. In Claire's words, "If he lied to me once before about who he was, how do I know what he is truthful about?"

Shared Nonverbal Signals

Another similarity between FTF and EBC is the sharing of nonverbal signals in one's communication pattern. Nonverbal interactions in humans related to courtship seem to follow predictable patterns (Moore, 2010). Most research, which focuses primarily on heterosexual couples, supports the idea that women typically initiate the earlier nonverbal interactions; however, the signs that women give tend to be subtle and, when men respond, it appears as if the man is making the first move. Then men and women both respond in reciprocal ways, each interaction building on the next until one of two outcomes: successful relationship interaction, or one person stops reciprocating and opts out of the relationship.

These same patterns also seem to hold true in online interactions. Someone may initiate an interaction through an approach and then assess whether that invitation was received well. Women may play a more prominent role in the earlier stages of courtship whereas men play a more prominent role in latter stages, such as just prior to sexual interaction. Nonverbal signals such as smiling and leaning forward to indicate interest seem to have emerged across multiple studies as playing an important role in the nonverbal courtship process (Moore, 2010).

In addition to verbal interactions, couples do indeed grow when they can assess and make meaning of one another's nonverbal interactions. Yet a main difference between FTF and EBC, however, is the way in which nonverbal signals are communicated. In online interactions, nonverbal signals are communicated by emoticons rather than by someone's facial expressions or body positioning. Emoticons can enhance communication through technology when one can accurately display a general nonverbal reaction to the communication that fits the circumstance and, moreover, can give the other person added information about the context in which one's message was received. For example, one couple was discussing the most recent argument they had. Since the couple had the argument over a chat function, the wife brought in a print out of the argument. During the argument, one issue was the use of one partner's emoticons in communication. After a comment where the wife was trying to diffuse the powerful emotions that were building up, inserting a smiling face emoticon. In his state of upset, her partner misinterpreted the smile as her attempt to mock him, thus fueling his anger and escalating the conflict.

Problematic implications for online relationships are that users of communicative technologies may insert an emoticon to display a certain nonverbal signal that (a) may not be accurate to their true experience, and/or (b) may be misinterpreted by the receiver. Holly and Damien came into session arguing about an interaction they had over a text message earlier that day. In the message, Holly stated that she wanted Damien to be mindful of the time so that he would be on time for the session, especially given his tendency to run late. Since the message was not accompanied by any nonverbal signals, Damien took the message as a directive and as an attack about his time-management skills. Consequently, he reacted by socializing with his boss after work, partially to prove a point that he could be on time for the session without her managing his schedule for him, but ended up late to the session. The nonverbal signals not communicated were that Holly was interested in Damien and attempting to build the relationship. She was not intending to be critical toward him, which most likely would have been reflected in tone and attitude had she spoken to him in person rather than sending a text message.

Development of Rituals and Sense of Everydayness

Another area in which FTF and EBC are similar is the development of rituals and sense of everydayness that the couple shares. Rituals, defined as repetitive yet meaningful interactions, are a key piece of the relationship dynamic. Because of the positive impact of rituals on a sense of satisfaction and stability in the relationship (Bruess & Pearson, 2002), rituals can be a useful adjunct in treatment (Olson, 1993). Couples have found rituals useful as a way to process such events as forgiveness (Barnett & Youngberg, 2004) and infidelity (Winek & Craven, 2003). Examples include renewing their vows or engaging in some ritual creating a sense of having a unique boundary around their relationship. The rituals contribute to a couple's sense of shared couple identity (Berg-Cross, Daniels, & Carr, 1993) and can be used as a way to bind the couple together, provide a sense of predictability in their relationship, and identify elements of family life that they want to transmit to future generations (Crespo, Davide, Costa, & Fletcher, 2008). The establishment of rituals in relationships is also associated with increases in marital satisfaction for newer parents (Crespo et al., 2008). Various types of rituals have been identified in both married and unmarried couples. In married couples, rituals include those related to time, symbols, daily routines, communication, habits, intimacy, and spirituality (Bruess & Pearson, 1997). Unmarried couples have rituals distinct from those for married couples, such as gift giving, assistance giving, visiting with extended family, and planning for the future (Campbell, Silva, & Wright, 2011).

One way in which rituals differ in computer-mediated relationships is the use of the Internet is a mechanism for conducting the ritual. For example, one couple's ritual was to hold hands and pray together before dinner each night. When the couple was separated by distance, however, they were unable to continue this ritual. Therefore the ritual transitioned from praying together while touching to praying together without touching but over the webcam. This type of ritual can be evident in offline relationships as well, but the difference is that the Internet is not the form of mediation in the ritual. Further, the ritual can be compromised if there are technical difficulties in the participation in the ritual. Dysfunctional rituals may also emerge in couples (Olson, 1993). For example, each member of the couple may play out a part in their dynamic that they admit is nonproductive and unhealthy, but in the moment, they cannot manage to do anything different. For example, Mark and Tina left a therapy session feeling hopeful about their relationship and worked to develop a plan for what they would do differently daily, weekly, and monthly for one another. At the end of the first week, however, neither one had participated in doing anything differently. In the second week, the couple decided on a ritual to designate every Tuesday night as "cooking class night" where they selected a new recipe they had never made before and spent time together working through the recipe.

Similarly, the concept of "everydayness" refers to the unstructured interactions and experiences people have with each other on a daily or regular basis. This includes seeing each other in less contrived ways, such as experiencing daily chores together, and negotiating aspects of the relations as they emerge. In both FTF and EBC relationships, a sense of everydayness is shared. The difference, however, is that in relationships characterized by EBC, the everydayness is structured. In other words, individuals in the relationship have to organize a time in which they share the everydayness with one another. Without this negotiation of time, an individual member of a couple is not privy to the day-to-day interactions, feelings, and experiences of another without an explicit invitation to do so.

Is Technology Good or Bad for Relationships?

Attention to the differences between EBC and FTF communication has led to a discussion of the valuation of this mode of communication on relationships. Specifically, the involvement of technology in relationships has created controversy among whether technology is good or bad for relationships (Hertlein & Webster, 2008). Both anecdotal and empirical evidence from couples in treatment highlight the issue in relationships associated with technology usage, including a redefining of what it means to be unfaithful (Hertlein & Piercy, 2012; Schneider, 2000). The truth is technology may be both good and bad for relationships: the ways in which technology can strengthen a relationship may also be ways in which it interferes with a relationship.

The determination as to whether technology interferes with relationships or supports them is largely dependent on the couple and how each individual and the couple use technology. In one case, Derek came to treatment seeking assistance with his habit of viewing online pornography. Assessment revealed part of Derek's concern with his porn-viewing behavior was less about the actual content of what he was viewing and more about the fact that he was staying up after his wife went to bed to watch porn. Derek's decision to not join his wife in bed at the same time had immediate implications for both his personal and the couple's sexual relationship and satisfaction. It was clear to Derek this type of Internet usage was something that created problems in his relationship. In another case, Hadas and Aharon, a couple in their 20s who identified as Orthodox Jewish, were commended for their strengths as a couple by others, which in part included their regular habit of seeking information online for the betterment of their relationship. They reported that they had almost developed a pre-Shabbat ritual of looking at the Internet together for date night ideas before disengaging from technology. After the close of Shabbat they would go on a date to the place they had explored before their day of rest. This was a practice they planned to continue once they were married. Here, the role of the Internet was a supportive one in the relationship and actually functioned as a protective mechanism.

Motivation for Participation in Interactive Communication Technologies

A significant body of literature explores the motivation surrounding electronic communication. Early investigations have found motivations such as information, entertainment, convenience, and interpersonal utility (defined as affection, social interaction, and monitoring) play a key role in understanding computer usage (Papacharissi & Rubin, 2000). Other studies have acknowledged the role of social motivations (such as conversation, support, and interactions with friends), economic reasons (such as comparison shopping and less expensive ways to conduct personal and professional business), and the sense of control (Ko, Cho, & Roberts, 2005; Korgaonkar & Wolin, 1999; Parker & Plank, 2000). More personal motivators include social escapism (Kargaonkar & Wolin, 1999), diversion, surveillance, and the potential to change one's mood (Roy, 2008). These personal factors could be akin to the factor termed "self-development," as identified by Roy (2008). Yet the most common experiences in adulthood are those of e-mailing and conducting online searches with six out of ten adults who use the Internet engaging in these behaviors daily (Zickuhr & Smith, 2012). Most adults are engaging in e-mailing with their school instructors or work professionals, as well as with friends and family as a means of keeping in consistent communication (Adams & Stevenson, 2004). In addition, many adults are conducting online searches with the purpose of seeking information or resources and/or to disseminate information to others (Scherer, 1997).

Motivations for computer use are also somewhat dependent on the degree to which one is associated with a minority and/or socially disadvantaged group. The social diversification hypothesis (Mesch & Talmud, 2010) posits that the computer and new media, due to its increased accessibility to people of a wide variety of ethnic and socioeconomic backgrounds, allows one to form interpersonal relationships with people who would otherwise be outside of their social network. To some degree, the accessibility that one has to using web-based technologies is related to the amount of social capital one has: with more social capital comes more access and vice versa. In the case of how social capital impacts motivation for use, those individuals who hold more of a minority status in a given location are more likely to use a computer's communicative abilities to improve their social capital via expansion of their social network through use of chatrooms and weblogs whereas those in the majority are more likely to use the computer for maintaining social ties, occurring primarily through the use of social networking sites (Mesch, 2012).

Another way people understand computer usage is through particular perspectives. One of the more well-cited approaches is the uses and gratification (U & G) approach. This approach is predicated on the assumption that media users select to participate in certain media or computer-based activities (uses) as a way to fulfill a psychological need (gratification) (Lin, 1999; Stafford, 2008). Stafford (2003, 2008) contends the U & G approach in understanding choices in Internet usage differ from its application to television media in that understanding Internet usage contains three motivational dimensions—process motivations, content motivations, and social motivations. It is within these dimensions where differences between light and heavy Internet users emerge. Heavy users are more inclined to use the Internet for social gratification and are driven by social motivation more so than light users; light users are more driven by process usage such as using the Internet for resources and surfing than heavy users (Stafford, 2008). This framework is supported by the research of Ko et al. (2005), who found people who value social motivation are more likely by engaging in FTF interactions than those who place a high value in information motivation, who are more likely to participate in EBC methods.

Approximately one-third of users use social media for the development of new relationships, with another 20% using social networking sites to maintain their existing friendships (Brandtzæg & Heim, 2009). Fourteen percent of the sample used social networking sites for socializing, part of which includes garnering social support when one is distressed. The categories of usage included those who use social networking for seeking information (10%), debating (6.5%), sending short messages (3%), passing time (3.5%), sharing content (3%), fun (2%), surfing profiles (1.5%), and contacting family (1%). These motivations for participation in social networking were classified into the U & G theory into four areas: information seeking, entertainment, social interactions, and personal identity (Brandtzæg & Heim, 2009). Further, the type of social networking user can be classified into one of four types: Sporadics (using it sporadically), Lurkers (using social networks but not interacting with people), Socializers (those who socialize with others), Debaters (those who debate with others), and Advanced users (those who use electronic networks for a variety of reasons; Brandtzæg, 2010).

Some of the differences in usage of social networking are dependent on gender. Women's attitude of social networking is dependent on their self-esteem and need to belong. According to Brandtzæg (2012),

> SNS usage seems to be a much more important tool for socializing among females in comparison to males; therefore, being outside SNSs may have a socially excluding effect on females but not on males. According to a large-scale adoption study in the US, females are more likely to use SNSs than their male counterparts (Hargittai, 2007). This gender skew is also confirmed in this study: females use SNSs more frequently and interact more socially than males. (p. 483)

For men, the only variable affecting this particular attitude toward social networking sites was the efficacy regarding Internet usage (Gangadharbatla, 2009). Women also seem to consider communication over e-mail as having a higher degree of social presence than men (Gefen & Straub, 1997).

Once a relationship is established, however, more specific usages emerge with regard to interactions with the primary partner. Most commonly, partners use computer-mediated technology in relationships to express affection (Coyne, Stockdale, Busby, Iverson, & Grant, 2011). Others use technology for discussing serious issues (25%). Relatedly, another 6% use technology to introduce an issue that might be confrontational into the relationship. Three percent of people indicated using new media to hurt their partner (something women were more likely to do than men) and a bit more (12%) used new media to apologize to their partner. Women were also more likely to engage in interactions with other people at the same time as they were communicating with their partner over new media (Coyne et al., 2011).

The motivation for usage also has implications for relationships. Couples who have at least one partner who is a heavy user and, therefore, more motivated by social interactions, may experience a problem that is self-reinforcing. The more time the heavy user spends online, for example, the greater the chances are that the user will interact with others outside of the relationship, thus resulting in more opportunities for interactions, both appropriate and inappropriate. As one's context for relating with others moves more online than offline, one may find oneself spending increasing amounts of time online than offline to interact with people. According to Stafford (2008), "the more you learn about the Internet, the more you use it, and the more you find to use it for" (p. 14). In cases where heavy users may be paired with light users, the motivations for computer usage will remain a mystery to one who does not use the computer as often and/or who uses the computer differently. It may be difficult for partners to understand the difference in motivation. This was true for Connie and Dave. As a person who worked in the website services field, Connie found herself a heavy Internet user. As a result, she became more knowledgeable about various websites and interactional tools. The difference in knowledge level created an issue between the pair because Dave was suspicious about Connie's online interactions but was not knowledgeable enough about the computer himself to be able to be reassured, thus fueling his suspicions and leaving him feeling as if he could not meet his partner's needs.

Other theorists have applied a social-cognitive lens to describing Internet usage (LaRose, Mastro, & Eastin, 2001). Based on Bandura's work, a social-cognitive lens articulates the relationship between people and their environments and, moreover, posits that interactions with new media influence what new media promotes. Consequently, these interactions influence what the media puts forth and reforms expectations about what is received. One of the key concepts within this paradigm is the concept of enactive learning. This means people understand rules about particular environments without actually playing a role in the environment other than as an observer. This concept applies directly to online behavior as Internet users can develop an understanding of online rules without necessarily participating in the specific online behavior (LaRose et al., 2001). Some of these rules may affect online socialization and can result in a questioning of motivation when the rules developed for Internet interactions differ from the interactions and rules in the couple's offline relationship. For example, one of the rules on social networking sites such as Facebook may be to post photos of oneself as a profile picture, regardless of one's family or relationship status. In the case of Darius and Cherelle, a dating couple in their 20s, conflict emerged when Darius posted a picture of himself on a social media site instead of a picture of he and Cherelle, an unexpressed rule about which Cherelle felt strongly but had never communicated to Darius. As a result, Darius's anger to the unexpressed (and seemingly unilateral) rule Cherelle iterated was defensiveness, thus reinforcing Cherelle's belief that she had a solid rationale for generating this particular rule. Through discussion it emerged that the issue at the core of the rule was Cherelle's belief that Darius's placement of photos of only himself as profile pictures was motivated by an intention to portray himself as single. Similar motivations may also be ascribed to situations where one member of a couple posts photos that are physically revealing.

Motivations Toward Participation in Synchronous Versus Asynchronous Communication

Another key concept related to motivation is incentives and Internet behavior. People perform a behavior because they will receive a certain outcome from it (LaRose et al., 2001). For many, the incentives gained from participation in online coupling (such as ease of expression, protection of being vulnerable) are not necessarily obvious but still powerful. In fact, both the synchronous and asynchronous nature of interactive communicative technologies adds particular incentives to online communication and couple relationships. Synchronous communication is communication occurring at the same time—for example, chat rooms, text messaging, and other interactions conducted simultaneously. Asynchronous communications refer to communication occurring over time, such as e-mail or instant messages not received immediately by the intended recipient. Synchronous communication has a built-in incentive of immediate response. Inquiries about one's whereabouts, activities, and directives can be effectively transmitted instantly.

Research in the field of education suggests a key incentive in the usage of asynchronous communication is the ability to be more thoughtful about one's message; having a chance to correspond at greater levels of depth (with the receiver focusing more on the message than the presenter (Ocker & Yaverbaum, 1999). Further, those with a tendency to be shy may find more comfort in and be more motivated to participate in asynchronous than synchronous communicative methods (Bures, Amundsen, & Abrami, 2002), so those uncomfortable in larger social surroundings may be drawn to forms of asynchronous communication and may communicate at a deeper level than those opting for synchronous communication. This was certainly true for Donte, a 35-year-old Italian American man, and Marisa, a 30-year-old Indonesian American woman. Donte had initiated contact with Marisa through exchanging e-mails in a work context, and over the course of several months they pursued a relationship with one another outside of the work environment. One of the qualities Marisa stated initially drew her to Donte was his ability to be genuine, open, and emotionally expressive in ways she had not encountered with other men, particularly those sharing her cultural background. The two began to travel to one another's residences to spend weekends together and it was during this time Marisa found herself with someone who did not appear to have the same level of self-confidence as the person with whom she had communicated over e-mail. For Marisa, Donte's more subdued personality in real time (synchronous communication) seemed to contradict the confidence he displayed online in asynchronous methods. Marisa eventually came to the conclusion Donte was far more comfortable behind a computer or screen than he was in real time, and presented different challenges for them as a couple in their negotiations about how to spend time together.

Those who are motivated to participate in asynchronous situations, however, also have to come to a decision about the rules of engagement, namely, frequency and timing of messages (Ocker & Yaverbaum, 1999). Confusion around this issue may prevent couples from moving forward. For example, Issunboushi, a Japanese American man, was in therapy to address his pattern of selecting partners who he believed to be inappropriate because they were "out of his league." Over the course of counseling, he reported he had developed a romantic interest with another professional in a similar business. As their electronic interactions via e-mail (a predominately asynchronous method) shifted from a heavier work emphasis to a more personal one, Issunboushi was vigilant about the number of e-mails and timing of their correspondence. Over time, however, he noticed a decrease in the frequency and timing of his e-mails. This left Issunboushi in a quandary: whether to interpret his companion's shift in communication as evidence of a shift in feelings toward him (and consequently the definition of the relationship) or whether to attribute the changes to adjustments in his schedule and availability. The crux of the issue for Issunboushi was that since there were no rules around the communication, Issunboushi had pronounced difficulty in interpreting the message and constructing a response.

Other research in the field of education can be extrapolated to apply to interpersonal relationships. Much of the literature suggests the ability to process information presented through interactive communicative technology is dependent on the type of communication used. Synchronous communication may be more natural, but this style of communication may be more difficult to process because immediate responses are required to keep the conversation going. On the other hand, asynchronous communication may feel less natural and more purposive, but may be easier to process in some ways because there is little need to respond immediately (Hrastinski, 2008). Several studies have compared both modalities of communication in educational settings (see Hrastinski, 2008, for a complete analysis of studies) and, taken together, reveal a few important trends. First, many of the members who participated in online learning in synchronous chat formats had a greater sense of connection and social support with one another as compared to those who participated in asynchronous e-learning methods. Second, participation in asynchronous communication methods may be better when the focus of the communication is task-oriented. Third, asynchronous communication may be difficult to start when there are fewer people involved in the potential interaction; likewise, people interact more frequently when the communication method is synchronous (Hrastinski, 2008).

The differences described above have direct implications for couples, both positive and negative. In cases where the communication is problematic, it is often the case synchronous and asynchronous types of communication are used inappropriately—that is, couples use asynchronous communication for synchronous communication or use synchronous communication in times when asynchronous communication would be more fitting. This application is supported by research examining couple's conflict resolution strategies in computer-mediated versus FTF communication. From a sample of 47 couples, there seemed to be little difference in the satisfaction level of resolving a conflict through a computer versus FTF. The participant's own responses indicated the use of computer-mediated communication was effective because there were fewer nonverbal distractions. In other words, there was little way to become angry at one's tone or facial expressions because there were none. Another benefit cited by participants was the asynchronous communication allowed for someone to not respond in the heat of the moment (Perry & Werner-Wilson, 2011).

A clear example of this is demonstrated in Shana and Max, who sought treatment to address their constant fighting. As a professional couple, they both worked from 7 a.m. to 5 p.m. In addition, Max often had clients with whom he had to meet after working hours. As a result of these schedules, the couple often relied on text messages to communicate with one another during the day. While many of their interactions using text messaging were benign, some messages were intended to ostensibly resolve (but actually resulted in continuing) the conflict under question. In one instance, Shana showed the therapist her phone detailing the text message conversation attempting to resolve an argument between she and Max from earlier that day. Shana began the interaction by messaging Max she was upset by Max's attitude toward her, such as the way he spoke to her in front of his colleague. She then provided him directives specifically on what he should have said differently.

Despite her attempt to resolve the conflict by providing directives, Shana's tone in the text was clearly one of anger; her message could easily be characterized as critical in tone due to its word choice, symbols, and terse sentences, in that text messages generally tend to be abbreviated. Consequently, Max's text response to Shana's message was swift and angry. It blamed her for maintaining the problem in the relationship and seemed to respond more to her tone than to the content. In this event, Shana was attempting to resolve the problem synchronously through a text message characterized by brevity and a short directive leveled at Max. As a result, Max responded in a typical synchronous way—accusing Shana of not being empathetic or supportive rather than discussing the initial problem she introduced.

The bottom line is motivation for participation in synchronous versus asynchronous activities should be based on the couples' primary goal of the communication. If the goal of the communication is to transmit information, asynchronous communication may be sufficient. In the case of Max and Shana, for example, therapists could work with the couple to develop strategies for the use of text messaging to process an argument. This might mean the couple is not allowed to text message to resolve a disagreement unless there is agreement as to the nature and purpose of texting. If it was Shana's goal to use texting as a way to process the problem with Max, for example, it might be best if the couple can implement a rule prohibiting the receiver from responding immediately, thus allowing for time to process the complexities of the issue at hand (asynchronous).

If the goal of the communication is to have couples experience a satisfying intimate and collaborative interaction, FTF communication may be better (Ocker & Yaverbaum, 1999). For example, if it were the case that Shana was requesting support and desired a sense of connection with Max, it would make more sense for the couple to develop a rule around using text messaging as synchronous communication, with each recognizing the goal is to provide connection rather than to resolve a concern. Therapists may find using text messages in relationships to resolve communication difficulties can be exceedingly helpful if there are guidelines that can accompany the interaction. Ocker and Yaverbaum (1999) outline strategies for how to increase the satisfaction and sense of collaboration in computer-mediated communication. Among these are (a) educating those using the services on the benefits of each type of communication, (b) providing education on how to use the programs correctly, and (c) increasing exposure to these types of communication. In its application to couples, some activities a therapist may present might include some of these strategies. For example, therapists can describe the differences between synchronous and asynchronous communication among couples to help them to make an informed decision around how they want to design the use of technology in their relationship.

Another part of the conversation has to be the practicality of when to use which strategy. Debbie, a 28-year-old writer, and Nedka, a 39-year-old advertising executive, came to therapy. Debbie indicated she often felt ignored by Nedka during the workday, which resulted in her calling Nedka repeatedly during the day to get the time and attention she felt she deserved. Yet according to Nedka, the demands of her position did not leave her available to take Debbie's calls, and if she was able to take them, she was not generally located in a physical location to be able to conduct the kind of conversation Debbie wanted to have. Part of therapy helped the couple to have appropriate expectations around when Nedka would be able to talk, but also to heighten Nedka's awareness of Debbie's need for communication throughout the day. Further, couples should be aware of the circumstances when asynchronous communication would serve their relationship better than synchronous communication, and vice versa. For example, in times where Debbie desires social support and connection, Nedka should be aware of the need and identify times where communication could be synchronous.

Perceived Versus Actual Motivations

For many couples, the motivations to participate in interactive communicative technologies are well understood by their partner. For example, one may participate in online gaming for personal enjoyment and connection with distant friends and family members, an arrangement clearly understood by one's partner. Other motivations for posting of certain information online or in social networking contexts may be interpreted as entertainment, a show of support, or as information seeking. Yet there are also some circumstances in which motivations to participate in interactive communication technologies are not well understood (resulting from divergent assumptions about an individual's motivations) or may not be sanctioned by the relationship. Other motivations for interactive communication with others include entertainment and enjoyment (Hsu & Lu, 2007), curiosity, emotional support, romance, escape, social compensation, love, and sex (Wang & Chang, 2010). Yet some couple relationship contracts do not include the computer to be used in this way (a) if it takes significant time away from the attention to the primary relationship, and/or (b) if the entertainment, support, and social compensation are with others outside of the relationship who may threaten the relational intimacy.

In many cases, people's evaluation of their partner's online behavior is inaccurate: One partner may ascribe the other partner's online behavior as stemming from a need for social compensation or love when in actuality it may originate from a need for platonic emotional support. Some of the challenges associated with making accurate interpretations regarding one's motivation for engagement in interactive communicative technologies are the motivation varies depending on the theory and context (Yoo, 2010). Separate studies have been conducted on the motivations for participation in social networking (Kim, Shim, & Ahn, 2011), which differs in some ways from general Internet usage. Park, Jin, and Jin (2011), for example, proposed a model for explaining the interaction between motivational factors and self-disclosure on intimacy over Facebook. Part of their findings included information on what elements of intimacy, both in its online and offline formats, apply specifically to Facebook. One of the main differences may be in the need for affiliation—the authors proposed the need for affiliation inspires people to disclose more. Previous research has found self-disclosure occurs online more quickly; it would thus appear to follow the need for affiliation would inspire greater self-disclosures in an online social networking context such as Facebook, thus inspiring greater degrees of intimacy. The results, however, did not support the need for affiliation in Facebook users as directly contributing to intimacy.

Despite the lack of evidence for the need for affiliation relating directly to intimacy development on Facebook or related social networking sites, many couples view their partner's interactions on Facebook as demonstrating a need for affiliation from people other than the primary partner. This is an example of one of the two key misattributions couples make in regard to motivation and in each case, the perceived motivation can be quite distinct from the actual motivations. First, as in the example above, one partner may ascribe the incorrect motivations (need for affiliation) to their partner's interactions (behavior on Facebook). In many cases, the same evidence is provided to support each partner's discrepant perception of motivations. Some of these reasons may be due to the associations online: "If greater attractiveness is perceived for males who misbehave, confirmatory and rewarding reactions by others might reinforce such behaviors or set observational learning dynamics into play encouraging others to behave in a similar manner" (Walther, Van der Heide, Kim, Westerman, & Tong, 2008, p. 45). For example, Robin believed Chuck's motivation to use his Facebook account was to get positive feedback about his looks from online female friends since it was the very same motivation driving his peers. This issue evolved into two conflicts for the couple: an issue about the rules of Facebook, and another issue regarding the appropriateness of friends. Second, in cases where there is little discrepancy on the differences in motivation, partners may disagree about the extent a particular motivating factor contributes to the behavior. Jimmy and Bianca came to session divided about the appropriateness of Jimmy's online behavior. Bianca stated she was upset about Jimmy communicating with his friends online, particularly as Bianca viewed his behavior as stemming from a lack of desire to build up a solid relationship with her. In short, she thought he spent more time with his online friends than her, and believed this was the result of being "bored" with their home life.

Finally, couples may misattribute motivations because they lack an ability to conceptualize the complexity of the multiplicity of motivations. One motivation may be accurate in describing a piece of the puzzle, but generally the behavior is underwritten by a complex interplay of personal, relational, and environmental motivators. Another example is in the case of online gaming. Escapism may be one reason people participate in online gaming (Kwon, Chung, & Lee, 2011), yet this reason may be one of many (socialization, enjoyment, stress relief, etc.). Yet escapism may be the only reason acknowledged by the partner. Therefore, directives to stop the behavior are often met with resistance because the cause of the behavior is not as simple as a lone motivating factor. Conflict, then, emerges as each member of the couple tries to convince the other to adopt his or her perspective of the motivator.

Characteristics of Those Meeting and Relating Online

Demographic Characteristics

Previous literature in the field of information systems and computer usage sought to identify the "who," "what," and "when" of computer and Internet usage. The statistics of who participates in online dating varies slightly from study to study. A number of studies have discovered a significant proportion of individuals using online dating services are within the 40-year range (Valkenburg & Peter, 2009), though the age range of who participates in online dating may depend on the region in which one lives (Hitsch, Hortacsu, & Ariely, 2005). The majority of those who participate in online dating report they are single. Approximately one-quarter to one-third of users is divorced. In the United States, those who use online dating services tend to mirror the characteristics of Internet users in general insomuch as they are more highly educated with higher incomes (Hitsch et al., 2005; Valkenburg & Peter, 2009). Relatedly, those who perform more tasks on the Internet are more likely to participate in online dating, suggesting one's comfort with Internet technologies leads into usage of other Internet technologies (Kang & Hoffman, 2011). Gender might also have some effect on participation in online dating. Female initiators of FTF dating may feel less secure and confident, but express more compassion and cooperation. Men, on the other hand, feel more confident but less cooperation and compassion (Gutkin, Pinho, Robinson, & Curtis, 2010). Men also are more likely than women to browse profiles or potential partners and send messages to potential partners—for example, 19% of women using online dating services never received a first contact e-mail from a man where such was true for 54% of men (Hitsch et al., 2005).

Socioemotional Characteristics

Barraket and Henry-Waring (2008) note the increase in the literature regarding the psychological and sociological variables affecting online interactions. For example, Birnie and Horvath (2006) explored psychological predictors of interacting with others online and found people who have a tendency to participate in more intimate communications offline are more likely to participate in interactions characterized by intimacy online. Another finding is people who are better writers are better at online relationship formation (Baker, 2008). Kang and Hoffman (2011) indicated people who generally trust people are less likely to participate in online dating because of the inability to authenticate the information shared with them. Further, social changes in life correlate with the resurgence of online dating, including an increase in single-parent households, more demand in the workplace, and increased sensitivity in the workplace for sexual harassment claims (Barraket & Henry-Waring, 2008).

Another topic of investigation is how these sociological attributes influence one's participation in online dating. Consistent with the theory posed by Bures et al. (2000), Valkenburg and Peter (2009) cited the social compensation theory and posited individuals with higher levels of anxiety are more likely to participate in online dating because of the ease of accessibility. Though not explicitly tied to the accessibility of the Internet, other research has also cited the association between one's usage of the Internet for dating or relating purposes and their level of general anxiety. One rationale for this is those who are shyer or socially anxious may feel they have greater control over an asynchronous environment, or an environment where they control what other people observe about them (Scharlott & Christ, 1995). In fact, it is also well documented the need for escapism is one reason factoring into one's decision to participate in online activities (Wang & Chang, 2010). This notion is also supported by research in online gaming (Koo, 2009) as well as the generic literature on computer usage in general (Korgaonkar & Wolin, 1999).

One study shedding some light into the complexity of this issue was performed by Birnie and Horvath (2006). They found shyness seems to be related to people's using the Internet to connect with others socially, though they selected more anonymous mechanisms though which to interact with others. In this way, research by McKenna et al. (2002) and Morahan-Martin and Schumacher (2003) is consistent with this finding as shy people do seem to use the Internet for relationship formation; shy people, however, tend not to utilize channels that may promote more intimacy. More recent research conducted by Brandtzæg (2012) found men who use social networking sites experience greater degrees of loneliness than men who do not use such sites. On the other hand, at least one other research study has found that those with higher levels of anxiety or loneliness do not necessarily contribute to ones' use of the computer as a tool for engaging in online relationships (Bonebrake, 2002). One of the proposed explanations is that the Internet allows for users to find specialized groups with similar interests easier.

Valkenburg and Peter (2009) also cited an alternative hypothesis, the "rich-get-richer" hypothesis, which posits those highly adept at dating use the Internet as another avenue in which to experience success. Their results in a Dutch sample supported the "rich-get-richer" hypotheses—that is, people with low levels of anxiety around dating are the ones who are more likely to be on dating websites.

Kang and Hoffman (2011) indicated individuals who generally trust others are less likely to participate in online dating. This finding could be explained by the predominant belief that those who participate in online dating may have something to hide and therefore cannot be trusted. Identifying who can be trusted in online dating situations may be achieved through a warranting process (Gibbs, Ellison, & Lai, 2011). Warranting refers to how people check to ensure the personal identify information provided to them from other Internet users is verifiable. In this process, Internet users generally will search for information about the person with whom they are communicating in other venues (such as by third parties who do not manipulate the information) to corroborate the information received (Gibbs et al., 2011). This may be one of the first blocks a new couple has to navigate within their relationship. After the initial interaction, each individual has to determine to what extent one will assess the accuracy of one's partner's self-presentation. In other words, does one test the accuracy of the information prior to a relationship developing further, or does one make a decision about whether to pursue that after a series of interactions?

Another issue is control. The Internet provides ways people can control action in the relationship, particularly if the interactions are conducted asynchronously. According to Barraket and Henry-Waring (2008),

> A high level of personal control over the pace and nature of electronically mediated communication has been identified as a distinguishing feature of relationships initiated online (Ben-Ze'ev, 2004; Hardey, 2002; McCown et al., 2001; Van Acker, 2001), which produces new norms of interaction. The level of perceived control available to online dating users was identified as a significant benefit of this form of dating by the majority of participants in our study. While our respondents clearly identified this sense of agency as a benefit of the medium, many of them described feeling a heightened sense of vulnerability as they became the subject of others' exercise of personal control in online interactions. (p. 159)

The other facet of online dating is when people are in control of searching for a romantic partner they are able to connect and expose themselves to networks they would not normally connect to. This exposure to other groups is purposeful, as one wants to widen one's connections to the most number of people possible (Barraket & Henry-Waring, 2008). This notion is further supported by research findings indicating a primary reason for social networking usage is to meet new people (Brandtzæg & Heim, 2009).

Types of Online Relationships

Part of the issue for motivation toward participating in electronic romantic relationships is there may be certain motivations corresponding with certain classifications of relationship types. Over 1/3 of people who participate in online dating are seeking a long-term relationship (39%; Hitsch et al., 2005). Three main types of online relationships exist: virtual, developmental, and maintenance (Griffiths, 2001). The virtual online relationship refers to those relationships where the couple who communicates online keeps their relationship in the virtual plane—in other words, they do not meet. These relationships are generally not long term but may involve a wide variety of behaviors from casual communication to sharing sexually explicit messages. Developmental online relationships are those relationships beginning online with the intention of moving offline at some point in the future. These relationships are characterized by the exchange of emotional interactions with one another, which develops a lasting and meaningful relationship. Finally, maintenance relationships are those beginning offline and shift to online as a way to maintain the relationship (Griffiths, 2001).

The different couple typologies have varied clinical implications for relating. For example, couples in the maintenance typology would be the type who did not necessarily have to go through the warranting process since the initial interaction is offline. Likewise, the couples who meet online and never have to move the relationship offline, as in the virtual relationship, may participate in more risky behavior since there is limited chance they will have an actual physical encounter. The middle group, those who met online and transitioned to an offline relationship, may have already developed the skills to be able to use technology to advance their relationship, potentially in ways similar to those used at the beginning of the relationship.

Predictors of Satisfaction in Online Relationships

There are several areas which contribute to overall intimate relationship satisfaction: intimacy, agreement, independence, and sexuality (Hassebrauck & Fehr, 2002). Of these, intimacy was rated highest and sexuality rated the lowest of the four. Qualities associated with relationship satisfaction on which people place the least importance include harmony-seeking, similarity in goals, and whether there were few conflicts (Hassebrauck & Fehr, 2002). This also makes sense within the context of computers, as it is hard to assess for harmony when two people are having a typed exchange. Further, information exchanged online between two parties is more likely to reflect disclosures rather than goal setting.

Some of these areas associated with relationship satisfaction in offline relationships may also predict satisfaction with online relationships (Anderson & Emmers-Sommer, 2006). These include intimacy (Hian, Chuan, Trevor, & Detenber, 2004; Walther, 1996), trust (Hardey, 2004; Henderson & Gilding, 2004; Feng, Lazar, & Preece, 2004) and communication satisfaction (Emmers-Sommer, 2004). One of the explanations for this finding was that intimacy and trust tend to be linked together. For example, in online interactions in a networked work setting, people are expected to have the same access to private data and to maintain the integrity of the data. In order to accomplish this, those who work together have to operate from an assumption of being able to trust one another (Feng, Lazar, & Preece, 2004). This is in spite of Rumbough's (2001) finding that nearly 1/3 of chatroom users fictionalize who they are online.

Though not supported by empirical data, other authors have suggested that there are three other variables that contribute to relational satisfaction in online relationships. Similarity (Barnes, 2003), for example, connects people together because of the vast array of groups and communities provided by the Internet. Additionally, empathy and liking appear to be important variables to the establishment of trust, both in online and offline scenarios (Feng, Lazar, & Preece, 2004). Commitment is another factor thought to be related to the enhancement of intimacy and the experience of a greater degree of relationship satisfaction (Parks & Floyd, 1996). Because online interactions are characterized by greater degrees of self-disclosure, each partner, upon learning of other's details, may experience themselves as being bound to other because of the sharing of that information, thus experiencing a higher level of commitment. Finally, attributional satisfaction and uncertainty reduction processes may also be key components to online relationship satisfaction (Anderson & Emmers-Sommer, 2006; Pratt, Wiseman, Cody, & Wendt, 1999). In other words, the more we can remove feelings of ambiguity and uncertainty and the more we can predict someone's behavior, the greater the likelihood that we will feel close and connected to them and that our relationship is on solid ground. In online interactions and with technology in our relationships, we have the ability to cross-reference what others say about us as well as retain records of conversations as a way to enhance our prediction abilities, thus resulting in more satisfaction.

Phases of Online Dating

Whitty (2009) outlines phases of online dating by drawing from her previous research on phases in offline dating. Givens (as cited in Whitty & Joinson, 2009) outlines five phases of dating not specific to the Internet: attention, recognition, interaction, sexual arousal, and resolution. These steps have been adapted by Abuvia and Adelman and are specific to matchmaking but have some overlap with Givens' stages. Yet, according to Whitty and Joinson (2009), "Internet dating does seem to include the three phases highlighted by Abuvia and Adelman. However, these phases do not necessarily neatly fit into the sequential order they propose" (p. 281). Whitty and Joinson's stages include attention, recognition, interaction, FTF meeting, and resolution. In the attention phase, those who want to meet people offline take great care to construct a personal profile that will be attractive to the population of interest (Whitty & Joinson, 2009). The development of an appropriate personal profile (complete with photo) is critical in relationships originating on the Internet. Research focused on heterosexual couples has demonstrated that women are more likely to respond to men who have what they consider "attractive" profiles, whereas men tend to write more detailed introductory and grammatically correct e-mails to women who they consider attractive than those they consider less attractive (Guéguen, Lourel, Charron, Fischer-Lokou, & Lamy, 2009). Additionally, those who have more attractive photos are considered having more attractive self-descriptions (Brand, Bonatsos, D'Orazio, & DeShong, 2012).

Recognition in the context of online dating can take many forms (Whitty & Joinson, 2009). Some types of recognition can include winking at someone's profile, "poking" someone, or having someone view your profile. Some of these recognition strategies also apply to online social networking. For example, Facebook allows one to "poke" someone or "like" their comment, a form of recognition that does not require a complicated interaction, but does provide acknowledgement of the relationship.

The interaction phase can take many forms, and some of this may depend on the gender of the individual initiating the interaction (Whitty, 2004). Because of the numerous ways people can interact online (e-mails, instant message, etc.), this phase may encompass a broad range of activities over a short duration of time before the couple moves into the FTF meeting phase. Many online daters believe the FTF meeting is part of the screening process and may occur in a public place due to the anonymity of who is on the other end of the computer (Whitty & Joinson, 2009). In the resolution phase, the couples will make a determination as to whether to continue to see one another while potentially vetting other online options.

Another perspective on the development of electronic dating relationships is provided by Romm-Livermore and Somers (2009), with different paths for men and women. The main stages in heterosexual relationships include: "(a) constructing a profile, (b) searching, (c) initiating communication, (d) receiving communication, (e) setting FTF dates, (f) conducting dates, and (g) concluding the e-dating process" (p. 305). Men generally initiate the interactions, will do so earlier than women, and will put forth more energy and time. Women will receive significantly more winks, e-mails, and hits on their profiles than men.

References

Adams, R., & Stevenson, M. (2004). A lifetime of relationships mediated by technology. In F. Lang & K. Fingerman (Eds.), *Growing together: Personal relationships across the life span* (pp. 368–393). New York: Cambridge University Press.

Anderson, N. (2007). Video gaming to be twice as big as music by 2011. Retrieved March 20, 2011 from: http://arstechnica.com/gaming/news/2007/08/gaming-to-surge-50-percent-in-four-years-possibly.ars

Anderson, T. L., & Emmers-Sommer, T. M. (2006). Predictors of relationship satisfaction in online romantic relationships. *Communication Studies, 57*(2), 153-172.

Baker, A. (2008). Down the rabbit hole: The role of place in the initiation and development of online relationships. In A. Barak (Ed.), *Psychological aspects of cyberspace: Theory, research, applications* (pp. 163–184). Cambridge, England: Cambridge University Press.

Barnes, S. (2003). *Computer-mediated communication: Human-to-human communication across the Internet.* Boston: Allyn & Bacon.

Barnett, J. K., & Youngberg, C. (2004). Forgiveness as a ritual in couples therapy. *The Family Journal, 12*(1), 14–20. doi:10.1177/1066480703258613

Barraket, J., & Henry-Waring, M. S. (2008). Getting it on (line): Sociological perspectives on e-dating. *Journal of Sociology, 44*(2), 149–165. doi:10.1177/1440783308089167

Ben-Ze'ev, A. (2004). *Love online: Emotions on the Internet.* New York: Cambridge University Press.

Berg-Cross, L., Daniels, C., & Carr, P. (1993). Marital rituals among divorced and married couples. *Journal of Divorce & Remarriage, 18*(1–2), 1–30. doi:10.1300/J087v18n01_01

Birnie, S. A., & Horvath, P. (2006). Psychological predictors of Internet social communication. *Journal of Computer-Mediated Communication, 7*(4), 0. doi:10.1111/j.1083-6101.2002.tb00154.x

Bonebrake, K. (2002). College students' Internet use, relationship formation, and personality correlates. *CyberPsychology & Behavior, 5*(6), 551–557. doi:10.1089/109493102321018196.

Brand, R. J., Bonatsos, A., D'Orazio, R., & DeShong, H. (2012). What is beautiful is good, even online: Correlations between photo attractiveness and text attractiveness in men's online dating profiles. *Computers in Human Behavior, 28*(1), 166–170. doi:10.1016/j.chb.2011.08.023

Brandtzæg, P. B. (2010). Towards a unified Media-User Typology (MUT): A meta-analysis and review of the research literature on media-user typologies. *Computers in Human Behavior, 26*(4), 940–956. doi:10.1016/j.chb.2010.02.008

Brandtzæg, P. B. (2012). Social networking sites: Their users and social implications—a longitudinal study. *Journal of Computer-Mediated Communication, 17*(4), 467–488. doi:10.1111/j.1083-6101.2012.01580.x

Brandtzæg, P. B., & Heim, J. (2009). Why people use social networking sites. *Online Communities and Social Computing, II,* 143–152. doi:10.1007/978-3-642-02774–1_16

Bruess, C. J. S., & Pearson, J. C. (1997). Interpersonal rituals in marriage and adult friendship. *Communication Monographs, 64*(1), 25–46. doi:10.1080/03637759709376403

Bruess, J. S. C., & Pearson, C. J. (2002). The function of mundane ritualizing in adult friendship and marriage. *Communication Research Reports, 19*(4), 314–326. doi:10.1080/08824090209384860

Bures, E. M., Amundsen, C. C., & Abrami, P. C. (2002). Motivation to learn via computer conferencing: Exploring how task-specific motivation and CC expectations are related to student acceptance of learning via CC. *Journal of Educational Computing Research, 27*(3), 249–264. doi:10.2190/R4WG-88TJ-C3VF-YQJ0

Campbell, K., Silva, L. C., & Wright, D. W. (2011). Rituals in unmarried couple relationships: An exploratory study. *Family and Consumer Sciences Research Journal, 40*(1), 45–57. doi:10.1111/j.1552-3934.2011.02087.x

Coyne, S. M., Stockdale, L., Busby, D., Iverson, B., & Grant, D. M. (2011). "I luv U :)!": A descriptive study of the media use of individuals in romantic relationships. *Family Relations, 60*(2), 150–162. doi:10.1111/j.1741-3729.2010.00639.x

Crespo, C., Davide, I. N., Costa, M. E., & Fletcher, G. J. O. (2008). Family rituals in married couples: Links with attachment, relationship quality, and closeness. *Personal Relationships, 15*(2), 191–203. doi: 10.1111/j.1475-6811.2008.00193.x

Donn, J. E., & Sherman, R. C. (2002). Attitudes and practices regarding the formation of romantic relationships on the Internet. *CyberPsychology Behavior, 5*(2), 107–123. doi:10.1089/109493102753770499

Emmers-Sommer, T. M. (2004). The effect of communication quality and quantity indicators on intimacy and relational satisfaction. *Journal of Social and Personal Relationships, 21,* 399–411.

Feng, J. F., Lazar, J., & Preece, J. (2004). Empathy and online interpersonal trust: A fragile relationship. *Behavior & Information Technology, 23,* 97–106.

Gangadharbatla, H. (2009). Individual differences in social networking site adoption. In C. Romm-Livermore & K. Setzekorn (Eds.), *Social networking communities and e–dating services: Concepts and implications* (pp. 1–17). Hershey, NY: Information Science Reference.

Gefen, D., & Straub, D. W. (1997). Gender differences in the perception and use of email: An extension to the technology acceptance model. *MIS Quarterly, 21*(4), 389–400. doi:10.2307/249720

Gibbs, J. L., Ellison, N. B., & Lai, C. (2011). First comes love, then comes Google: An investigation of uncertainty reduction strategies and self-disclosure in online dating. *Communication Research, 38*(1), 70–100. doi:10.1177/0093650210377091

Griffiths, M. (2001). Sex on the Internet: Observations and implications for Internet sex addiction. *Journal of Sex Research, 38*(4), 333–342. doi:10.1080/00224490109552104

Guéguen, N., Lourel, M., Charron, C., Fischer-Lokou, J., & Lamy, L. (2009). A web replication of Snyder, Decker, and Bersheid's (1977) experiment on the self-fulfilling nature of social stereotypes. *Journal of Social Psychology, 149*(5), 600–602. doi:10.1080/00224540903238503

Gutkin, R., Pinho, S. T., Robinson, P., & Curtis, P. T. (2010). On the transition from shear-driven fibre compressive failure to fibre kinking in notched CFRP laminates under longitudinal compression. *Composites Science and Technology, 70*(8), 1223–1231. doi:10.1016/j.compscietch.2010.03.010

Hall, J. A., Park, N., Song, H., & Cody, M. J. (2010). Strategic misrepresentation in online dating: The effects of gender, self-monitoring, and personality traits. *Journal of Social & Personal Relationships, 27*(1), 117–135. doi:10.1177/0265407509349633

Hardey, M. (2002). Life beyond the screen: Embodiment and identity through the Internet. *Sociological Review, 50*(4), 570–585. doi:10.1111/1467-954X.00399

Hardey, M. (2004). Mediated relationships. *Information Communication & Society, 7,* 207–222.

Hassebrauck, M. & Fehr, B. (2002). Dimensions of relationship quality. *Personal Relationships, 9,* 253–270.

Heino, R. D., Ellison, N. B., & Gibbs, J. L. (2010). Relationshopping: Investigating the market metaphor in online dating. *Journal of Social and Personal Relationships, 27*(4), 427–447.

Henderson, S. & Gilding, M. (2004). "I've never clicked this much with anyone in my life": Trust and hyperpersonal communication in online friendships. *New Media & Society, 6,* 487–506.

Hertlein, K. M., & Nelson, T. (2006, October). Designing an Internet infidelity treatment framework. Workshop presentation at the annual meeting of the American Association for Marriage and Family Therapy Conference, Austin, TX.

Hertlein, K. M., & Piercy, F. P. (2012). Essential elements of Internet infidelity treatment. *Journal of Marital and Family Therapy, 38*(1), 257–270. doi:10.1111/j.17520606.2011.00275.x.

Hertlein, K. M., & Webster, M. (2008). Technology, relationships, and problems: A research synthesis. *Journal of Marital and Family Therapy, 34*(4), 445–460. doi:10.1111/j.1752-0606.2008.00087.x

Hian, L. B., Chuan, S. L., Trevor, T. M. K., & Detenber, B. H. (2004). Getting to know you: Exploring the development of relational intimacy in computer-mediated communication. *Journal of Computer-Mediated Communication, 9*(3).

Hitsch, G., Hortacsu, A., & Ariely, D. (2005, January). What makes you click: An empirical analysis of online dating. In *2005 Meeting Papers* (Vol. 207, pp. 1–51). St. Louis, MO: Society for Economic Dynamics.

Houran, J., Lange, R., Rentfrow, P. J., & Bruckner, K. H. (2004). Do online matchmaking tests work? An assessment of preliminary evidence for a publicized "predictive model of marital success." *North American Journal of Psychology*, 6(3), 507-526.

Hrastinski, S. (2008). The potential of synchronous communication to enhance participation in online discussions: A case study of two e-learning courses. *Information & Management, 45*(7), 499–506. doi:10.1016/j.im.2008.07.005

Hsu, C., & Lu, H. (2007). Consumer behavior in online game communities: A motivational factor perspective. *Computers in Human Behavior, 23*(3), 1642–1659. doi:10.1016/j.chb.2005.09.001

Kang, T., & Hoffman, L. H. (2011). Why would you decide to use an online dating site? Factors that lead to online dating. *Communication Research Reports, 28*(3), 205–213. doi:10.1080/08824096.2011.566109

Kim, J., Shim, J., & Ahn, K. (2011). Social networking service: Motivation, pleasure, and behavioral intention to use. *Journal of Computer Information Systems, 51*(4), 92–101.

Ko, H., Cho, C. H., & Roberts, M. S. (2005). Internet uses and gratifications: A structural equation model of interactive advertising. *Journal of Advertising, 34*(2), 57–70.

Koo, D. (2009). The moderating role of locus of control on the links between experiential motives and intention to play online games. *Computers in Human Behavior, 25*(2), 466–474. doi:10.1016/j.chb.2008.10.010

Korgaonkar, P. K., & Wolin, L. D. (1999). A multivariate analysis of web usage. *Journal of Advertising Research, 39*(2), 53–68.

Kwon, J., Chung, C., & Lee, J. (2011). The effects of escape from self and interpersonal relationship on the pathological use of Internet games. *Community Mental Health Journal, 47*(1), 113–121. doi:10.1007/s10597-009-9236-1

LaRose, R., Mastro, D., & Eastin, M. S. (2001). Understanding Internet usage. *Social Science Computer Review, 19*(4), 395–413 doi:10.1177/089443930101900401

Lin, N. (1999). Building a network theory of social capital. *Connections, 22*(1), 28–51.

McKenna, K. Y., Green, A., & Gleason, M. (2002). Relationship formation on the Internet: What's the big attraction? *Journal of Social Issues, 58*, 9–31.

Mesch, G. S. (2012). Minority status and the use of computer-mediated communication: A test of the social diversification hypothesis. *Communication Research, 39*(3), 317–337.

Mesch, G. S., & Talmud, I. (2010). *Wired youth: The social world of youth in the information age*. Oxford, UK: Routledge.

Moore, M. M. (2010). Human nonverbal courtship behavior—a brief historical review. *Journal of Sex Research, 47*(2/3), 171–180. doi:10.1080/00224490903402520

Morahan-Martin, J., & Schumacher, P. (2003). Loneliness and social uses of the Internet. *Computers in Human Behavior, 19*(6), 659–671. doi:10.1016/S0747-5632(03)00040-2

Ocker, R. J., & Yaverbaum, G. J. (1999). Asynchronous computer-mediated communication versus face-to-face collaboration: Results on student learning, quality and satisfaction. *Group Decision and Negotiation, 8*(5), 427–440. doi:10.1023/A:1008621827601

Olson, F. (1993). The development and impact of ritual in couple counseling. *Counseling and Values, 38*(1), 12–20. doi:10.1002/j.2161-007X.1993.tb00816.x

Papacharissi, Z., & Rubin, A. M. (2000). Predictors of Internet use. *Journal of Broadcasting & Electronic Media, 44*(2), 175–196. doi:10.1207/s15506878jobem4402_2

Park, N., Jin, B., & Jin, S. A. (2011). Effects of self-disclosure on relational intimacy in Facebook. *Computers in Human Behavior, 27*(5), 1974–1983. doi:10.1016/j.chb.2011.05.004

Parker, B. J., & Plank, R. E. (2000). A uses and gratifications perspective on the Internet as a new information source. *American Business Review, 18*(2), 43–49.

Parks, M. R. & Floyd, K. (1996). Making friends in cyberspace. *Journal of Communication, 46,* 80–97.

Peris, R., Gimeno, M. A., Pinazo, D., Ortet, G., Carrero, V., Sanchiz, M., & Ibanez, I. (2002). Online chat rooms: Virtual spaces of interaction for socially oriented people. *CyberPsychology & Behavior, 5*(1), 43–51.

Perry, M. S., & Werner-Wilson, R. J. (2011). Couples and computer-mediated communication: A closer look at the affordances and use of the channel. *Family and Consumer Sciences Research Journal, 40*(2), 120–134. doi:10.1111/j.1552-3934.2011.02099.x

Pratt, L., Wiseman, R. L., Cody, M. L., & Wendt, P. F. (1999). Interrogative strategies and information exchange in computer-mediated communication. *Communication Quarterly, 47*, 46–66

Romm-Livermore, C., & Somers, T. (2009). How e-daters behave online: Theory and empirical observations. In C. Romm Livermore & K. Setzekorn (Eds.), *Social networking communities and e-dating services: Concepts and implications* (pp. 292–313). Hershey, PA: Information Science Reference.

Roy, S. K. (2008). Determining the uses and gratifications for Indian users. *CS-BIGS, 2*(2), 78–91. Retrieved from http://www.bentley.edu/csbigs/vol2–1/roy.pdf

Rumbough, T. (2001). The development and maintenance of interpersonal relationships through computer-mediated communication. *Communication Research Reports, 18,* 223–230.

Scharlott, B. W., & Christ, W. G. (1995). Overcoming relationship-initiation barriers: The impact of a computer-dating system on sex role, shyness, and appearance inhibitions. *Computers in Human Behavior, 11*(2), 191–204. doi:10.1016/0747-5632(94)00028-G

Scherer, K. (1997). College life on-line: Healthy and unhealthy Internet use. *Journal of College Student Development, 38*(6), 655–665.

Schneider, J. (2000). Effects of cybersex addiction on the family: Results of a survey. *Sexual Addiction and Compulsivity, 7,* 31–58. doi:10.1080/10720160008400206

Stafford, T. F. (2003). Differentiating between adopter categories in the uses and gratifications for Internet services. *IEEE Transactions on Engineering Management, 50*(4), 427–435. doi:10.1109/TEM.2003.819652

Stafford, T. F. (2008). Social and usage-process motivations for consumer Internet access. *Journal of Organizational and End User Computing, 20*(3), 1–21. doi:10.4018/joeuc.2008070101

Valkenburg, P. M., & Peter, J. (2009). Social consequences of the Internet for adolescents A decade of research. *Current Directions in Psychological Science, 18*(1), 1–5. doi: 10.1111/j.1467-8721.2009.01595.x

Van Acker, E. (2001). Contradictory possibilities of cyberspace for generating romance. *Australian Journal of Communication, 28*(3), 103–116.

Walther, J. B. (1996). Computer-mediated communication: Impersonal, interpersonal, and hyperpersonal interaction. *Communication Research, 23*, 3–43.

Walther, J. B., Van Der Heide, B., Hamel, L., & Shulman, H. (2009). Self-generated versus other-generated statements and impressions in computer-mediated communication: A test of warranting theory using Facebook. *Communication Research, 36*, 229–253. doi:10.1177/0093650208330251

Walther, J. B., Van Der Heide, B., Kim, S.-Y., Westerman, D., & Tong, S. T. (2008). The role of friends' appearance and behavior on evaluations of individuals on Facebook: Are we known by the company we keep? *Human Communication Research, 34*(1), 28–49. doi:10.1111/j.1468-2958.2007.00312.x

Wang, C., & Chang, Y. (2010). Cyber relationship motives: Scale development and validation. *Social Behavior and Personality, 38*(3), 289–300. doi:10.2224/sbp.2010.38.3.289

Whitty, M.T. (2004). Cyber-flirting: An examination of men's and women's flirting behaviour both offline and on the Internet. *Behaviour Change, 21*(2), 115–126.

Whitty, M. T., & Carr, A. N. (2006). New rules in the workplace: Applying object-relations theory to explain problem Internet and email behaviour in the workplace. *Computers in Human Behavior, 22*(2), 235–250.

Whitty, M. T., & Joinson, A. N. (2009). *Truth, lies and trust on the Internet.* New York: Routledge.

Wildermuth, S. M. (2004). The effect of stigmatizing discourse on the quality of on-line relationships. *Cybersychology and Behavior, 7*(1), 73–84.

Winek, J. L., & Craven, P. A. (2003). Healing rituals for couples recovering from adultery. *Contemporary Family Therapy, 25*(3), 249–266. doi:10.1023/A:1024518719817

Yoo, C. S. (2010). The changing patterns of Internet usage. *Federal Communications Law Journal, 63*(1), 11–16.

Zickuhr, K., & Smith, A. (2012). *Digital differences.* Retrieved from http://pewinternet.org/Reports/2012/Digital-differences.aspx

3 Issues E-merging in Couple Life

The Internet is like alcohol in some sense. It accentuates what you would do anyway. If you want to be a loner, you can be more alone. If you want to connect, it makes it easier to connect.

—*Esther Dyson*

Current technology and new media reintroduces couples to age-old issues in relationship formation and maintenance as well as introduces couple's new issues. Issues emerging in relationships related to technology and new media include but are not limited to: how the couple has organized to spend time with one another, how power is experienced in the relationship, and how couples handle the idiosyncrasies around each partner's usage of technology and new media. Each of these issues (shared time, cybersex, online infidelity, and online gaming) introduces challenges into relationships. The areas presented in this chapter are to help the readers orient themselves to the potential positive and negative factors introduced into relationships. A treatment model that can be applied to the issues below will be introduced in a later chapter.

Shared Time Together

Individuals move together into the coupling phase in a myriad of ways. In many cases, relationships develop through common interests, experiences, and activities. There are two current views on shared couple time. First, couples are now, more than ever, experiencing interferes in their day-to-day life, which can complicate their ability to spend time with one another. At the same time, there is an increased importance placed upon shared time in relationships (Voorpostel, Lippe, & Gershuny, 2009). A change in shared time together for couples has also changed over the years. Between 1965 and 2003, individuals reported spending more minutes on leisure activities, from 171 and 179 minutes for women and men, respectively, to 206 and 230 minutes (an increase of 20% for men and 28% for women). Men generally reported the proportion of time they spent with a partner seems to be about 68%, a percentage that stayed fairly constant over the 38 years of data; women, on the other hand, increased the proportion of time spent with the presence of a partner, from 53% in 1965 to 65% in 2003 (Voorpostel et al., 2009).

Partners who spend time together participating in shared activities report higher levels of relational satisfaction and more stability as compared to time where couples engage in individual pursuits (Hill, 1988; Holman & Jaquart, 1988; Johnson, Zabriskie, & Hill, 2006; Rogers & Amato, 1997; Sullivan, 1996). On the other hand, relationships where the participants actively spend more time together are also associated with feelings of the time as not being enough. This can result in one feeling upset the time spent did not meet their expectations and they were somehow disillusioned (Daly, 2001). Further, when couples participate in individual activities, wives in heterosexual relationships are more likely than husbands to report relationship dissatisfaction specifically in those cases where the extracurricular activity is disliked by the wife (Crawford, Houts, Huston, & George, 2002).

In some cases, the selection of the shared activity may depend on each partner's value system (Kalmijn & Bernasco, 2001). For example, some couples may discover participating in a shared religious ideology or particular traditions might enhance the meaning of these activities and enjoyment each receives within the relationship. In other cases, however, there is an inherit risk to moving to a place of greater leisure time in the couple relationship. In a study on fathers and leisure time negotiation, it was found that fathers are most often the people in the relationship initiating the adoption of leisure time. Most often, this is intended as a way to relieve the partner of her responsibilities. Yet even with the invitation, the female partner has difficulty giving up the role because of the power associated with being the person who runs the household schedule (Dyck & Daly, 2006). It is also possible a resistance to engage in leisure time may also emerge from a fear (real or imagined) that bad things will happen should the person who is in charge leave that position to participate in leisure time without assisting with household duties. One of Jennie's main complaints with her husband Scott was her belief that she was the person who was always caring for the couple's dogs and that Scott had little to no ownership in the process. Scott's request of Jennie was framed around her adopting more positive a view of the couple's relationship and the expectation of one another. Part of this was complicated by a resentment that Jennie held against Scott: After not having enough money coming in from his business, the couple struggled to make ends meet and ultimately ended up losing their home to foreclosure. In Jennie's view, Scott's whole life (sole employee of his own freelance business as well as a coach for a local youth sports team) was one of leisure and she did not trust him to participate more in their relationship in exchange for her participation in more leisure activities.

Researchers have sought to understand the circumstances under which couples fare better with regard to separate versus shared activities. One longitudinal study (Crawford et al., 2002) demonstrated the dissatisfaction in relationships where each member of a couple participates in different activities is more problematic for the wife and relationship when husbands participate in activities disliked by wives. In addition, the dissatisfaction experienced by the wives contributed positively to the participation of their spouse in continuing to participate in that particular activity. In another study (Johnson, 2005), couples were asked to complete a survey composed of a number of questionnaires, including the Marital Activity Profile, the Satisfaction of Married Life Scale, and demographic information. "Overall, couples in this study indicated it was not the level or amount of couple leisure involvement or the satisfaction with the amount of time spent together, but the satisfaction with couple" (Johnson, 2005, p. 20). There also seem to be differences in how individuals in different couple types (dual-earner versus one-earner, versus both unemployed) spend time together and the impact on their relationship. Men in dual-earner couples indicated they spend less time with their partners, whereas for women the opposite was true. When both members of a couple, however, were unemployed, women were less likely than men to spend their leisure time in the presence of their partner (Voorpostel et al., 2009).

The extent to which one in an intimate relationship participates in individually based electronic activities has much validity in an electronic age. In most cases, participation in online activities occurs at one computer or device, most likely because these machines are too small to afford space for multiple users. Individual/separate leisure activities may sometimes be a source of contention in cases where one partner participates in online activities and the other partner is not interested or included.

There are many instances when couple time together is compromised by independent electronic activities. This was true for the case of Mandy and Joe. Mandy and Joe met online via participation in an online game. As they became close, Mandy and Joe moved in together and continued to play the online game. Over time, Mandy stopped playing the game, which brought them together and ended up becoming interested in other activities online while Joe maintained his involvement in the same game. The couple developed a tempo in their relationship where they would spend time together engaged in parallel play—each at their different games at the same time, but no interaction between them.

Online Video Gaming

Potential Relational Benefits

Online video gaming is now considered a mainstream activity in everyday life. As noted in Chapter 1, the sheer number of people participating in online gaming is growing at an astonishing rate. Couples have to make decisions about how this entity will play a part their lives. In 2011, I (K.H.) went to a large online gaming conference to recruit participants for a study on online gaming and relationships. As I handed out my advertisements for the survey, the conference attendees asked what I was researching. I responded I was interested to find out the ways in which gaming added to and complicated couple relationships. This reply was usually met with a story about how they or someone they knew was in a relationship where online gaming contributed substantially to the relationship's disillusion or success. For those who shared, it seemed there was not a middle ground—online gaming seemed to have one effect on the relationship or the opposite. The information I received at the conference lent support to some research already found: just over a third of couples disagree about whether online gaming was acceptable in their relationships (Helsper & Whitty, 2010). Certainly, the information mentioned above was acquired from casual conversations soliciting research participants and thus, it would not be appropriate to draw any scientific conclusions. But one theme became apparent: The impact of gaming in online relationships was also on the minds of the gamers attending the conference, not just the lone family researcher present.

Participating in the online gaming world may present particular challenges to couple relationships (Hertlein & Webster, 2008). Online video games are just one area in which couples may choose to participate independently and collectively (Taylor, 2006; Zhong, 2011) as well as with each other or with other people. Online video games refer to video games couples play interactively to the online role playing games. In some ways, online gaming can be helpful to couple relationships. It provides a safe place for the exploration of social interactions. For example, in some of the games that allow for text-based communication to other players, users can present their written text in a way that would present them most favorably. Other ways where games may be beneficial is in assisting people in developing relationships outside of a reliance on physical attributes because the users are generally only able to see one another's avatars (or characters) instead of the gamer. There may also be a sense of togetherness that is generated when playing with another partner or family members (Mitchell, 1985).

There is also some evidence to suggest that couple relationships are helped by online gaming because to be successful in the games, one has to be able to navigate social situations to collaborate with others to accomplish tasks in the game (Hertlein & Hawkins, 2012). Part of the way a gamer successfully navigates these social interactions is through developing a heightened understanding around gender roles. In online gaming, an avatar may or may not represent the characteristics of its owner. Additionally, the gender gap in an online role playing game might disappear altogether since women can adopt masculine characters and vice versa. In some ways, the online world may provide a more equal playing field. Another benefit is the exposure to others who are geographically distant with the same or similar interests. Finally, those who participate in online fantasy games may have higher levels of creativity and ability to fantasize outside of the gaming realm, namely, within their physical relationship with a partner (Hawkins & Hertlein, 2013).

Potential Relational Challenge

Despite the benefits of online gaming in relationships, MMORPG games have become vulnerable to attack because of their association with addiction characteristics, issues of player versus partner loyalty, number of hours spent on the game in one sitting, and one's willingness to pay for the service (Lu & Wang, 2008). One study cites problematic Internet behavior as presenting problems in clinical practice (Mitchell, Becker-Blease, & Finkelhor, 2005), one element of which is online gaming.

One of the issues is around the elements of online gaming considered collective play. According to Zhong (2011), "frequent participation in collective actions increases the chance of social interactions. However, it is unavoidable that sometimes online social interactions are accompanied with selfish, deceptive or ulterior motivations" (p. 2353). In this way, one may observe his or her partner interacting with others with increasing frequency and may develop suspicion around their partner's motives. It may also be the case one's motives are trusted by his or her partner but there is not the same assumption of good intent of the other gamer's motives.

The challenges associated with online video gaming could be explained by social presence theory (Short, Williams & Christie, 1976). This theory posits that people who share experiences together are more likely than others to feel more close to one another because of the immediacy in their interaction. For example, Uma and Amar both came from large families of East Indian descent, and it was through their families they met. When the therapist inquired as to the development of their relationship over time, Amar cited that Uma was generally the first one who responded to his e-mails and he, in turn, responded to her quickly. They experienced each other as being reliable in their communication, more so than most others in their lives, and felt the two of them immediately shared a bond characterized by mutual respect and shared family values.

The structure of online video gaming really makes social presence theory relevant. Online video gaming is characterized by (a) a specific number of challenges that have to be overcome in a game to be successful in progressing through the game's levels, and (b) the accomplishment of such tasks primarily through working in a group—thus, an embedded opportunity for social interaction. Issues emerge when the online gamer is participating in online gaming and developing immediacy and intimacy with someone else and not providing those things to their partner. The net result may be the gamer being accused of spending more time and energy and have more positive feelings for online relations than a primary partner. This can be even more problematic when one considers the online associations for which the immediacy and intimacy may be developing are ones with whom the player may potentially develop a romantic interest.

A highly developed sense of fantasy was previously classified as something online gaming may contribute to the positive nature of relationship. In some cases, however, when online video games are utilized as a strategy to avoid the tension and stress in one's offline life, it may interfere with problem solving, flexibility, creative problem solving, and other issues, setting couples up to present with the issue of online gaming in treatment (Mitchell & Wells, 2007). In addition, some non-game-playing partners may fear that their partners engaging in MMPORGs in which symbolic taboo activities (STAs; e.g., killing, torture, rape) are a part of the play, is a sign of them being psychological unhealthy, and may also mean that they are unable to separate engagement in STAs in gamespace versus offline real world space (Whitty, Young, & Goodings, 2011; Young & Whitty, 2010, 2011). Current research is demonstrating that most adult gamers can easily separate engagement in STAs online from engagement in these kinds of activities in the real world (Whitty et al., 2011). In addition, most can psychologically cope with witnessing and/or engaging in STAs in MMORPGs (Whitty et al., 2011).

Accountability

One of the primary issues associated with technology in intimate relationships is the issue of accountability. This issue is one of the few that transcends various topical areas but may still be a major player in interactions. Accountability is a key issue in relationship maintenance. As couples struggle to navigate the use of power within the relationship, each individual has to take accountability for their own behavior. Though little has been written about accountability in clinical literature, accountability has been identified as critical in infidelity treatment (Bird, Butler, & Fife, 2007).

To some degree, accountability relies on one being aware of their own online behavior. Researchers to date have only focused on awareness of technology usage in adolescents (Cheong, 2008; Heim, Brandtzæg, Kaare, Endestad, & Torgersen, 2007; Hundley & Shyles, 2010; Ling, 2004). Hundley and Shyles (2010) found teens experienced a high degree of temporal displacement while using technological devices—meaning that they were frequently not aware of the amount of time spent with their technology. In its application to technology in couples, accountability is an issue on two main levels. First, each member of the couple is accountable for his/her own behavior related to using electronically based communication to interact with others outside of their relationship. This includes regulation of who each partner is contacting via outgoing messages as well as managing incoming contacts. Second, accountability also applies to people's online behavior regarding interactions with their own partner. According to Postmes, Spears, and Lea (1998), "the notion that [computer-mediated communication] gives people a strategic freedom to express themselves because they are unaccountable has been identified as the cause of an ostensible increase in antinormative behavior in CMC compared to face-to-face conditions" (p. 694). In other words, the more people you can communicate with relates to the sense of limited accountability.

One client in treatment indicated he was angry at his partner for some of the conversations she had with a third party. During the course of the conversation, it emerged that he had logged onto her e-mail without her knowledge or permission, a clear violation of their relational contract. Such behavior complicates a case because those who place themselves in the position of monitoring their partner often assert the end justifies the means. Further, in cases where infidelity is discovered, both couple and therapist experience the dilemma of knowing the partner logging into accounts did breach the trust, but is forced to attend to the more egregious issue of sense of betrayal emerging from the problematic behavior. Margaret was distressed by her husband's participation in flirtatious chats with a coworker and began monitoring his e-mail communications. A conversation about accountability in violating the relationship contract goes by the wayside to manage the fidelity issue. Another dimension of the accountability problem is the decision around the degree to which a partner is required to report his or her behavior to the other partner. It is not unusual for couples to have inconsistencies with regard to what rules around password usage should they implement in their relationships.

The accountability of one's behavior shifts, however, when there has been a breach of the relationship contract. One partner may feel the need to monitor their partner's interactions, which can have pronounced implications for the couple. In many ways, the desire to observe and monitor one's behavior while placing the accountability for such action on the other party is adaptive and protective. Typically, this dynamic emerges in a relationship where one party has been hurt or betrayed by the other's online activities and believes their partner's behavior warrants monitoring. For example, Angie logged onto her boyfriend's Facebook account to ensure he was not maintaining communication with a woman for whom he had previously expressed a strong level of attraction, despite his assurances that all communication had stopped. In other cases, this adaptive behavior may also be central to creating more issues for couples. In Angie's case, she and her boyfriend had a very clear agreement about the nature through which he would share his online activities with her—and her logging onto his accounts without his knowledge was not one of them. The pair of them had agreed to be forthcoming with specific and potentially contentious issues and to have the flexibility in their relationship to pose questions to one another appropriately. While Angie knew that her secretly logging into accounts would result in the termination of the relationship per her boyfriend, her fear about his online activities, its consequences, and what meaning he gave it prevented her from adhering to her relationship agreement. The bottom line is that inattention to accountability may create an environment ripe for the development of a problematic power struggle in the couple's relationship, which can further contribute to relational discord. In short, just because you can do something does not necessarily mean you should.

Suspicion and Jealousy

A related issue to online activities and couples is the emerging issue of suspicion and jealousy. Jealousy is a fact of couple like that emerges with regard to both offline and online behavior. This is particularly true for women's observations of their partner's electronic behavior. In a study on jealousy in offline versus online circumstance, female undergraduates rated sharing of feeling via the Internet or cell phone as creating more jealousy than offline "suspicious" behaviors such as dancing or fantasizing about another partner. Women also rated their partner's involvement with someone else over technology and new media as "more distressing" than men (Dijkstra, Barelds, & Groothof, 2010, p. 340). Jealousy may occur more globally in the context of relational and family life. As each partner in a relationship goes to participate in individual interactions online, some couples may develop concerns around their partner's individual behaviors. Part of this issue may be related to the amount of time one partner devotes to the game versus what is devoted to the relationship. An individual may identify their partner stays online gaming with others for a number of hours, while the time spent with their offline family members or partner remains relatively limited. Suspicion is particularly likely to emerge if the game playing is characterized by a shift in one's personality and can become a slippery slope—as suspicion grows and partners feel less secure about their relationship, suspicion continues to increase (Acker, 2003).

Behaviors specific to the Internet contributing to jealousy in a couple's life surround the use of social networking sites. For example, one is more likely to experience jealousy if their partner is on Facebook trading information with a potential love interest, if one has a higher level of trait jealousy, and if there is lower trust in the relationship (Muise, Christofides, & Desmarais, 2009). Though similar research has yet to be conducted on other social networking sites, findings indicate that Facebook intrusion (a concept associated to some degree with the amount of time one spends on Facebook), is related to reduced relationship satisfaction and an increase in jealousy (Elphinston & Noller, 2011).

And though men's use of social networking sites seems to generally be more task oriented as opposed to developing interpersonal relationships (see, e.g., Guadagno & Cialdini, 2002; Williams, Consolvo, Caplan, & Yee, 2009), men also use social networking more frequently than women to develop potential dating relationships (Mazman & Usluel, 2011; Muscanell & Guadagno, 2012; Raacke & Bonds-Raacke, 2008). There are three main characteristics described in the literature outlining why social networking sites may contribute to higher levels of jealousy in relationships (Utz & Beukeboom, 2011):

1. The fact that activity on the site may be viewed by a number of "friends" means personal interactions in which one participates with individuals other than one's partner can be viewed by many, which may be threatening to someone prone to jealousy.
2. The increased amount of information a user shares is disseminated to a large number of people, rendered the romantic partner as one of many instead of someone specific.
3. The monitoring of a partner can occur with greater frequency through a social networking site in socially-acceptable ways. (Tokunaga, 2011)

Further, individuals with lower levels of self-esteem are more likely to experience jealousy with regard to their partner's behaviors on social networking sites, specifically if those individuals have a higher level of trait jealousy (Utz & Beukeboom, 2011). Overall, findings support the notion that what one does on social networking sites is more important to relationships than how much time is spent on the sites.

Furthermore, akin to traditional infidelity cases, the desire to monitor the offending partner's behavior is a normal feeling after the revelation of infidelity. When infidelity has been conducted using Internet-based communication; however, the ecological elements of accessibility, affordability, and anonymity all play a part in maintaining the power imbalance in the relationship when one partner monitor the others behavior. Once some of the problematic behavior is discovered, the accessibility of web-based communications makes it easy to continue to monitor someone's accounts and communications (see Chapter 4 for a further discussion of these concepts).

Cybersex

Cybersex is becoming increasingly common with the integration of new media in our lives. As Dryer and Lijtmaer (2007) note, "the Internet's unique characteristics express dynamics that are both like and unlike other material" (p. 39). The exact proportion of who participates in sexual activity online varies from study to study with a range of 20% of Internet users participating in this all the way up to 83% (Cooper, Mansson, Daneback, Tikkanen, & Ross, 2003; Cooper, Putnam, Planchon, & Boies, 1999; Cooper, Scherer, & Mathy, 2001). A large majority (70%) of those using the Internet for sexual activities keep their activities a secret (Cooper, Scherer, Boies, & Gordon, 1999).

Cybersex broadly refers to a wide variety of behaviors and activities that the term, according to one scholar, "is of practically no use for the social scientific discourse as long as individual phenomena are not differentiated from one another" (Döring, 2000, p. 864). Part of the issue rests in the fact that the definition of cybersex is based largely on self-report to one item on a survey (Shaughnessy, Byers, & Thornton, 2011). In some cases, cybersex is broadly defined as activities involving the Internet that result in sexual gratification (Cooper & Griffin-Shelley, 2002); other authors, however, indicate interactive activities as being a necessary piece to the definition (see, e.g., Daneback, Cooper, & Månsson, 2005). Reid (as cited in Waskul, Douglass, & Edgley, 2000) framed cybersex as "a form of coauthored interactive erotica" (p. 384). This contention has also gained some empirical support (Shaughnessy, Byers, & Thornton, 2011).

Cybersex is "a sexual communication between at least two people that is focused on sexual relations and occurs via synchronous Internet modes" (Shaughnessy et al., 2011, p. 86). A more narrow definition regarding being sexually satisfied is provided by Döring (2000): "a social interaction between at least two persons who are exchanging real-time digital messages to become sexually aroused and satisfied" (p. 863). According to Griffiths (2001), these interactions are text-based fantasies where each person masturbates to the activity. The actual behaviors constituting cybersex, though, can be anywhere on a continuum, from viewing of sexual content to actual interactions with someone via webcams (Delmonico & Griffin, 2008; Ferree, 2003).

Three different types of cybersexual interactions are described in the literature (Döring, 2000). One type is known as virtually based reality cybersex. This form of cybersex relies on real-time stimulation of a partner from technological distance. Marketed as teledildonics, it allows users to plug into their computer and stimulate themselves and a partner using the device without personal physical contact with one another. The second type is called video-based cybersex and consists of people sharing sexual activity via video-based communication services. This includes undressing in front of one another, touching oneself, and watching each other masturbate in front of the camera. The final form of cybersex is the text-based form. This type of messaging is the form most likely discussed in literature. It is based on the thick, rich description of sexual acts each person would perform on the other as well as what they are doing to themselves as they read the messages on the screen and think about the person on the other end of the texts. It is a sibling of phone sex, the main difference being the descriptions uttered over the phone are instead composed into lines of text, allowing the individual typing to create a more thoughtful and sensual experience.

The different types of cybersex forms have different implications for a couple's relationship. The text-based form of messaging sexual intentions are characterized by thought, edits, and specific ways of self-presentation. As a result, it can be great for couples to participate in it together. Amanda and Josh discovered in the early part of Josh's deployment that cybersex was an integral part of their distant sexual relationship. During the course of the couple cybertexting with one another, Amanda reported she felt she was able to do more sexually for Josh because of the barrier of the computer; she could experiment with words in a way that she did not feel comfortable doing in person, thereby opening up their sexual repertoire in a more broad way online than they had even been able to experience in their offline lives. As a result, Josh was pleasantly surprised when he returned from his deployment to see Amanda was now ready to try some of the things she had experimented with online that Josh had been very receptive to. In this way, the wall that the computer put up between the couple actually helped Amanda try on a different sexual persona, resulting in positive changes in their sexual and relational satisfaction.

On the other hand, the discovery of a cybersex relationship between two individuals that is focused on text-only communication can be more damaging than some of the visual types of cybersex if one member of the couple is participating in it with someone other than their primary partner. One client, for example, discovered her partner's saved chat sessions with someone else while looking for some bank records on his computer.

Another relatively recent phenomenon related to sex and technology is the concept of sexting, defined as one's use of cell or smartphones to access sexually explicit materials and applications (Cooper, Delmonico, & Burg, 2000) or the sending and receiving of text messages with pictures or written content that depicts nudity, sexuality, and/or sexual activities (Galvin, Bylund, & Brommel, 2012). There is little research on sexting, and even less is known about parent-child and parent adult-child communications around this behavior (Galvin et al., 2012). In an online panel study, researchers interviewed 1,247 youth between the ages of 14 and 24 and found that sexting is more common in the age group of 18 to 24 year olds, but is still occurring in people aged 14 to 17 (Associated Press & MTV, 2009). For young adults in college it appears that most are engaging in sexting behaviors with people they define as "friends with benefits" (Bisson & Levine, 2009), or partners, or who they are dating, or those with whom they are "hooking up" with or plan to "hook up" with in the future (Owen, Rhodes, Stanley, & Fincham, 2007).

Impact of Cybersex on the Couple

There are also different types of cybersex users. At-risk users (Cooper et al., 1999) are those users who would not have a problem with pornography and the Internet without the presence of the Internet. Cavaglion and Rashty (2010) describe the process of the at-risk user developing problems as beginning with a slow decline in the quantity and quality of interactions with others, including an eventual decline in work performance. A second type of user is defined as recreational (Cooper et al., 1999). This means the Internet provides a way to seek out cybersexual activities or facilitates the viewing of porn, but the person uses this strictly for entertainment value and is in no way addicted to either the Internet or the sexual activity. This type can be the most difficult for couples to understand because one partner's usage might be recreational, but because of its sexual nature, it may be classified by their partner as being and addiction or compulsion problem. Couples entering therapy with this dynamic will often pit the therapist in the position of deciding which partner is correct, thus complicating the treatment process from the beginning. A third type of user is known as the compulsive user. Implications for couples where one partner is a compulsive user include a decrease in the amount of sex desired by the compulsive individual toward their spouse (Schneider, 2003), a decrease in one's sense of sexual desirability, a reduced frequency in sexual interaction, and a decrease in sexual satisfaction (Bergner & Bridges, 2002; Bridges, Bergner & Hesson-McInnis, 2003). Some of these consequences may explain Schneider's (2003) findings indicating nearly one quarter of couples she interviewed had divorced or separated as a result of cybersexual activities on the part of one of the partners.

One of the challenges associated with cybersex is the potential for problematic usage. Concerns that couples may have include the duration of time that one may spend online. In some ways, it may be a slippery slope where one individual starts chatting in a time and place convenient for them. On the other hand, the continued chats and online pursuits begin to interfere more with family life and functioning, such as that online involvement may limit one's involvement in family life. It also does not help that in some cases, one person may classify their partner's behavior as addictive. This classification may in turn create more defensiveness for the partner thus limiting the couple's ability to talk with one another effectively.

The implications specifically for women transcend across several categories: behavioral, physical, relational, personal, and spiritual (Ferree, 2003). In the behavioral dimension, implications might be that the participation in cybersexual activities could become problematic and interfere with one's relationship. The physical dimension details the implications of female cybersex users on their physical interactions with others, their body image, and other aspect of well-being should the cybersex activities turn into addiction and result in a neglect of self-care. The personal implications relate to the potential for women who have experienced abuse in the past to reenact the trauma in cyberspace. The relational dimension refers to the information presented earlier—that is, the impact of cybersex on a relationship in terms of the potential for reduced desire for one's partner. Spiritual implications refer to those where one ascribes particular meaning to their behavior in comparison with their value system (Ferree, 2003).

Internet and Sex Addiction

Internet addiction is a controversial topic for three main reasons. First, there is little empirical evidence regarding the development and classification of Internet sexual addiction. The classifications identified by Young (1999) have not been researched or supported by empirical evidence (Griffiths, 2001). In addition, Young et al. (2000) also produces a personality profile of those who participate in compulsive Internet sexual behavior consisting of persons with low self-esteem, a history of sexual or other addictions, the presence of a sexual dysfunction, or a problematic body image. Young, Griffin-Shelly, Cooper, O'Mara, and Buchanan (2000) also described a trajectory of the development of an Internet addiction problem, one resembling the development of some paraphilias. It is predicated on the assumption that the Internet is the mechanism by which unexpressed or unacknowledged sexual desire and fantasies are expressed. This expression is then reinforced by positive feelings accompanying the feelings associated with sexual expression, thus increasing the likelihood one will participate in the behavior again, but this time with more purpose and begin to organize their experiences to achieve a particular sexual end. While this may be a clinical reality for some cases, the lack of research on the development of Internet sex addiction is unclear because it is not supported by research (Griffiths, 2001).

Second, Internet sex addiction is not consistently defined by the either the general or scientific community. One attempt to define the Internet sex addict revolves around the classification of consumers of Internet sex into categories: information overload, cybersexual addictions, cyberrelationship addiction, net compulsions, and computer addiction (Young, 1999). This typology, however, presents challenges for couples in two ways. First, only three of the five make reference to the Internet specifically (Griffiths, 2000b): cybersexual addiction, cyberrelationship addiction, and net compulsions. An individual might have a compulsion to receive much information quickly and the Internet may facilitate a way to do that, but it does not automatically translate into a sexual or Internet compulsion. Second, couples who do not understand there are differences among various typologies may classify any perceived problematic Internet behavior as an addiction when it may not be the case. In fact, there are no fewer than six terms to describe problematic Internet behavior (Czincz & Hechanova, 2009), which can be confusing to both scholars and lay people.

The third reason for the controversy in the definition of an Internet sex addict is the belief by some that behavioral addictions are not addictions at all. Theresa and Mike, a middle-aged Christian couple, came to treatment because Theresa discovered a series of e-mails, text messages, chats and downloaded pornography on her partner Mike's computer. When Theresa confronted him about it, Mike disclosed that he was a sex addict, thus the reason for the behavior. Theresa had a very difficult time accepting Mike's explanation for the use of pornography, particularly as they were both what she called, "Good Christian people." In fact, his explanation produced more hurt in her than just his behavior. She explained that she believed his reliance on the addiction model communicated to her a lack of personal accountability in his own behavior, communicated the message that he had no control over his actions, and as a result she believed he had failed her and God. Theresa, a person who saw the world and people's behavior as either good or bad, did not "believe" in an addiction model that promotes a sense of powerlessness with regard to behavior. Despite the therapist's attempt to help Theresa understand the legitimacy of data supporting a physiological change in a certain proportion of addiction cases, Theresa failed to see behavioral compulsions as having those same characteristics.

Typically, the guidelines for the definition of addictions are subsumed under the substance abuse disorder section in the *Diagnostic and Statistical Manual of Mental Disorders, Fourth Edition, Text Revision* (DSM IV–TR; American Psychological Association, 2000). The criteria for such disorders note the use of a substance that interferes with daily and relational functioning. This definition, however, does not specify behavioral addictions, and this category will still not be included in the upcoming DSM as a category but instead included in the appendix (Curley, 2010). The category most akin to classifying behavioral addictions is as a compulsive disorder (Widyanto & Griffiths, 2006). In short, the term behavioral addiction is applied when someone sees the negative consequences of a particular behavior but still continues to participate in them (Heather, 1998; Kreek, Nielsen, Butelman, & LaForge, 2005; Nestler, 2000).

Couples have difficulty discussing cybersex. It also affects whether the online sexual activity is classified as an addiction: salience, mood modification, tolerance, withdrawal, conflict, and relapse (Griffiths, 2001). Of these six, three of them (tolerance, withdrawal, and relapse) are directly related to the characteristics of addiction (Kandell, 1998). Salience, mood modification, and conflict are related concepts that may not necessarily be diagnostic but can create challenges in couple relationships. Salience refers to the extent to which the cybersex activities are a part of someone's life. For example, James would feel anxious about his wife going to bed because it would be at that time he could resume his activities. For this individual, he has a high degree of salience. Mood modification means people experience particular mood states when engaging in Internet sex. For some this could mean using it as a coping skill. For others, it means they get an exhilarating feeling when participating in Internet sex.

Other criteria used to define Internet addiction as an issue include the number of hours one spends online (Byun et al., 2009). Yet much like the criteria discussed above, there is considerable variance in the amount of hours online would constitute an addiction (Czincz & Hechanova,

2009). Some authors noted 8 hours a week is sufficient to consider a diagnosis of Internet addiction; others see the number as being close to 38 hours per week (Grohol, 1999). One definition seems to include some of the elements characterized by addiction is provided by Beard and Wolf (2001) such as tolerance, withdrawal, becoming irritable when asked to cease activity, use it as a coping mechanism for uncomfortable emotions, and could potentially compromise employment, education, individual well-being, and relationships.

The ambiguity around a clinical definition also spills over into the couple's relationship. One partner may cite the number of hours spent as an issue, but two other areas include the activities one pursues online and the impact on one's daily normative functioning (Czincz & Hechanova, 2009). What becomes the most problematic for couples is that one person is using the Internet as a form of escapism and neglects daily duties and family life in lieu of participation of the Internet. When this occurs, there are two problems in a relationship. The first is the actual problematic behavior (i.e., whatever behavior is viewed as "taking away" from the relationship) and the couple's ability to spend time with one another. The other issue is the one person accused having the addiction may experience their partner's expression of concern as an attack and become defensive about their online behavior, thus increasing the criticism and defensiveness in the couple's interactions.

An additional issue with classifying behavior online as an addiction is it removes accountability (in some cases, inappropriately) from the person engaging in the problematic behavior. For example, Sue's husband was seeking individual treatment for what he conceptualized as a lifelong addiction to sex. Sue, who had been raised in a family who believed in the principles of being honest, honorable, and truthful, did not buy into what she termed the "addiction mentality." She viewed this as a "cop out" and believed such a label diminished her husband's accountability for his own behavior, thus impairing her ability to accurately assess his commitment to the relationship and the likelihood he would repeat this behavior.

This is not to say the label of addiction absolves someone of responsibility. Some studies have relied on sample self-definitions as to whether they were addicted to the Internet and found those who believed they were addicted reported experiencing negative consequences of their Internet use (e.g., guilt regarding going online, anticipating using the Internet, and receiving complaints from people close to them regarding their Internet behavior (Egger & Rauterberg, 1996)).

Online Infidelity

Mileham (2007) noted, "Never before has it been so easy to enjoy both the stability of marriage and the thrills of the dating scene at the same time" (p. 12). In other words, a person is able to have their cake and eat it, too, without the messiness and incredibly high risk of physically sneaking around their partner—all they need to do is delete their browser history. As a result, the expanding world of websites, social networking sites, and opportunities for connecting online increase the likelihood of developing deep and personal relationships with others, potentially to the exclusion of the primary partner. The development of such relationships has the potential to create lasting damage to the primary relationship (Underwood & Findlay, 2004).

Couples do not always agree on what it means to be unfaithful online (Parker & Wampler, 2003). Infidelity is broadly defined as behaviors that are in opposition to the established relational contract (Weeks, Gambescia, & Jenkins, 2003). Yet those who have experienced a breach in their contract with the involvement of the Internet have difficulty specifically pointing that the Internet behavior actually broke the contract. Therapists also struggle with the same thing. In a study examining how to treat Internet infidelity, Nelson (2000) found even experts in the field of infidelity could not agree on a common definition for Internet infidelity. The three most common scenarios depicting Internet infidelity include (a) one partner chatting with/exchanging flirtatious e-mails with someone other than the primary partner, (b) one partner meeting someone in person with whom s/he had exchanged flirtatious e-mails, and (c) individual viewing of pornography online. Any combination of these scenarios might represent infidelity to a particular couple. Therefore, regardless of the perceived breach of relationship contract, therapists must help the couple come to a common description and definition of the problem (Hertlein & Webster, 2008).

Reactions to Internet infidelity may mimic those of offline infidelity, including the perception that it is a negative event for the couple characterized by pain, guilt, shame, betrayal, and rejection, not to mention the impact to the trust and communication in the relationship (Henline & Lamke, 2003; Hertlein & Piercy, 2006; Parker & Wampler, 2003). Jealousy is also a reaction present in the experience of both offline and online infidelity (Guadagno & Sagarin, 2010). Despite the similarity in the presence of the responses, the severity of the problem differ between online and offline infidelity (Whitty, 2005). Whitty (2005) found women have a tendency to focus on the emotional consequences of online infidelity (such as hurt, loss of trust, and time invested outside of the relationship) more than men. This is consistent with the findings of Roscoe, Cavanaugh, and Kennedy (1988), who found that men are more likely to classify physical interactions with another person as infidelity whereas women are more likely to consider emotional relationships with another as infidelity.

Finally, distinguishing infidelity from addiction is also an emerging issue. Celebrities such as Tiger Woods, Charlie Sheen, and Jesse James have all cited "sex addiction" as the motivating factor for their infidelity.

It is unclear, however, to what extent addiction is used as a scapegoat to addressing one's infidelity. According to Hertlein and Jones (2012),

> practicing therapists often find it difficult to distinguish between addiction and infidelity in practice, further complicated by the empirically-supported relationship between chemical (e.g., alcohol, drugs) and process addictions (e.g., sexual addiction, addictive gambling, Internet addiction) (Ledgerwood & Downey, 2002; Merta, 2001; Potenza, 2002; Rowan & Galasso, 2000). (p. 115)

Therapists have to walk a fine line between understanding the difference between addiction and infidelity as it may have serious consequences in one's ability to continue in the relationship. Vicki and Luke came to treatment upon the revelation of Luke's numerous sexual encounters with other women throughout the course of their relationship. In the first session, Vicki was very clear with the therapist: She wanted to know what inspired Luke's behavior because the motivations dictated whether she would stay in the relationship—if Luke was an addict, she would end the relationship because she believed it meant he would not change. If Luke was not an addict and acting out for other reasons, she indicated that she would make a commitment to the relationship.

Gender

Men and women are generally expected to adhere to different standards of behavior based on societal norms (Hare-Mustin & Marecek, 1990; McGoldrick, Carter, & Gracia-Preto, 2010). Such norms vary from culture to culture around the globe, and include gendered expectations with regard to daily living tasks like shopping, cooking, caretaking, sexual practices, Internet usage, communicating, and work, to name but a few. Research tells us that there are even 'standards' in the way people are to be viewed in the context of therapy with regard to their gender. This includes what is considered healthy and unhealthy behaviors and identities as they relate to the gender (Blumer, Ansara, & Watson, 2012; Broverman, Broverman, Clarkson, Rosenkrantz, & Vogel, 1972 Rieker & Carmen, 1984).

For instance, in a dated, yet still relevant study, Broverman et al. (1972), administered a Sex-Role Stereotype Questionnaire to 79 mental health care providers asking about the characteristics that make a person more or less mentally healthy. Participants were asked to describe these characteristics for either an adult with sex unspecified, sex specified male, or sex specified female. The results indicated a significantly high degree of agreement among clinicians (both male and female identifying) as to the attributes that characterize health in adults. The clinicians' concept of who is a healthy and mature adult is the same for adult men and adults with sex unspecified. The clinicians' concept of a mature healthy woman, however, differed in that they were less likely to attribute traits of being healthy to women. Clinicians have different concepts of health for men and women, and these differences parallel the sex-role stereotypes that remain prevalent in our society today. Yet other investigations have found flaws with Broverman et al's 1974 work, suggesting that gender differences and sex roles are less pronounced, particularly outside of Euro American contexts (Kelley & Blashfield, 2009). For example, in a study exploring whether African American men and women endorse sex-role stereotypes differently than Euro American men and women, results indicated that African Americans did not endorse these stereotypes in the same way, though there were still differences between African American men and women (Dade & Sloan, 2000).

In some cases, the ways that people express their gender may have implications for treatment and result in discriminant practices in terms of a clinician's viewing of a client's adjustment to the environment, and overall mental wellness (Blumer et al., 2012; Rieker & Carmen, 1984). Some investigations have found that clients who act consistent with their sex-role stereotypes are viewed more positively by therapists (Seem & Johnson, 1998; Sherman, 1980). In addition, researchers indicated clients who present outside of gender binary (i.e., male or female, man or woman) have their mental health called into question, and it is not uncommon for them to be labeled as having gender identity issues or being "gender dysphoric" (Ansara & Hegarty, 2012; Blumer, Green, Knowles, & Williams, 2012).

Expectations around gender also often affect who clients view as being easier to therapeutically bond with, and as more clinically helpful (Blumer & Barbachano, 2008). For instance, in general, male-identifying clinicians tend to talk more in session and interrupt clients more frequently than female-identifying therapists (Shields & McDaniel, 1992; Werner-Wilson, Price, Zimmerman, & Murphy, 1997). Additional research has shown there are benefits for therapists in adopting a gender style that is more androgynous (Blier, Atkinson, & Geer, 1987; Harvey & Hansen, 1999; Nelson, 1993). Androgynous clinicians are perceived as being more clinically flexible and adaptable to clients of many gender orientations (e.g., male, female, transgender; Harvey & Hansen, 1999). Androgynous therapists also have been rated higher on certain therapeutic process variables like the ability to elicit self-disclosure from clients (Blier et al., 1987). In addition, regardless of their gender, clients have reported finding speaking to someone more androgynous or slightly feminine less threatening (Blier et al., 1987; Harvey & Hansen, 1999; Nelson, 1993).

Gendered findings like those presented in this chapter underscore the notion that a different therapy context is experienced through differences in therapist and client genders, and that gender is a variable that needs to be attended to in clinical practice when addressing any issues couples present with (Avis, 1991; Sheinberg & Penn, 1991) including technology related ones (Hertlein & Piercy, 2006). For instance, consider the role of gender in the context of couples presenting for issues around cybersex. Despite research by Meston and Buss (2009) that reports there are over 200 reasons women provide for participating in sexual activity, a statistic which challenges the conventional sex roles ascribed to women, there are clear gender stereotypes around Internet sex. In regard to Internet sex, Ferree (2003) claimed, "Standards for feminine behaviour limit women's expressions of sexuality more than men's practices, and women's participation in Internet sex is far outside the stereotypical boundaries" (p. 386). This contention was supported by my (K.H.) research on therapist's assessment and treatment of Internet infidelity cases. I examined whether the social background characteristics, such as gender, age, religion, and so on, of the client and therapist made a difference in the treatment of Internet infidelity cases. Therapists perceived women who viewed pornography online were more likely to be viewed as more atypical than men participating in the same behavior (Hertlein & Piercy, 2008).

Ferree (2003) proposes other reasons that women are not considered as participating in cybersex is that it is a behavior historically attributed only to men. Cybersexual activities are divided into two types: solitary and interactive. Solitary activities involve viewing pornography and reading erotic materials. Interactive activities included communicating with others online through e-mail, chat rooms, and engaging in masturbatory practices while engaging in cybersex online. Ferree (2003) acknowledges women generally participate in the interactive forms, although women also participate in the solitary activities although less frequent. This is due to the emphasis women place on courtship as a result of their "relational" wiring. In some ways, the Internet actually makes it easier for women to pursue sexual desires because of the content-based format.

Gender Socialization

Another issue emerging for couples regarding the use of electronic media is the expectation around socialization of computer and technology usage. Srite, Thatcher, and Galy (2008) found perceptions of one's masculinity and/or femininity contributed to one's level of anxiety around computer usage, self-efficacy with regard to the use of technology, and innovation in application and usage of technology. Specifically, those who identified with a more masculine identity had high degrees of self-efficacy with regard to their Internet usage, were more innovative with regard to their computer usage, and less anxious about technology than those who ascribed to a more feminine identity. This is consistent with research that indicates that, regardless of the woman's employment status, power in a relationship stems from the sex roles to which the partners adhere (Tichenor, 1999).

While gender self-identification can differ from biological sex, these findings are consistent with the findings from a study on the usage of technology among male and female postgraduate students, where male students were more likely to participate in advanced searches on the computer than were female students (Horvat, Oreski, & Markic, 2011). The gender socialization aspect of technology usage has implications for couples in one of two ways. In couples where one ascribes to a masculine gender orientation, they may experience greater efficacy with regard to technology. Those who ascribe to a more feminine gender may experience a level of reduced efficacy with computer use and an increase in anxiety around technology usage for themselves and/or their partner(s). Such anxiety may translate to anxiety about their partner's interactions and activities online. In relationships where both parties ascribe to a feminine orientation, each partner may feel uncertainty about the online activities of their partner, and uninformed about how to approach the other person when there are questions about their partner's technology usage.

Therapeutically, this can be managed through (a) acknowledgment of the role gender plays in technology usage and (b) adjustment of one's clinical model to address the differences in socialization, if necessary. This will mean encouraging partners who identify with a feminine orientation to encourage application, innovation, and familiarity with computers and software applications as a way to reduce their anxiety about what things are going on in their partner's lives. For example, Joan, who identified as being relatively feminine, and Mitchell, who was more masculine in his gender orientation, were in therapy to work on communication issues. One notable struggle was Joan's perception that Mitchell could communicate with others online with relative ease where she did not feel that she could communicate online in the same way. In this case, by increasing the more feminine-identifying partner's self-efficacy and ability to explore computer life, an opportunity was created for her and her partner to experience a more pronounced sense of control over technology usage, thus encouraging what could be a more egalitarian power base in the relationship. Despite the relevance of considering gender in clinical practice, it remains a variable that is largely ignored in family therapy (Hare-Mustin & Marecek, 1990).

References

Acker, M. (2003). Precursors of suspicion in marriage. *Australian Journal of Psychology, 55*, 32.

American Psychological Association. (2000). *Diagnostic and statistical manual of mental disorders* (4th ed., text revision). Washington, DC: American Psychological Association.

Ansara, Y. G., & Hegarty, P. (2012). Cisgenderism in psychology: Pathologizing and misgendering children from 1999 to 2008. *Psychology & Sexuality, 3*, 137–160. doi:10.1080/19419899.2011.576696.

Associated Press & MTV. (2009, September 23). *AP-MTV Digital abuse study, executive summary.* Retrieved from http://www.athinline.org/MTVAP_Digital_Abuse_Study_Executive_Summary.pdf

Avis, J. M. (1991). Power politics in therapy with women. In T. J. Goodrich (Ed.), *Women and power: Perspectives for family therapy* (pp. 183–200). New York: W. W. Norton.

Beard, K., & Wolf, E. (2001). Modification in the proposed diagnostic criteria for Internet addiction. *Cyberpsychology and Behavior, 4,* 377–383. doi:10.1089/109493101300210286

Bergner, R. M., & Bridges, A. J. (2002). The significance of heavy pornography involvement for romantic partners: Research and clinical implications. *Journal of Sex & Marital Therapy, 28*(3), 193–206. doi:10.1080/009262302760328235

Bird, M. H., Butler, M. H., & Fife, S. T. (2007). The process of couple healing following infidelity: A qualitative study. *Journal of Couple & Relationship Therapy, 6*(4), 1–25. doi:0.1300/J398v06n04_01

Bisson, M. A., & Levine, T. R. (2009). Negotiating a friends with benefits relationship. *Archives of Sexual Behavior, 38*(1), 66–73. doi:10.1007/s10508-007-9211-2

Blier, M. J., Atkinson, D. R., & Geer, C. A. (1987). Effect of client gender and counselor gender and sex roles on willingness to see the counselor. *Journal of Counseling Psychology, 34,* 27–30. doi:10.1037/0022-0167.34.1.27

Blumer, M. L. C., Ansara, Y. G., & Watson, C. M. (2012). *Cisgenderism in family therapy: How everyday practices delegitimize people's gender self-designations* (Unpublished manuscript).

Blumer, M. L. C., & Barbachano, J. M. (2008). Valuing the gender-variant therapist: Therapeutic experiences, tools, and implications of a female-to-male trans-variant clinician. *Journal of Feminist Family Therapy: An International Forum, 20*(1), 46–65. doi:10.1080/08952800801907135

Blumer, M. L. C., Green, M. S., Knowles, S. J., & Williams, A. (2012). Shedding light on thirteen years of darkness: Content analysis of articles pertaining to transgender issues in marriage/couple and family therapy journals. *Journal of Marital and Family Therapy, 38*(S1), 244–256. doi:10.1111/j.1752-0606.2012.00317.x

Bridges, A. J., Bergner, R. M., & Hesson-McInnis, M. (2003). Romantic partners' use of pornography: Its significance for women. *Journal of Sex & Marital Therapy, 29*(1), 1–14.

Broverman, I. K., Broverman, D. M., Clarkson, F. E., Rosenkrantz, P. S., & Vogel, S. R. (1970). Sex-role stereotypes and clinical judgments of mental health. *Journal of Consulting and Clinical Psychology, 34,* 1–7.

Broverman, I. K., Vogel, S. R., Broverman, D. M., Clarkson, F. E., & Rosenkrantz, P. S. (1972). Sex-role stereotypes: A current appraisal. *Journal of Social Issues, 28*(2), 59–78.

Byun,S., Ruffini, C., Mills, J., Douglas, A., Niang, M., Stepchenkova, S., Lee, S., Loutfi, J., Lee, J., Atallah, M., & Blanton, M. (2009). Internet addiction: Metasynthesis of 1996–2006 quantitative research. *CyberPsychology & Behavior, 12*(2), 203–207. doi:10.1089/cpb.2008.0102

Cavaglion, G., & Rashty, E. (2010). Narratives of suffering among Italian female partners of cybersex and cyber-porn dependents. *Sexual Addiction and Compulsivity: The Journal of Treatment, 17*(4), 270–287. doi:10.1080/10720162.2010.535690

Cheong, P. H. (2008). The young and techless? Investigating Internet use and problem-solving behaviors of young adults in Singapore. *New Media & Society, 10*(5), 771–791. doi:10.1177/1461444808094356

Cooper, A., Delmonico, D. L., & Burg, R. (2000). Cybersex users, abusers, and compulsives: New findings and implications. *Sexual Addiction & Compulsivity, 7*(1-2), 5-29. doi: 10.1080/10720160008400205

Cooper, A., & Griffin-Shelley, E. (2002). Introduction. The Internet: The next sexual revolution. In A. Cooper (Ed.), *Sex and the Internet: A guidebook for clinicians* (pp. 1–15). New York: Brunner-Routledge.

Cooper, A., Mansson, S. A., Daneback, K., Tikkanen, R., & Ross, M. W. (2003). Predicting the future of Internet sex: Online sexual activities in Sweden. *Sexual and Relationship Therapy, 18,* 277–291.

Cooper, A., Putnam, D., Planchon, L., & Boies, S. (1999). Online sexual compulsivity: Getting tangles in the net. *Sexual Addiction and Compulsivity: Journal of Treatment and Prevention, 6*(2), 70–104.

Cooper, A., Scherer, C., Boies, S., & Gordon, B. (1999). Sexuality on the Internet: From sexual exploration to pathological expression. *Professional Psychology: Research and Practice, 30*(2), 154–164.

Cooper, A., Scherer, C., & Mathy, R. (2001). Overcoming methodological concerns in the investigating of online sexual activities. *CyberPsychology & Behavior, 4*(4), 437–447. doi:10.1089/109493101750526999

Crawford, D. W., Houts, R. M., Huston, T. L., & George, L. J. (2002). Compatibility, leisure, and satisfaction in marital relationships. *Journal of Marriage & Family, 64*(2), 433–449. doi:10.1111/j.1741-3737.2002.00433.x

Curley, B. (2010). *DSM-V draft includes major changes to addictive disease classifications*. Retrieved from http://www.jointogether.org/news/features/2010/dsm-v-draft-includes-major.html

Czincz, J., & Hechanova, R. (2009). Internet addiction: Debating the diagnosis. *Journal of Technology in Human Services, 27*(4), 257–272. doi:10.1080/15228830903329815

Dade, L. R., & Sloan, L. R. (2000). An investigation of sex-role stereotypes in African Americans. *Journal of Black Studies, 30*(5), 676–690. doi:10.1177/002193470003000503

Daly, K. J. (2001). Deconstructing family time: From ideology to lived experience. *Journal of Marriage & Family, 63*(2), 283–294. doi:10.1111/j.1741-3737.2001.00283.x

Daneback, K., Cooper, A., & Månsson, S. A. (2005). An Internet study of cybersex participants. *Archives of Sexual Behavior, 34,* 321–328. doi:10.1007/s10508-005-3120-z

Delmonico, D. L., & Griffin, E. J. (2008). Cybersex and the E-teen: What marriage and family therapists should know. *Journal of Marital & Family Therapy, 34*(4), 431–444. doi:10.1111/j.1752-0606.2008.00086.x

Dijkstra, P., Barelds, D. P. H., & Groothof, H. A. K. (2010). An inventory and update of jealousy-evoking partner behaviours in modern society. *Clinical Psychology and Psychotherapy, 17,* 329–345.

Döring, N. (2000). Feminist views of cybersex: Victimization, liberation and empowerment. *CyberPsychology & Behavior, 3,* 863–884. doi:10.1089/10949310050191845

Dryer, J. A., & Lijtmaer, R. M. (2007). Cyber-sex as twilight zone between virtual reality and virtual fantasy: Creative play space or destructive addiction? *Psychoanalytic Review, 94*(1), 39–61. doi:10.1521/prev.2007.94.1.39

Dyck, V., & Daly, K. (2006). Rising to the challenge: Fathers' role in the negotiation of couple time. *Leisure Studies, 25*(2), 201–217. doi:10.1080/02614360500418589

Egger, O., & Rauterberg, M. (1996). *Internet behaviour and addiction* (Technical Report No. AP-01–96). Zurich: Swiss Federal Institute of Technology.

Elphinston, R. A., & Noller, P. (2011). Time to face it! Facebook intrusion and the implications for romantic jealousy and relationship satisfaction.

CyberPsychology, Behavior & Social Networking, 14(11), 631–635. doi:10.1089/cyber.2010.0318

Ferree, M. C. (2003). Women and the web: Cybersex activity and implications. *Sexual and Relationship Therapy, 18*(3), 385–393. doi:10.1080/1468199031000153973

Galvin, K., Bylund, C. L., & Brommel, B. J. (2012). *Family communication: Cohesion and change* (8th ed.). Upper Saddle River, NJ: Pearson.

Griffiths, M. D. (2000b). Internet addiction—Time to be taken seriously? *Addiction Research, 8*, 413–418. doi:10.3109/16066350009005587

Griffiths, M. D. (2001). Sex on the Internet: Observations and implications for Internet sex addictions. *Journal of Sex Research, 38*(4), 333–342. doi:10.3109/16066359.2011.588351

Grohol, J. M. (1999). Too much time online: Internet addiction or healthy social interactions. *Cyberpsychology and Behavior, 2*(5), 395–401.

Guadagno, R. E., & Cialdini, R. B. (2002). Online persuasion: An examination of gender differences in computer-mediated interpersonal influence. *Group Dynamics: Theory, Research, and Practice, 6*(1), 38–51. doi:10.1037/1089-2699.6.1.38

Guadagno, R. E., & Sagarin, B. J. (2010). Sex differences in jealousy: An evolutionary perspective on online infidelity. *Journal of Applied Social Psychology, 40*(10), 2636–2655. doi:10.1111/j.1559-1816.2010.00674.x

Hare-Mustin, R. T., & Marecek, J. (1990). Gender and the meaning of difference: Postmodernism and psychology. In R. T. Hare-Mustin & J. Marecek (Eds.), *Making a difference: Psychology and the construction of gender* (pp. 22–64). New Haven, CT: Yale University Press.

Harvey, J. A., & Hansen, C. E. (1999). Gender role of male therapists in both professional and personal life. *Sex Roles, 41*, 105–113. doi:10.1023/A:1018841909632

Hawkins, B. P., & Hertlein, K. M. (2013). Treatment strategies for couple problems related to massively multiplayer online games. *Journal of Couple and Relationship Therapy, 12(2)* 150–167.

Heather, N. (1998). A conceptual framework for explaining drug addiction. *Journal of Psychopharmacology, 12*(1), 3–7. doi:10.1177/026988119801200101

Heim, J., Brandtzæg, P. B., Kaare, B. H., Endestad, T., & Torgersen, L. (2007). Children's usage of media technologies and psychosocial factors. *New Media & Society, 9*(3), 425–454. doi:10.1177/1461444807076971

Helsper, E. J., & Whitty, M. T. (2010). Netiquette within married couples: Agreement about acceptable online behavior and surveillance between partners. *Computers in Human Behavior, 26*(5), 916–926. doi:10.1016/j.chb.2010.02.006

Henline, B. H., & Lamke, L. K. (2003, November 19–22). *The experience of sexual and emotional online infidelity.* Poster presented at the 65th annual conference of the National Council on Family Relations, Vancouver, British Columbia, Canada.

Hertlein, K. M., & Hawkins, B. P. (2012). Online gaming issues in offline couple relationships: A primer for marriage and family therapists (mfts). *The Qualitative Report, 17*(15), 1–48.

Hertlein, K. M., & Jones, K. E. (2012). Four key dimensions for distinguishing Internet infidelity from Internet and sex addiction: Concepts and clinical application. *American Journal of Family Therapy, 40*(2), 115–125. doi:10.1080/01926187.2011.600677

Hertlein, K. M., & Webster, M. (2008). Technology, relationships, and problems: A research synthesis. *Journal of Marital and Family Therapy, 34*, 445–460. doi:10.1111/j.1752- 606.2008.00087.x

Hertlein, K. M., & Piercy, F. P. (2006). Internet infidelity: A critical review of the literature. *The Family Journal, 14*(3), 366–371. doi:10.1177/1066480706290508

Hill, M. S. (1988). Marital stability and spouses' shared leisure time: A multidisciplinary hypothesis. *Journal of Family Issues, 9,* 427–451.

Holman, T. B., & Jaquart, M. (1988). Leisure–activity patterns and marital satisfaction: A further test. *Journal of Marriage and the Family, 50,* 60–77.

Horvat, J., Oreski, D., & Markic, D. (2011). Gender differences in the Internet usage among postgraduate students. In V. Luzar-Stiffler, I. Jarec, & Z. Bekic (Eds.), *Information Technology Interfaces (ITI): Proceedings of the ITI 2011 33rd International Conference on* Information Technology Interfaces (pp. 281–286). Dubrovnik, Croatia: IEEE.

Hundley, H. L., & Shyles, L. (2010). US teenagers' perceptions and awareness of digital technology: A focus group approach. *New Media & Society, 12*(3), 417–433. doi:10.1177/1461444809342558

Johnson, D. (2005). Two-wave panel analysis: Comparing statistical methods for studying the effects of transitions. *Journal of Marriage and Family, 67,* 1061–1075. doi:10.1111/j.1741-3737.2005.00194.x

Johnson, H. A., Zabriskie, R. B., & Hill, B. (2006). The contribution of couple leisure involvement, leisure time, and leisure satisfaction to marital satisfaction. *Marriage and Family Review, 40,* 69–91. doi:10.1300/J002v40n01_05

Kalmijn, M., & Bernasco, W. (2001). Joint and separated lifestyles in couple relationships. *Journal of Marriage and Family, 63,* 639–654.

Kandell, J. J. (1998). Internet addiction on campus: The vulnerability of college students. *Cyberpsychology and Behavior, 1,* 11–17. doi:10.1089/cpb.1998.1.11

Kelley, L. P., & Blashfield, R. K. (2009). An example of psychological science's failure to self-correct. *Review of General Psychology, 13*(2), 122–129. doi:10.1037/a0015287

Kreek, J. K., Nielsen, D. A., Butelman, E. R., & LaForge, K. S. (2005). Genetic influence on impulsivity, risk taking, stress responsivity and vulnerability to drug abuse and addiction. *Neurobiology of Addiction, 8*(11), 1450–1457. doi:10.1038/nn1583.

Ledgerwood, D. M., & Downey, K. K. (2002). Relationship between problem gambling and substance use in a methadone maintenance population. *Addictive Behaviors, 27,* 483–491. doi:10.1016/S0306-4603(01)00187-3

Ling, R. (2004). *The mobile connection: The cell phone's impact on society.* San Francisco, CA: Morgan Kaufmann.

Lu, H. P., & Wang, S. M. (2008). The role of Internet addiction in online game loyalty: An exploratory study. *Internet Research, 18*(5), 499–519. doi:10.1108/10662240810912756

Mazman, S. G., & Usluel, Y. K. (2011). Gender differences in using social networks. *The Turkish Online Journal of Educational Technology, 10*(2), 133–139.

McGoldrick, M., Carter, B., & Gracia-Preto, N. (2010). *The expanded family life cycle: Individual, family, and social perspectives* (4th ed.). Boston, MA: Allyn and Bacon.

Merta, R. J. (2001). Addictions counseling. *Counseling and Human Development, 33,* 1–15.

Meston, C., & Buss, D. (2009). *Why women have sex.* New York: Henry Holt.

Mileham, B. L. (2007). Online infidelity in Internet chat rooms: An ethnographic exploration. *Computers in Human Behavior, 23*(1), 11–31. doi:10.1016/j.chb.2004.03.033

Mitchell, E. (1985). The dynamics of family interaction around home video games. *Marriage and Family Review, 8*(1–2), 121–135.

Mitchell, K. J., Becker-Blease, K., & Finkelhor, D. (2005). Inventory of problematic Internet experiences encountered in clinical practice. *Professional Psychology: Research & Practice, 36*(5), 498–509. doi:10.1037/0735-7028.36.5.498

Mitchell, K., & Wells, M. (2007). Problematic Internet experiences: Primary or secondary presenting problems in persons seeking mental health care? *Social Science & Medicine, 65*(6), 1136–1141. doi:10.1016/j.socscimed.2007.05.015

Muise, A., Christofides, E., & Desmarais, S. (2009). More information than you ever wanted: Does Facebook bring out the green-eyed monster of jealousy? *CyberPsychology & Behavior, 12,* 441–444. doi:10.1089 = cpb.2008.0263

Muscanell, N. L., & Guadagno, R. E. (2012). Make new friends or keep the old: Gender and personality differences in social networking use. *Computers in Human Behavior, 28*(1), 107–112. doi:10.1016/j.chb.2011.08.016

Nelson, M. L. (1993). A current perspective of gender differences: Implications for research in counseling. *Journal of Counseling Psychology, 40,* 200–209. doi:10.1037/0022-0167.40.2.200

Nelson, T. S. (2000). *Internet infidelity: A modified Delphi study* (Unpublished doctoral dissertation). Purdue University.

Nestler, E. J. (2000). Genes and addiction. *Nature Genetics, 26,* 277–281. doi:10.1038/81570

Owen, J. J., Rhodes, G. K., Stanley, S. M., & Fincham, F. D. (2007). "Hooking up" among college students: Demographic and psychosocial correlates. *Archives of Sexual Behavior, 39,* 653–663. doi:10.1007/s10508-008-9414-1

Parker, T. S., & Wampler, K. S. (2003). How bad is it? Perceptions of the relationships impact of different types of Internet sexual activities. *Contemporary Family Therapy, 25*(4), 415–429. doi:10.1023/A:1027360703099.

Postmes, T., Spears, R., & Lea, M. (1998). Breaching or building social boundaries? SIDE-effects of computer-mediated communication. *Communication Research, 25,* 689–715.

Potenza, M. N. (2002). A perspective on future directions in the prevention, treatment, and research of pathological gambling. *Psychiatric Annals, 2,* 203–207. doi:10.1046/j.1525-1497.2002.10812.x

Raacke, J., & Bonds-Raacke, J. (2008). MySpace and Facebook: Applying the uses and gratifications theory to exploring friend-networking sites. *Cyberpsychology, Behavior, and Social Networking, 11*(2), 169–174.

Rieker, P. P., & Carmen, E. (1984). *The gender gap in psychotherapy.* New York: Plenum Press.

Rogers, S. J., & Amato, P. R. (1997). Is marital quality declining? The evidence from two generations. *Social Forces, 75*(3), 1089–1100.

Roscoe, B., Cavanaugh, L. E., & Kennedy, D. R. (1988). Dating infidelity: Behaviors, reasons and consequences. *Adolescence, 23,* 35–43.

Rowan, M. S., & Galasso, C. S. (2000). Identifying office resource needs of Canadian physicians to help prevent, assess and treat patients with substance use and pathological gambling disorders. *Journal of Addictive Diseases, 19,* 43–58. doi:10.1300/J069v19n02_04

Schneider, J. P. (2003). The impact of compulsive cybersex behaviours on the family. *Sexual and Relationship Therapy, 18*(3), 329–354. doi:10.1080/1468199031001539 46

Seem, S. R., & Johnson, E. (1998). Gender bias among counseling trainees: A study of case conceptualization. *Counselor Education and Supervision, 37,* 257–268. doi:10.1002/j.1556-6978.1998.tb00549.x

Shaughnessy, K., Byers, S., & Thornton, S. J. (2011). What is cybersex? heterosexual students' definitions. *International Journal of Sexual Health, 23*(2), 79–89. doi:10.1080/19317611.2010.546945

Sheinberg, M., & Penn, P. (1991). Gender dilemmas, gender questions and the gender mantra. *Journal of Marital and Family Therapy, 17,* 33–44. doi:10.1111/j.1752-0606.1991.tb00862.x

Sherman, J. (1980). Therapists' attitudes and sex-role stereotyping of women. In A. Brodsky & R. Hare-Mustin (Eds.), *Psychotherapy and women* (pp. 35–66. New York: Guilford.

Shields, C. G., & McDaniel, S. H. (1992). Process differences between male and female therapists in a first family interview. *Journal of Marital and Family Therapy, 18,* 143–151. doi:10.1111/j.1752-0606.1992.tb00925.x

Short, J., Williams, E., & Christie, B. (1976). *The social psychology of telecommunications.* Hoboken, NJ: John Wiley.

Srite, M., Thatcher, J. B., & Galy, E. (2008). Does within-culture variation matter? An empirical study of computer usage. *Journal of Global Information Management, 16*(1), 1–25.

Sullivan, O. (1996). Time co-ordination, the domestic division of labour and affective relations: Time use and the enjoyment of activities within couples. *Sociology, 30,* 79–100.

Taylor, T. L. (2006). *Play between worlds: Exploring online game culture.* Cambridge, MA: MIT Press.

Tichenor, V. J. (1999). Status and income as gendered resources: The case of marital power. *Journal of Marriage & Family, 61*(3), 638–650.

Tokunaga, R. S. (2011). Social networking site or social surveillance site? Understanding the use of interpersonal electronic surveillance in romantic relationships. *Computers in Human Behavior, 27*(2), 705–713. doi:10.1016/j.chb.2010.08.014

Underwood, H., & Findlay, B. (2004). Internet relationships and their impact on primary relationships. *Behaviour Change, 21*(02), 127-140. Retrieved from http://www.ic.unicamp.br/~wainer/cursos/2s2008/impactos/casamento1.pdf

Utz, S., & Beukeboom, C. J. (2011). The role of social network sites in romantic relationships: Effects on jealousy and relationship happiness. *Journal of Computer-Mediated Communication, 16*(4), 511–527. doi:10.1111/j.1083-6101.2011.01552.x

Voorpostel, M., Lippe, T., & Gershuny, J. (2009). Trends in free time with a partner: A transformation of intimacy? *Social Indicators Research, 93*(1), 165–169. doi:10.1007/s11205-008-9383-8

Waskul, D., Douglass, M., & Edgley, C. (2000). Cybersex: Outercourse and the enselfment of the body. *Symbolic Interaction, 23,* 375–397.

Weeks, G., Gambescia, N., & Jenkins, R. (2003). *Treating infidelity: Therapeutic dilemmas and effective strategies.* New York: Guilford.

Werner-Wilson, R. J., Price, S. J., Zimmerman, T. S., & Murphy, M. J. (1997). Client gender as a process variable in marriage and family therapy: Are women clients interrupted more than men clients? *Journal of Family Psychotherapy, 11,* 373–377. doi:10.1037/0893-3200.11.3.373

Whitty, M. T. (2005). The realness of cybercheating: Men's and women's representations of unfaithful Internet relationships. *Social Science Computer Review, 23*(1), 57–67.

Whitty, M. T., Young, G., & Goodings, L. (2011). What I won't do in pixels: Examining the limits of taboo violation in MMORPGs. *Computers in Human Behavior, 27,* 268–275.

Widyanto, L., & Griffiths, M. (2006). "Internet Addiction": A critical review. *International Journal of Mental Health & Addiction, 4,* 31–51.

Williams, D., Consalvo, M., Caplan, S., & Yee, N. (2009). Looking for gender (LFG): Gender roles and behaviors among online gamers. *Journal of Communication, 59,* 700–725.

Young, G., & Whitty, M. T. (2010). Games without frontiers: On the moral and psychological implications of violating taboos within multi-player virtual spaces. *Computers in Human Behavior, 26*(6), 1228–1236.

Young, G., & Whitty, M. T. (2011). Should gamespace be a taboo-free zone? Moral and psychological implications for single-player video games. *Theory & Psychology, 21*(6), 802–820.

Young, K. S. (1999). The evaluation and treatment of Internet addiction. In L. VandeCreek & T. Jackson (Eds.), *Innovations in clinical practice: A source book* (pp. 19–31). Sarasota, FL: Professional Resource Press.

Young, K. S., Griffin-Shelly, E., Cooper, A., O'Mara, J., & Buchanan, J. (2000). Online infidelity: A new dimension in couple relationships with implications for evaluation and treatment. *Sexual Addiction & Compulsivity: The Journal of Treatment & Prevention, 7*(1–2), 59–74. doi:10.1080/10720160008400207

Zhong, Z. (2011). The effects of collective MMORPG (massively multiplayer online role-playing games) play on gamers' online and offline social capital. *Computers in Human Behavior, 27*(6), 2352–2363.

4 The Couple and Family Technology Framework

When I got my first television set, I stopped caring so much about having close relationships.

—Andy Warhol

The Development of the CFT Framework

Some years ago, I (K.H.) conducted a workshop at a national conference. The topic was Internet infidelity, with specific attention to the facets of a therapist's values that contribute to and/or detract from successful resolution in these cases. As my copresenter and I presented the self-of-therapist concepts related to treatment, a workshop attendee posed a question about the difference between Internet infidelity and addiction. My copresenter and I briefly distinguished the difference and moved onto another topic. Shortly after, a related question arose: "Well isn't it like having an alcoholic go to a bar?" Several attendees nodded in agreement. As we responded to the question, each response outlining the differences between the two was met with assertions from the attendees that the two phenomena were the same. No matter what we said, many workshop attendees were convinced there was no separation between Internet infidelity and addiction.

As I returned home from the conference, I could not get the responses from the attendees out of my head, primarily because it mirrored the comments and questions that I was receiving from clients. In many cases, clients had approached me about the addiction to the computer that seemed to be emerging with their partner. It was a problem that had never before emerged within the couple's relationship until a computer or another electronic device entered the picture. I considered the ways in which I could better present the training material in such a way that would teach others the distinct differences between Internet addiction, sex addiction, and Internet infidelity. Improving my training around this topic meant understanding the etiology of the disconnect. For example, practicing therapists seem very well capable of treating the conventionally understood type of infidelity. They can articulate their assessment procedures, their strategies, the multiple dimensions of the problem (Weeks, Gambescia, & Jenkins, 2003), understanding the relational climate in which the infidelity was born, the importance of forgiveness, and the manner in which couples make decisions about their relationship.

Enter the computer. The same assessment strategies, interventions, case conceptualization, and treatment structure seem to no longer be considered by practicing therapists. In other words, the default, which once was "here is what I do in every other infidelity case," shifts to "this must be an addiction." This sentiment was not only expressed in the conferences and workshop questions, but also in empirical data. Hertlein and Piercy (2008) found that therapists generally considered a couple's infidelity experience to emerge in the context of relational deficits. Yet when asked about the treatment strategies for Internet infidelity, some of the initial strategies mentioned revolved around implementing first-order changes (i.e., managing the environment around the computer, such as moving the computer to another room where its usage could be monitored).

These observations as well as others, experienced over the course of a short period of time, caused me to think about the way in which a computer's structure has shifted the way the conference attendees, and ultimately clients, think about relationships and technology. Why would the introduction of a computer change the way people think about their cases? And, more importantly, how can I articulate the manner in which these impacts occur? Certain elements about the computer and new media (i.e., the ecological elements) to be discussed in Chapter 5 bear some responsibility in some specific ways. One way is they change the structure (defined as roles, rules, and boundaries) of couple and family relationships. These ecological elements also change the processes (defined as relationship initiation, relationship maintenance, and relationship dissolution) in relationships. In an earlier draft of this book, we elected to spend one chapter discussing the structural changes driven by the ecological elements and in a subsequent chapter, discuss the changes to process. Yet, as the writing process emerged, it became clear that we could not discuss the impact to roles, rules, and boundaries without also identifying how these shifts in structure had both direct and indirect implications for relational processes. In fact, the framework as outlined in Figure 4.1 notes feedback between structure and process changes. Therefore, in this chapter we will highlight (a) specific structural issues related to technology and new media, (b) processes in relationships related to technology and new media, and (c) how the structural changes influence process changes, and vice versa.

The Couple and Family Technology (CFT) Framework is based on the integration of three broad perspectives in family science: the family ecology perspective, the structural-functional perspective, and the interaction-constructionist perspective. This model was originally published in *Family Relations* (Hertlein, 2012) but has been updated to more

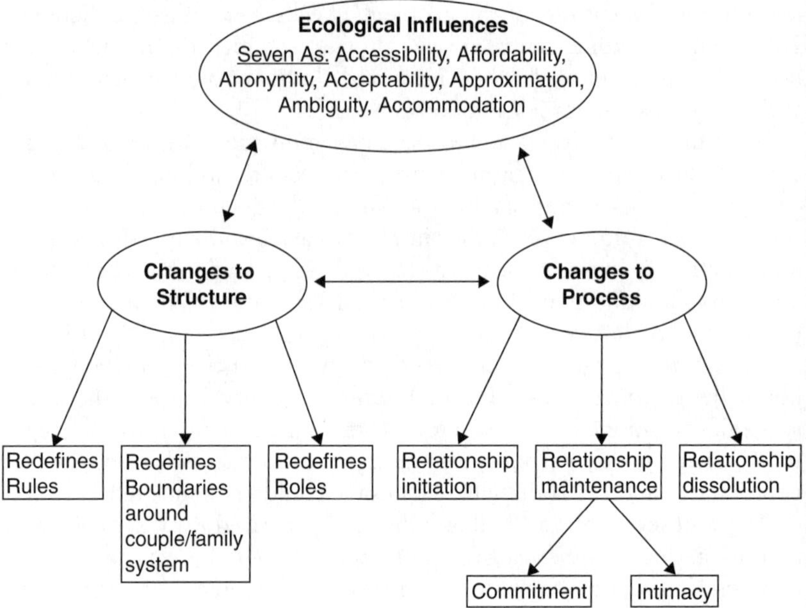

Figure 4.1 The CFT framework.

accurately reflect the relationship processes. The seven As, or ecological elements in relationship to be described in Chapter 5, are driven by the family ecology perspective, which addresses the ways in which one's environment and context influence individual/relational systems. In the CFT framework, the ecological elements drive a couple's structure and processes, specifically with regard to rules, roles, boundaries, intimacy, commitment, and others. Further, changes to only one level of structure do not necessarily mean there are changes to one level of process; rather, changes to one level of structure (roles, for example) can inspire changes in many levels of process, such as commitment, intimacy building, trust, and others. In other words, one specific change to structure does not predict a change in a specific process; rather, the specific changes to process are influenced by the structural changes as well as the couple's context, history, stressors, and other pertinent information.

The CFT framework is more aligned with domestication theory (Haddon, 2006; Silverstone, Hirsch, & Morley, 1992) than it is the Technology Acceptance Model (TAM; Davis, 1989). As a general framework applied to understanding usage of a variety of applications, TAM describes the processes by which computer users adopt various emerging technologies, but was initially designed to address what affected technology usage in the workplace (Lu, Yu, Liu, & Yao, 2003). TAM is based on the assumption that people have particular beliefs about the ease of computer usage, which in turn affect their attitudes about computer and technology, thus affecting their behavior (i.e., increased intention to use that technology, which leads to actual usage of the technology; Davis, 1989; Lu et al., 2003). The belief held related to the extent to which the technology in question is useful or easy to use is dictated to some degree by the external variables surrounding it. For example, Mary learns that there is a new computer program that can help her manage her weight. She believes this program is easy to learn and therefore, has developed a positive attitude with regard to the program. This positive attitude corresponds with an increased intention to use this type of technology (Burton-Jones & Hubona, 2006). Of the four stages identified (external variables influencing perceived usefulness and perceived ease of use, leading to attitude and behavioral intentions for usage), the most important relationship is that between the perceived usefulness and behavioral intentions (Hynes & Rommes, 2005; King & He, 2006). Specific variables appear to have a meditating relationship on the perceived usefulness and perceived ease of usage of technology (King & He, 2006). Some examples include: age, level of education, and prior experience (Agarwal & Prasad, 1999; King & He, 2006).

Alternately, domestication theory focuses on how families adapt to and, consequently, incorporate technology into their day-to-day life. As couples and families adopt technology into their lives, the developments made to technology change in response to enhance its utilities for families (Haddon, 2006). This approach fits more with our conceptualization of the role of technology and new media in family life because we see the integration of technology into people's lives as something that influences people's behavior rather than focusing on narrowing on intention of usage. In describing the process by which the Internet entered our homes, Bakardjieva (2006) noted,

> The boundaries between the world beyond the doorstep and the 'private' life of the household were ceaselessly cracking and shifting. People were bringing in work from their offices and schools, friends and relatives were coming and staying, giving remote input and advice, demanding time and attention. The physical household was in actuality only a node in a much larger network of significant others, which, to a large extent, determined the nature and rhythms of its preoccupations. . . . Objects such as computers and modems were flowing across the public-private divide and along the interpersonal networks reaching far beyond the doorstep so that it was difficult to say exactly which object belonged to the particular household. (p. 66)

The same process is true for the CFT framework. First, the three components of the model recursively influence one another. The ecological elements affect how structure and processes in relationships manifest because they affect both the structure and process of relationships. Further, the shifts in structure can affect changes to process and changes to process can subsequently affect changes to structure, such as changes to boundaries, and consequently, couple and family processes. According to Spears and Lea (1994), "CMC [computer-mediated communication] introduces the possibility of revolutionary social and structural changes in the ways that people communicate and relate to each other" (p. 427). One primary example is in the issue of accessibility (an ecological element) within computer-mediated communication as it relates to boundaries (a structural component), and power (a relational process) as described in the SIDE model proposed by Spears and Lea (1994). The SIDE model "is a theory of situated self-categorization, and tries to specify the situational conditions under which different self-categories will be salient and under which behavior normative to that category will be appropriate and possible" (Spears & Lea, 1994, p. 441).

One of the areas in which this is more prevalent is in the area of increased accessibility in our digital world. Computers, new media, and technology make the ability to communicate with many groups of people at any given time easier than ever before in history because it increases accessibility (Spears & Lea, 1994). With increased accessibility, users of computers and other new media are afforded the opportunity to connect with others more broadly outside of their traditional social circle. New media allows users to transcend the typical boundaries and adopt new roles in other structures and groups that they would not be able to otherwise. For example, as the Internet creates equal opportunity for both men and women to cheat (Hertlein & Stevenson, 2010), it creates an equalizing phenomenon (Dubrovsky, Kiesler, & Sethna, 1991), specifically in terms of power with regard to sex outside of the relationship. This phenomenon is related to the Foucault concept of panopticon, or the concept that specific structural features of something contribute to control, surveillance, and equality (Spears & Lea, 1994). Another prime example of an ecological element's influence on the process and structure of relationships is in the case of anonymity. Postmes, Spears, and Lea (1998) discussed the concept of anonymity in computer-mediated communication and proposed that anonymous users may have a tendency to become deindividuated, meaning they more closely follow the norms of the group. The impact could also be opposite on the process: Haines and Mann (2011) found that anonymity changed the group dynamics when awareness was involved—in other words, in groups with more awareness of other's actions, there was a higher likelihood to feel indispensable. In either case, the implementation of new media and technology into relationships results in people's views of their role in the relationships, which can have direct implications for the subsequent actions and behavior within that group context.

Another characteristic of the domestication model is the importance of symbolism and meaning. In other words, users of technology and new media will ascribe meanings to certain technology functions (Hynes & Rommes, 2005). This, too, corresponds with the CFT framework. In many cases, couples ascribe meaning to the applications, programs, and technologies used by their partners, particularly when it accompanies behaviors viewed negatively by the other partner.

The Flexibility of the CFT Framework

The interaction of ecological elements, structure, and process is certainly a complicated one. It will also vary for each couple depending on the unique elements and dynamics within the couple's relationship. One of the advantages to the CFT framework is that it is succinct enough to be able to accurately describe the process for couple and families, but broad enough to be able to account for the many ways in which the couple might present. It functions as a meta-perspective to already existing theories. In other words, therapists working with couples from this perspective can continue to use the theories that best fit them, but do so underneath the umbrella of the CFT approach. It is a way to conceptualize how technology affects couple (and family) life rather than being prescriptive with regard to theoretical orientation.

Part of its flexibility rests on the fact that, as a way to think about cases, the CFT framework is broad enough to be adapted to couples of varied cultural and ethnic backgrounds. Every couple has differences in their values, rules, and the way that they define their relationship. For example, Sergi and Nadia, both originally from Siberia but now residing in the United States, stated the computer is accessible and allows for affordable interaction, which leads them to feel more connected and supported in their relationship with family members in their country of origin; yet that same accessibility and affordability is concerning for others, like more rural couples. For instance, Johona and Lynxton, two individuals from Native American descent, live in a remote area in the Desert Southwest of the United States. They tend to view the accessibility that technology brings into their home with more suspicion and have developed more stringent rules with regard to its usage in the relationship.

Case Conceptualization: Using the CFT Framework

The Case of Jake and Bella

Jake and Bella sought treatment to recover from infidelity. Jake, a 35-year-old male who worked in the financial industry, had been discovered by his 34-year-old wife Bella as having a year-long affair with a previous girlfriend. While Jake's relationship with his ex-girlfriend prior to meeting Bella had been conducted offline, his more recent affair had been facilitated primarily online with a few meetings offline in a hotel in another city where they consummated their relationship. Bella discovered the relationship through text messages she found on Jake's phone. She received confirmation when she logged into his e-mail account and read the e-mails exchanged between Jake and his ex-girlfriend.

This case, as conceptualized with the CFT framework, occurred on three levels and an understanding of the ecological elements of the relationship and its effects on both structure and process of the relationship. First, the accessibility to communication mechanisms such as Jake's cell phone made it easier for him to communicate with his ex-girlfriend. The accessibility of devices and specific applications translated into Jake being accessible to his former partner as well as she being accessible to him. In fact, her ability to locate him through a social networking site is how they were able to reconnect. Next, once they were able to be accessible to one another through a social networking site, they exchanged contact information and were then accessible to one another through text messaging, e-mailing, and phone calls via mobile phones. Finally, because the communication through cell phone and e-mail are already paid for in monthly charges, the communication was affordable. Jake also used the relationship as a way to approximate what he wanted to do in his real life that he did not feel that he could do with his wife. One of the most disturbing aspects of the affair according to Bella was that the e-mails sounded as if Jake's true voice and genuine personality were coming through—a side that she had not seen in him in a while. She indicated that she believed that this is who he really was in real life and that he was hiding these things from her. She stated that she was concerned that he was able to reveal himself to this ex-girlfriend and not to her, which spelled out more danger for the relationship.

All of these things together altered the structure of the relationship. The boundaries that used to be around the couple became more diffuse. Suddenly, the boundary of the relationship went outside of the family home and invited people in ways that were not expected or agreed on by the couple. It also included people in Jake's electronic social networking circle in a way that the couple had not discussed. Further, the infidelity prompted a role change in Bella with which she was uncomfortable. Bella described herself as always priding herself in having a relationship where her partner played an equal part. She did not enjoy being in the position of being the person who had to check up on her husband, and her discomfort in her new role as someone who had to investigate her partner's behavior. Because the infidelity was primarily conducted online in Bella and Jake's home (and in some cases, right next to her) she felt as if her role transitioned into one of policing Jake's behavior. Bella's new role was further confirmed by the new rules that were developed in the relationship: She demanded and monitored the construction of a letter indicating that he was ending the relationship. Further, Bella and Jake had decided to sit down and develop rules within their relationship.

The structural changes had specific impacts on the process of the relationship. Suddenly, Bella began to question all of his connections and with this she experienced a profound level of jealousy and torment. In other times, when one experiences infidelity, the triggers seemed to be more direct. With Internet infidelity, Bella found that she was reacting to everything that Jake was doing and was being triggered all of the time. The fact that he was texting to someone on his phone, using the computer, or responding to a phone call all were triggers in addition to mentions of the city where Jake had gone to meet his lover and songs on the radio that reminded Bella of her husband's infidelity. This experience negatively impacted her experience of the relationship to the point where Jake was left to do all of the maintenance on the relationship because Bella was constantly being triggered. This resulted in her being more agitated and angry with Jake, who was beginning to feel like he could never catch a break.

The Case of Charisse and David

Charisse, 28, and David, 32, sought premarital counseling. Both described their relationship as healthy and were very much looking forward to the wedding. The couple had been together for 8 years, living together for the past 5 years. They became engaged a year ago and both reported that the process of premarital counseling for them was something that they wanted to do to have a stronger relationship. They did not note any concerns in the relationship they particularly felt a need to address in treatment.

In conversation with the couple, the therapist asked about computer and Internet usage. Both looked at each other and acknowledged that they had not yet had a conversation about the role that it played in their lives. Charisse reported that she had not had any issues or even desire to "check in" on David's e-mail accounts as some of her friends felt that they had to do in their relationships. David stated that technology actually made it easier for him to communicate with her and their mutual friends as a way to organize schedules and make plans with one another since both of them were typically on the run at their jobs. Charisse added that David was frequently good at communicating with her during their busy days through short text messages. She also stated she believed the fact that he was able to connect with her in that way was one of the things that drew the two of them together because they were able to share details of their daily life quickly and rather effortlessly.

These two case conceptualizations demonstrate that the CFT framework provides a way of viewing technology in relation to couples and families that is both flexible and concrete, making it easy to have a time efficient and effective way to quickly assess and better understand the part technology is playing in relationships, whether this part is viewed as more positive or negative.

References

Agarwal, R., & Prasad, J. (1999). Are individual differences germane to the acceptance of new information technologies? *Decision Sciences, 30*(2), 361–391.

Bakardjieva, M. (2006). Domestication running wild. From the moral economy of the household to the mores of culture. In T. Berker, M. Hartmann, Y. Punie, & K. Ward (Eds.), *Domestication of media and technologies* (pp. 62–79). Maidenhead, England: Open University Press.

Burton-Jones, A., & Hubona, G. S. (2006). The mediation of external variables in the technology acceptance model. *Information & Management, 43*(6), 706–717. doi:10.1016/j.im.2006.03.007

Davis, F. D. (1989). Perceived usefulness, perceived ease of use, and user acceptance of information technology. *MIS Quarterly, 13*(3), 319–340.

Dubrovsky, J., Kiesler, S., & Sethna, B. (1991). The equalization phenomenon: Status effects in computer-mediated and face-to-face decision-making groups. *Human–Computer Interaction, 6*(2), 119–146. doi:10.1207/s15327051hci0602_2

Haddon, L. (2006). The contribution of domestication research to in-home computing and media consumption. *The Information Society, 22*, 195–203. doi:10.1080/01972240600791325

Haines, R., & Mann, J. E. C. (2011). A new perspective on de-individuation via computer-mediated communication. *European Journal of Information Systems, 20*(2), 156–167. doi:10.1057/ejis.2010.70

Hertlein, K. M. (2012). Digital dwelling: Technology in couple and family relationships. *Family Relations, 61*(3), 374–387. doi:10.1111/j.1741-3729.2012.00702.x

Hertlein, K. M., & Piercy, F. P. (2008). Therapists' assessment and treatment of Internet infidelity cases. *Journal of Marital & Family Therapy, 34*(4), 481–497. doi:10.1111/j.1752-0606.2008.00090.x

Hertlein, K. M., & Stevenson, A. (2010). The seven "As" contributing to Internet-related intimacy problems: A literature review. *Cyberpsychology: Journal of Psychosocial Research on Cyberspace, 4*(1). Retrieved from http://cyberpsychology.eu/view.php?cisloclanku = 2010050202&article = 3

Hynes, D., & Rommes, E. (2005). "Fitting the Internet into our lives": IT courses for disadvantaged users. In T. Berker, Y. Punie, & M. Hartmann (Eds.), *Domestication of media and technology* (pp. 123-144). Berkshire, England: McGraw-Hill Education.

King, W. R., & He, J. (2006). A meta-analysis of the technology acceptance model. *Information & Management, 43*(6), 740–755. doi:10.1016/j.im.2006.05.003

Lu, J., Yu, C. S., Liu, C., & Yao, J. E. (2003). Technology acceptance model for wireless Internet. *Internet Research, 13*(3), 206–222. doi:10.1108/10662240310478222

Postmes, T., Spears, R., & Lea, M. (1998). Breaching or building social boundaries? SIDE-effects of computer-mediated communication. *Communication Research, 25*, 689–715. doi:10.1177/009365098025006006

Silverstone, R., Hirsch, E., & Morley, D. (1992). Information and communication technologies and the moral economy of the household. In Silverstone, R. and Hirsch, E. (eds.) Consuming Technologies, Consuming Technologies (pp. 15–31). London: Routledge.

Spears, R., & Lea, M. (1994). Panacea or panopticon? The hidden power in computer-mediated communication. *Communication Research, 21*(4), 427–459. doi:10.1177/009365094021004001

Weeks, G. R., Gambescia, N., & Jenkins, R. E. (2003). *Treating infidelity: Therapeutic dilemmas and effective strategies.* New York: W. W. Norton.

5 Ecological Influences on the Couple System

Human beings, viewed as behaving systems, are quite simple. The apparent complexity of our behavior over time is largely a reflection of the complexity of the environment in which we find ourselves.

—*Herbert Simon*

Acceptability

The Internet, engagement in new media, and ownership of more advanced technological gadgets is becoming more acceptable, both within our work and personal lives. For example, it is not uncommon for people in a place of employment to attend work meetings with a writing instrument, pad of paper, and a smartphone or other portable electronic device. The placement of mobile phone numbers on business cards in addition to the office number is another example of how acceptable technologies are becoming in one's work life.

Other aspects of new media that are becoming acceptable include the presence of an account on Facebook, Twitter, and other sites that provide opportunity for social engagement. People may be part of support groups online or chat rooms where they are dedicated to dealing with a particular topic and issue. For example, participation in online dating is increasing as an acceptable practice (McCown, Fischer, Page, & Homant, 2001). It may increase with age, suggesting that this phenomenon is becoming more acceptable with older persons (Stephure, Boon, MacKinnon, & Deveau, 2009). Using the Internet to pursue sexual interests is also becoming more acceptable (Daneback, Cooper, & Månsson, 2005).

As acceptability of ownership becomes more prevalent, the behaviors couples adopt also center around the meaning of what is acceptable for their peer group. This can raise serious issues for couples. Bob and Nancy came to treatment due to the experience of infidelity in their relationship. Because the communication with the third party was carried on via Facebook, the couple discussed and agreed they would both delete their Facebook accounts completely. This raised a secondary issue in the couple relationship: how was each member of the couple going to explain they were no longer participating in Facebook, a very acceptable practice, to other people without describing the incident that brought them to therapy? In the end, the acceptability of Facebook in their lives (and the lives of their friends) heavily influenced the couple to reinstate the Facebook accounts and led them to develop different strategies to protect their relationship and maintain an intimate connection.

Acceptability refers to both the practice of using the Internet and web-based services for a variety of functions but also the extent to which the new relationships formed from an online interaction are becoming more acceptable themselves. Regardless of the application or form of new media, Madden and Lenhart (2006) wrote specifically about how common the Internet is becoming for the initiation and development of romantic relationships. The initiation of such relationships can occur within social networking sites, but is certainly not limited to these sites.

Implicit in the practice of forming relationships online is the acceptable nature of participating in an intimate relationship maintained primarily online. Because couples are able to interact virtually, there may be fewer instances where they actually get a sense of each other in day-to-day life. One of the things evading couples is the sense of "everydayness" present in face-to-face relationships. This has resulted in an alternative model of couple development (which is discussed in Chapter 9) where the couple spends time feeling each other out, then going on a trip as their first physical encounter or meeting up for the weekend, and then making a decision whether to proceed with the relationship. In some cases, this might make sense for a wide variety of couple relationships.

In some cases, this acceptable practice can also create complications for couples. Ben and Lisa came to treatment because they were struggling in their relationship. Upon intake, the couple noted they had met online and pursued the relationship through instant messaging over one of the messaging systems. As time grew, they decided to meet for the first time on a week-long vacation to Hawaii. While no one could doubt the couple was crazy about one another, she stated her friends were concerned about her going for two main reasons: (a) personal safety and (b) the only physical interactions they would have and real-time opportunities to experience one another would be only in a vacation setting. This pattern in the relationship continued over time, with the couple going on vacation with each other twice more over an 8-month period and spending the rest of the time online. At the last trip, he asked her to marry him and the couple married 3 months later and she moved with him from a Midwestern state to a location in the Pacific Northwest. Within months of marrying him, she indicated that she began to see sides of him she had not previously seen on their trips and, after 5 years, found herself desperately unhappy without a clear idea of what had gone wrong; in this case, it was the acceptability of carrying the bulk of the relationship through web communication and leaving the physical interactions to occur while the couple was vacationing. Vacationing, of course, has very different characteristics than everyday life.

The acceptability of online relating has also increased the acceptability of being in a long-distance relationship and living away from extended family. Additionally, with the advent of video phoning and other similar capabilities, it is becoming more acceptable to move away from one's birthplace and central hub. As Bacigalupe and Lambe (2011) note, "technology is used first to maintain preexisting relationships (e.g., children moving away from their parents, who remain in the home region) and then to build on their existing relationship despite the lack of a common place" (p. 17). The acceptability of incorporating these issues in a couple's life also requires some negotiation. For which families is it more acceptable to participate in online interactions? Are there some families that actually require or value significantly more highly the physical face-to-face time instead of face-to-face time conducted over the Internet?

Likewise, there are also certain other expectations within families affecting the couple with regard to Internet time. For example, a family's participation in online gaming may be an important point of sharing and family connection that they experience. Many people participate in the massively multiplayer online role playing games (MMORPGs), games facilitated by social networking sites that they can play with their friends and similar games on their cell phones. This provides an opportunity to interact with extended family and friends in a way that maintains the connection but that does not necessarily entail sending individual messages or e-mails to them. In short, it is a way of being connected while being disconnected. The acceptable nature of such gaming within one's social life often has direct and indirect implications for couple life. A direct implication relates to with whom the interaction is with; the other implication is what is said and communicated within these games. For example, one partner may feel conflicted about their partner's daily contact with a former partner through these games—on the one hand, the partner is communicating little in the way of emotion and personal thought through playing games. On the other hand, there are many people with whom the game could be played—why choose one person who is a former partner?

The acceptability of these gadgets also has implications for boundaries and acceptable behavior within relationships. With regard to infidelity, women are more likely to cheat when they were in the same social group as other women who cheated (Atwater, 1979; Buunk, 1980). In its application to families and children, it is more becoming the norm that teens and kids have their own cell phones (Campbell & Ling, 2009). Though this research was conducted in the late 70s and early 80s, it begs the question as to whether the same thing occurs for men, or for gay, lesbian, or bisexual identifying persons, or whether the same phenomenon occur if you know people online who cheat and socialize with that group.

One result of the notion that people who know others who cheat online and accept infidelity behavior is it may create hyper vigilance for one partner in the relationship. Part and parcel with this hyper vigilance is an increased sense of justification and with regard to hacking one's partner's account. In a world that is getting exponentially more technological, it is becoming more acceptable to tap into your partner's personal account should you become suspect of their activities. For example, Molly and Desmond met through an online dating portal. After a few months of exchanging e-mails and texting, they began meeting up for dates—first, group dates with friends and later, dates with just one other. Within 8 months of their first online encounter, the couple decided Desmond would move into Molly's apartment. Shortly after moving, Desmond demanded that Molly provide him with her passwords for her e-mail and social networking accounts and, likewise, provided her with his account information. While Molly was not interested in logging into his accounts, she began to notice periodically that he would log into her accounts and monitor the activity and behavior with her friends and colleagues.

Another element of acceptability is the fact that some websites are geared toward and create an acceptable environment for couples to participate in hurtful or damaging behavior. For example, some sites have been created to advertise that someone is a poor partner. Other sites advertise they are a site that develops acceptability around the practice of cheating on one's partner. Certainly, the people using these sites do not have to be married or even in a relationship; however, the idea there are sites which create a context of acceptability for either cheating or potentially slandering one's partner certainly do not necessarily contribute to the health of a relationship.

Anonymity

Anonymity means users can present themselves to be in any way they desire to someone on the other end of an electronic communication (Cooper, 2002). Using the Internet and other forms of new media present one with the ability to present particular aspects about themselves to others without being challenged by the other people online with whom they are communicating or interacting. Because of this, the person who is anonymous has a higher degree of control in his or her self-presentation:

> Those engaging in online relationships can choose to present a detached attachment or absent presence characterized by features of oppositionality: distance/immediacy; anonymity/disclosure; deception/sincerity . . . in one line of text, an individual can transmit confessional self-disclosure while remaining anonymous. (Hertlein & Sendak, 2007, p. 2)

Retaining anonymity in Internet relationships can take many forms. Some people might choose to conceal their relationship status, their physical characteristics, or their immediate responses within interactions. In some cases, one may choose to omit or embellish physical characteristics of themselves, particularly if a face-to-face meeting does not appear to be on the horizon for a great deal of time. Further, if photos are exchanged, it is worth noting these photos may be edited by someone with a computer program as to appear perfect. This allows people developing relationships to be able to test the waters and gain acceptance prior to becoming completely vulnerable in a relationship. This is critical in relationship initiation, where often the physical characteristics block the development of any type of relationship from the start (McKenna, Green, & Gleason, 2002).

Most of the examples here detail the fact that anonymity refers to the sender of the message. Anonymity, however, can also refer to the description of the person receiving the transmission and can have important implications for couple relationships. Carl's partner Lindsey was in another area of their house when her phone beeped to indicate she has just received a message. As Carl grabbed the phone to bring it to her, he glanced at the message and noticed it seemed suspicious. Carl began to respond to the person as if he was Lindsey, and through this interaction discovered she was having a relationship with someone else.

In addition to one's ability to hide personal attributes from others, anonymity also refers to when users can be anonymous with their exchanges and interactions. Unlike face-to-face interactions, communication via a keyboard allows the person typing to edit their responses as they interact with others. Nonverbal reactions of a receiver are not automatically communicated to the sender as they are in face-to-face interactions (Cooper, 2002). Instead, any communication or reaction by the receiver that is communicated back to the original sender can be carefully crafted as to hide any reactions that may not be viewed favorably by the other party. The ability for online interactions to provide users with a way to edit, delete, backspace, and think about messages before hitting "send" provides a cloak of anonymity with regard to their emotions, reactions, and, in some ways, their authentic self.

The use of anonymity and limited disclosure of authentic reactions as a protective mechanism in relationships may assist a relationship in getting off the ground in the early stages until such a time where the relationship is safe enough to handle how each person honestly feels about certain issues. Part of this may be due to the fact that as each person is getting to know the other, messages eliciting a negative reaction by the reader may be given the benefit of the doubt that the sender was not aware of how the message came across. For example, Anna and Sonja, a same-sex couple in a committed relationship, came to treatment to manage Anna's recent anger outburst. When the therapist asked about their use of technology, Anna stated that her partner Sonja's communications with her over e-mail are short, abrupt, and read rather harshly. Anna, however, decided to look past the tone of the messages because she believed that Sonja was unaware of how the tone in the messages came across. After several months, however, Anna indicated the tone was becoming hurtful to her and that Sonja now needed to construct her messages differently and with a soft, supportive tone. Sonja expressed confusion at the new rules—if Anna was not upset before at her tone, why was she upset now? Clearly, if editing reactions continues beyond a certain point in a relationship, the couple may discover they do not have the level of intimacy or safety in the relationship they previously believed they had.

Anonymity has been tied directly to online infidelity. In research within an Internet chat room examining the key elements that contribute to affairs, Mileham (2007) found three: behavioral rationalization, effortless avoidance, and anonymous sexual interactionism. Anonymous sexual interactionism is the term used to describe the experience of treating the chat room as if it was a movie, watching things go by and, consequently, detaching themselves from their behavior in the process. When one becomes detached from their own behavior, the result may be a slippery slope, or progressively moving toward increasingly risky, problematic and/or hurtful behavior. The same situation occurs more broadly within online news articles with a comments section following the article. Consider the more recent article that you read in an online news source with a comments section after the article. It is likely that it did not take long for the comments to turn negative and personally attacking (perhaps three to four comments).

The concept of anonymity in this paradigm is no different from the paradigm offered in the Milgram experiments of the 1960s. Along with the demand characteristics of the experts instructing the research subjects to complete their tasks, the separation of the individual from the person to whom they were administering the shocks and the inherent anonymity within that structure contributed to the likelihood of administering the shocks (Badhwar, 2009). Anonymity has a rather prominent place in the decisions one makes about engaging in a particular behavior.

Accessibility

Recently, my (K.H.) husband was at a local car dealership waiting for a repair. In the waiting room with our 4-year-old son, he was joined by another man and his young child, approximately 2 1/2 years old. The man pulled out a tablet computer and put it in front of his son to occupy him while the man began to work on his laptop. The boy turned to look at my son and my son in turn turned to look at the boy. My son told my husband, "That boy is looking at me," and my husband went over to my son and saw what was on the tablet—Japanese anime pornography. The father of the other young boy noticed my son looking at the tablet and said to my husband: "Oh, he can watch that too if he wants." My husband politely declined and told my son to come with him. The other man peered out from his laptop screen and looked at the tablet. Upon realizing what was on it, he exclaimed "Oh my gosh! What are you watching?!?" and proceeded to change what was being portrayed on the computer.

This scenario exemplifies the concept of accessibility—just about anybody can access the Internet if given the proper connection and tools. Cooper (2002) described accessibility as the characteristic of the Internet allowing for individuals to be able to access a wide variety of material. While he described accessibility as related to the accessibility of sexual material online in his book "Sex and the Internet," it can refer to a wide variety of electronic material. One, for example, is the increased accessibility to our partners through e-mails, instant messaging, and other mechanisms (Cooper, 2002). Because of this accessibility, couples now have to negotiate the presence of media in their lives. Other elements of the Internet that have to be negotiated include access to others via social networking sites, blogs, chat rooms, and websites. Internet-based search engines exponentially increase our accessibility in its ability to find any number of people through posted addresses, phone records, and related contact information.

In addition to the accessibility provided by the Internet to the outside world, the reverse is also true: The Internet allows for us to be accessible to other people and entities. In other words, the Internet introduces people who are known to us and unknown to us into our couple and family relationships. Kyle and Laura came to treatment to address their constant bickering. Their latest argument centered on the connection Kyle made with a former partner online. Kyle indicated he did not seek out the contact with the former partner, but that the former partner had found him through an Internet search. Laura was critical of Kyle's handling of the situation. She indicated Kyle should have not at all accepted the communication—that is to say, not responded to the e-mail and pretended he never got it as a way to demonstrate a boundary around the couple's relationship.

The issue of others inviting themselves into daily life is no different and can occur in families as well. In another case, Morgan was able to access the information and e-mail address of her birth father, Ron—someone who had not played any part of her life in 16 years. With the accessibility of his information, she drafted and sent an e-mail inviting him into her life. This created complications for both Ron and his now-wife Monique, as well as their two children. Her ability to access them and invite him into their lives put Ron and Monique on a path to determining how best to handle the invitation, make a determination as to whether to present the information to their children and in what manner, and ultimately to decide whether to pursue a relationship with Morgan. After several weeks, Ron elected to respond to Morgan's e-mail and began a positive and fulfilling relationship for them both.

One being accessible to others is not always a positive thing for couple and family relationships. Though the couple above built a strong relationship with Morgan culminated by her moving to their hometown to live with them, Monique and Ron experienced tension with regard to their differences in how they saw the role Monique would play in Morgan's life. The couple also had to navigate and process Monique's jealousy at Ron's burgeoning and close relationship with Morgan, a sentiment that created several months of fighting and tension in the household. In another case, Guadalupe became aware of his wife, Rafaela's, amorous feelings for another man. He had received an anonymous e-mail from someone who knew about Rafaela's affections for someone else. In addition to the initial revelation, the stream of e-mails from the anonymous party continued to wreak havoc on the couple. Every time they seemed to make progress in recovery, another e-mail would inevitably arrive in his inbox and create an argument between the couple, trigger Rafaela's stomach pains, and prompt a panic attack in Guadalupe.

Not only are people accessible to others at any given time, they are also available in any given place. A couple called for therapy related to his infidelity in their relationship. His wife discovered a trail of phone calls and text messages to other women demonstrating a clear emotional connection. He indicated this behavior had gone on for years, but had become more pronounced and he had begun relationships with multiple women in the last year. After the first session, the couple seemed committed to making the relationship work. I (K.H.) felt pretty good about the case and was fairly hopeful they would be able to resolve these issues. The next week, the couple came in for their regularly scheduled session and I asked about their assignment over the week. It was clear there was some tension in the room. When I asked what happened, the wife said they had argued in the car ride home from the last session. The wife disclosed while she was driving on the way home from the therapy session, she discovered her husband in the seat next to her was texting his girlfriend messages about how much he loved her. I looked at him seated on the couch and said, "Dude—I'm trying to help you here." He just gave me a sheepish grin, looked down, and said, "I know." This example introduces one of the most problematic elements for couples related to access. Not only is the access itself problematic in the cases where it constitutes betrayal because of who is accessed, but the access to another in front of the primary partner generates a more complicated and secondary betrayal—activities conducted in secret, yet right out in the open. As the couple discussed in the paragraph above, the male partner was able to conduct his extramarital interactions outside of his partner's awareness while seated near her without drawing attention to himself.

This is especially problematic because one of the core components of infidelity is secrecy, and may very well be one of the first barriers couples need to navigate in their healing—processing the betrayal of the events in such a way that allows them to move forward without being suspicious of every action. In other words, accessibility may also be problematic for couples when one partner clearly does NOT have access to certain element of their partners' life, a phenomenon common with each person having an individual cell phone, logins, and e-mail addresses. Applications have even been developed to permit the saving of photos and messages in hidden locations on one's cell phone, detectable to no one but the owner of the phone. As a result, increased accessibility becomes synonymous with increased opportunities, a key variable in likelihood to engage in infidelity (Treas & Giesen, 2000).

We also believe that the definition of accessibility should be broadened. Cooper's (2002) definition of accessibility refers to the access that one in a relationship has to the outside world and its inhabitants. Accessibility can also refer to the fact that people in a relationship are accessible to others, not just that those in the relationship can access others. In other words, the Internet and other similar forms of new media introduce both people who are known to you and people who are not known to you in your relationship. For example, Chapter 10 discusses the circumstances around cyberbullying and cyberstalking, where those known and unknown to you contact you through email or cell phone.

Recent updates in cellular technology have the capability to pinpoint one's location. This can have positive or negative implications for a couple. On one hand, it can be used to promote the development of trust in an already-struggling relationship. Trez and Caitlin came to treatment to address Trez's constant infidelity throughout the duration of the relationship. One of the challenges to the couple's recovery process was that Trez's cheating happened while he was at work. Part of his job required that he travel to people's homes to conduct interviews. It was during these errands that he would also stop off to have sex with someone. The couple had to develop a solution to enable her to trust him enough so that he could still work and so that she could feel more trusting. The couple worked out an arrangement where when Caitlin needed him to respond to her or to check in, Trez would take a photo of where he was and respond immediately to her.

Affordability

To carry on relationships online is very affordable (Cooper, 2002). The ease with which one can communicate, the multiple methods, and the fact that it is acceptable to have a way through which to communicate can all create problems. It was not uncommon in couple relationships plagued by infidelity to be discovered by a receipt, a charge on a hotel, or a bill from a hotel. One couple that distinctly comes to mind is a couple who came to treatment to improve their relationship. They divulged in the early part of treatment that part of the issue was that even though they had an open relationship, which for them meant they each had physical encounters with other people outside of their relationship with the understanding that they were transparent about such encounters, she believed that he had violated their rules around the open nature of their relationship. She believed that he had hooked up with someone else and not told her. He denied hooking up with someone else and kept reminding her that if he had he would have told her. Every several weeks we would make progress on the couple's communication patterns and accessing their feelings, be able to help them to communicate their wants, needs, and hurts . . . and invariably, after the few weeks of growing closer, the female partner would once again begin to think about what she believed to be the discovery of an affair that was outside of their agreed upon relational parameters—this discovery was a receipt from an upscale restaurant that her husband clearly went to with someone other than her.

Affordability also relates to some of the programs developed to organize romantic relationships with others, including partners other than ourselves. Many applications, such as the ones described earlier, which allow you to hide photos and messages from others on your phone, can be downloaded for free. The same is true for opening virtually any e-mail account—all you need is a password and a username.

The cost, however, of participating in relationships that are affordable financially may not be affordable for relational health in the long run for certain couples. Recall the couple mentioned earlier in the chapter who had a relationship characterized but online interactions separately and then vacations together. Certainly, while financially feasible to carry on a long-distance relationship, the end result may be that one loses a sense of reality within the relationship. That being said, there are just as many couples, if not more, for whom financial affordability allows them to have relationships that they would not otherwise be able to have because of being separated by distance or circumstance. Marco and Brian, for example, began their relationship in the same town, but an academic opportunity opened up for Brian in another state. The affordability provided by the Internet and the ability to send each other daily journals complete with photos went a long way to sustaining the relationship and making it possible for them to develop a deeper level of commitment to one another, resulting in them deciding to live together and eventually marry upon Brian's return from out of state.

Approximation

Approximation refers to the quality of the Internet that approximates real-world situations (Ross & Kauth, 2002; Tikkanen & Ross, 2003). As graphics and computer technologies improve, the graphics and video projections become more lifelike and therefore more seductive.

There are a number of online mechanisms by which people replicate their offline lives. An article in *Time World*, for example, cites an incident where one woman filed for divorce after the revelation that her husband was having virtual sex with another avatar within the game Second Life (Adams, 2008). In this way, one's engagement in certain sexual interactions across a medium approximating the offline world can result in a blurring of the lines between fantasy and action (Ross, 2005).

To date, the main groups that have been examined with regard to the approximation phenomenon are men who seek same-sex partners online (Cooper, Galbreath, & Becker, 2004). The rationale provided by the participants in the study was that they were engaging in that behavior as a way to manage their stress or anxiety. The more they engaged in this practice, it became a self-reinforcing strategy. The researchers concluded people performed these behaviors online because they did not feel it was the appropriate behavior in which to participate in their offline lives, yet it is perceived as safe when it is online because it provides a way of having an authentic and realistic experience without specific unwanted consequences. For example, one can engage in cybersexual activities with someone without risk of becoming pregnant, or infected with viruses like the human immunodeficiency virus (HIV), or the contraction of any other sexually transmitted infections (STIs).

Approximation is a very powerful element of computer and web-based technologies that introduces a different dimension into couple relationships affecting both emotional and physical intimacy between partners. Participating in real-time conversations over instant messaging or text provides members of a couple with timely information about their partner's current emotions, motivations, thought processes, and feelings in a way that only phone calls could accomplish. Further, the ability to visually see one's partner (or others) through real-time Internet channels has important implications for couples. Particular programs currently advertised have the ability to provide some level of sexual gratification through their ability to provide real-time visual and tactile stimuli. For example, one can purchase devices with the ability to connect to computers or tablet computers with a USB that are designed to physically stimulate male genitalia. Upon connection, users visit a website to download or view short movies that are developed to move in sync with what is happening in the movie. Other developments to this same technology include a device for a partner to operate at their own computer to stimulate their partner remotely.

In some cases, approximation can interfere with relationships because the interactions with others online can be highly realistic. As mentioned above, the ability to have one see another in a real-time sexual situation can be appealing. When a physical partner cannot be found, options on pornographic websites such as live cameras can fill in the gap. For example, Whitty's (2005) research found approximation played a part in the experience of betrayal in online infidelity. Because communications on the Internet approximated real-world situations, the experience of online betrayal mimicked offline betrayal.

The quality or approximation contributes to our understanding of different types of motivations of computer users, particularly with regard to sex. Three types of cybersex users have been identified: recreational users, sexually compulsive users, and at-risk users (Cooper, Delmonico, & Burg, 2000). Recreational users are those who utilize the Internet as a way to entertain themselves or because they are curious about different aspects of sexual behavior. These cases are most often not brought to therapy as a presenting problem, nor are they addressed in treatment when this behavior is revealed. The category of compulsive users includes those who participate in pathological sexual expression and the Internet is just one manner in which this is accomplished. The third group represents a vulnerable portion of the population—a group of people that, without the Internet, would not have a problem with pathological sexual expression. Yet the Internet's accessibility creates opportunities for the at-risk user to participate in usage to gratify sexual needs. Individuals in this group are vulnerable to developing sexual compulsions when they are using the Internet to gratify themselves sexually in times of isolation (Delmonico, 1997).

Accommodation

As mentioned earlier, research conducted by Cooper et al. (2004) found the Internet is used to satisfy one's wants and needs when they cannot or do not believe they can get those needs met offline and related to using the Internet to approximate real-world situations; however, it is also evidence of the concept of accommodation in that it is likely these male participants felt constrained to participate in these sexual activities in their offline lives. This was similar to the findings of an earlier study on men who have sex with men, where the Internet was found to provide a way to experiment with having sex with someone of the same sex without having to identify as homosexual (Tikkanen & Ross, 2003) or gay. This desire to act in a certain way and the inability to do so creates a conflict between one's ideal and real self (Higgins, 1987), thus exhibit incongruent behavior (Ben-Ze'ev, 2004). According to Hertlein and Stevenson (2010),

> Many people feel the need for a secret life because they perceive their lives as rule-driven, confined, or constrained. Further, there are many who have the ability to risk or desire to seek out sensations which are now living routine (and by their report, "boring" lives). The Internet provides greater opportunity for one to act a certain way in "real time" but have a different persona when it comes to online behavior and activities, especially when there are no outward or obvious signs of this other, seemingly contradictory persona. (n.p.)

The crux of accommodation (in comparison to the previously mentioned ecological elements) is the distinction between one's "real" versus "ought" self as identified by Higgins (1987). Terrance and N'ysha came to treatment to improve the communication in their relationship. Over time, it became apparent that one of the issues in the relationship was N'ysha's report that she did not receive the same consideration from Terrance that he used to interact with his previous girlfriend. N'ysha indicated that she felt that Terrance was "two different people"—with his previous girlfriend, he was compassionate, respectful, and complimentary. With her, he was short, business-like, and somehow detached. This difference in interaction left her feeling as if she was "second place," a feeling that she wanted to resolve. The fact that people can construct their communication in ways consistent with a view of themselves they prefer rather than who they really are. This concept is defined as accommodation (Hertlein & Stevenson, 2010) and essentially refers to the Internet being another way in which people can portray themselves to be one way but really are another way.

Accommodation may not be a vulnerability for all couples. The extent to which it enhances or detracts from a couple's relationship is largely dependent on the extent to which each individual has a discrepancy between their real self and their ought self (see Table 5.1). For example, in couples where there is not observed discrepancy in real versus ought self,

Table 5.1 Implications for Stages of Accommodation

		Partner B	
		Discrepancy between real and ideal self	*Similarity between real and ideal self*
Partner A	*Discrepancy between real and ideal self*	Significant challenges to emotional intimacy and relating Electronically based communication might be more confusing to the couple because the way they relate online is variant from offline relating in many circumstances	Partner B may experience difficulty trusting Partner A's behavior, depending on the level of discrepancy May prefer to either communicate online or offline, depending upon which form of communication is the most desirable.
	Similarity between real and ideal self	Partner A may experience difficulty trusting Partner B's behavior, depending on the level of discrepancy May prefer to either communicate online or offline, depending upon which form of communication is the most describable.	Couple will experience satisfying relationship both on and offline Intimacy levels will grow more quickly and deeply than in the other couple forms because electronically based communication is used as an adjunct to the relationship and a way to continue to experience one another.

the implication is that the couple's relationship would be enhanced by electronic technologies. They would find more opportunities for interactions that are based on building emotional connections as well as building closeness through more frequent interactions. These couples learn to trust and be vulnerable to one another in any context, both online and offline. In other words, what you see is what you get with each partner in the relationship. Alternatively, the couple in which each partner experiences a discrepancy between their real and ought self is the opposite end of the continuum and more complex. One element of the complexity deals with the manner in which the computer is used to express oneself. In most circumstances, it is the case where people who use the computer find it is a suitable mechanism through which they can express their true selves when they feel constrained in their day-to-day offline lives. One partner in a relationship may feel more security in their ability to express themselves in ways that they would not normally. Examples of this can be found on virtually every news story or posting online that allows space for people to post opinions and feedback, comments tend to turn personally attacking others very quickly. One of these might occur under the concept of anonymity discussed earlier as it is easier to comment negatively on something when that feedback cannot directly be associated with you. Part of this, however, is also reflective of the concept of accommodation—there are things people really feel but are not appropriate to express in their day-to-day offline lives.

A final type of couple is one where one partner experiences the discrepancy to their online and offline lives and the other partner is more similar and therefore relatively consistent. This dynamic in a couple can cause conflict because of difficulty in understanding the other's perspective and the damage to the perception of trust in the relationship. The case of Reid and Toni exemplifies this. Reid and Toni came to treatment indicating Toni had discovered Reid's online communications with a woman in another country. Most of the e-mails were characterized by graphic sexual content, description of particular sexual activities (such as including other men in sexual interactions) and other behaviors that Toni had never known were of interest to Reid. Toni was sad and angry that Reid positioned himself to be one way to others online and act differently to her offline. In short, the computer allowed him to express what Toni came to believe as his true desires while he acted in a way that was socially prescribed in his day-to-day life with her.

In addition to the breakdown of trust in the couple relationship, the individual psyche of Toni was also damaged. She came to see herself as someone whose decisions could not be trusted and found herself waiting for the other shoe to drop with Reid. The end result was impairment to her self-esteem and a pronounced amount of shame, which prevented her from seeking the social support to get through the relationship problems she would have otherwise used.

Ambiguity

Relational Ambiguity

Ambiguity is another element related to technology and new media creating specific issues in couple relationships. This concept refers to one of two types: relational ambiguity and technological ambiguity. Relational ambiguity is any ambiguity around the evaluation of one's online behavior in regards to one's relationship. In many cases, members of a couple disagree on the valence of a behavior—that is, whether specific behavior occurring in the relationship related to the usage of Internet technologies is helpful, harmful, or neutral to the relationship. It is often the case that the partner participating in the behavior views it as neutral or positive, while the other partner evaluating it from a distance views it as neutral or harmful. The greater the degree to which a behavior is defined ambiguously in the couple's relationship, the greater the degree of harm and the greater the potential for a disruption to the couple's intimacy processes.

One of the things most striking about the notion of relational ambiguity is exactly how many behavior are ambiguous in the couples contract. In days prior to new media's insertion in everyday life, couples were pretty clear on what, for example, constituted infidelity: intimate physical contact with a person other than one's primary partner (Thompson, 1984). Emily Brown (1991), a renowned scholar on infidelity, was among the first to acknowledge the potential of emotional infidelity to soon emerge in relationships. In fact, the emotional component of infidelity (either online or offline) is recognized by couple and relationship scholars (see, e.g., Drigotas, Safstrom, & Gentilia, 1999). The advancements in technology, however, have increased the number of behaviors whose valence is quite ambiguous. Couples now have to make more decisions about what behaviors constitute appropriate behavior in the relationship and what behaviors cross the line. Despite the increasing amount of ambiguous online behavior, couples meeting today seem to fare no better at organizing conversations to either acknowledge or resolve the ambiguity prior to establishing a commitment with one another than couples who have committed together decades ago. For example, Ericka and Duane, both in their late 20s, sought premarital therapy 5 months prior to their wedding. The couple met through mutual friends and had spent approximately 3 years prior to becoming engaged, living together for the last 2 years. The conversations that emerged over the course of their premarital therapy revealed no areas where the couple seemed to have any problematic differences in opinion that would warrant further treatment or attention. Yet when the therapist introduced the area of infidelity and the definition as it relates to appropriate online behavior and boundaries in the relationship, the couple looked perplexed at one another and indicated they had not even thought about what those behaviors might entail. As the conversation unfolded, it became clear each had their own idea about how Internet infidelity would be conceptualized. The therapist assigned the couple to discuss the contract with one another over the week and return with some agreement this element of their relationship contract.

It is not only the couples who have a recent commitment that are not establishing the definitions for appropriate online behavior in their relationship. Couples who have had established relationships for some time generally do not revisit the original contracts they had with one another prior to the explosion of electronically based communication. In fact, many couples only revisit what would constitute appropriate behavior after there is some disagreement about the valuation of a particular behavior.

There are likely several reasons why couples, regardless of duration in their relationship, experiences challenges with regard to establishing clarity with their relational contract. The relational contract is defined as "as a set of implicit expectations that partners have concerning how they will define the relationship and interact with one another" (Birchler, Doumas, & Fals-Stewart, 1999, p. 256). First, the rapid development of software, systems, websites, and ways to communicate through electronic channels make it difficult to plan for every possible contingency within a relationship. For example, one cannot predict the amount of ways in which one might be contacted through the Internet by phone by others and what forms of interaction initiated by others will enter the couple's life. Secondly this is further compounded by the fact that evidence seems to indicate that couples do not seem to address contracts within their relationships (Birchler et al., 1999; Sager, 1976). The inattention to the relational contract can result in differences in expectations and discord.

The most common issues related to relational ambiguity revolve around issues of infidelity, namely, what are the electronic behaviors that constitute infidelity in a relationship? Some couples define infidelity solely as physical contact with another person outside of the primary relationship. When both partners hold this definition, the problems of whether or not someone cheated are relatively clear and any discord in couples seem to revolve around the betrayed partner claiming their partner participated in physical activity with another person outside the boundary of the relationship and the partner accused of such an activity denying there was any physical contact. Sal and Heather presented in treatment as a classic example of this phenomenon. Heather had discovered used condoms in their bedroom upon her return from a business trip. When she confronted Sal about her findings, he denied any involvement with someone else and claimed that he did not know how they got there.

In today's relationships, however, the clarity of the definition of infidelity behavior becomes murky when couples have to consider and agree upon the behaviors constituting infidelity. With more potential problematic behaviors, the likelihood each partner will agree on each behavior is reduced. In these cases, the discord in couples can revolve on one partner accusing of a behavior and the other denying, both partners agreeing that the behavior occurred but disagreeing about whether it constituted infidelity, or situations where both are true. For example, Nelda made an appointment for her and her husband for treatment regarding his infidelity. In speaking with Ray, it became apparent Nelda viewed his interactions with other women online as a breach in their relational contract. Ray confirmed he did talk to other women online, but indicated these were friends from high school with whom he did not have nor did he ever have any romantic interest or history. Furthermore, he viewed Nelda as having changed the rules in the contract and was angry that she did not trust him. In this case, the couples discord was less around the denial of events and more about the ambiguity around what constitutes stepping out of the relationship.

In some cases, the definition of infidelity can include the viewing of pornography by one partner. While pornography has been around for a long time, in the past people viewing pornographic magazines did not seem to be classified as cheating to the extent that viewing pornography online is viewed today. First, pornography online has the ability to be interactive, where magazines or movies did not have that same quality. Advances in technologies such as live webcams may make the pornography more real and, therefore, more of a threat.

Another striking characteristic of relational ambiguity with regard to technology and behavior in couple relationships is that ambiguity of the valuation of online behavior seems to occur with approximately the same frequency in online relationships as in offline relationships. Lynn and Jeff, both in their 40s, each had a pattern of participating in serially monogamous relationships for years that eventually fizzled out. They were both ready to find a person with whom to spend the rest of their life. They met each other online through a dating website and participated in a long-distance relationship for approximately a year and a half. The relationship started relatively slowly, but once clarification was made to be exclusively involved with one another, the couple developed rules around the frequency of their online contact with one another. They did not, however, include a discussion of rules around permissible online behavior. Thus, when Jeff observed certain activity and comments on Lynn's Facebook account from another, he categorized such behavior as a breach of the relationship contract; Lynn, on the other hand, held the position that rules around this behavior were never part of the contract and had she known about it, she would have done more to be clear with her friends about how to appropriately interact with her online.

This begs the question as to why couples whose relationships are conducted primarily online do not discuss the rules of the relationship with regard to online behavior despite the fact this is their primary mode of interaction with one another. One reason could be the tentative nature of communication facilitated online. In the case of Lynn and Jeff, a disagreement about rules with regard to online behavior could have three potential negative consequences. One might be that Lynn or Jeff might agree there are rules around the behavior but operate independent of those rules outside of the awareness of the other. Secondly, it might lead to the development of an argument between Lynn and Jeff, a couple who very much wants the relationship to be long lasting, but is also physically distant from one another. In this setting, Lynn may fear that it is easier for Jeff to end communication with her by walking away from the computer or ignoring texts/phone calls about the issue, a task more difficult to do when couples live in the same space. If she is not willing to take that risk, she may not be willing to start the conversation in the first place. A third consequence might be the development of a discussion lacking authenticity on the part of each partner. As described earlier in this chapter, one of the characteristics of online communication is that the user can type, write, backspace, and essentially alter their appearance. The sense of everydayness and spontaneity is lost as people think and organize what they want to say rather than being themselves and letting their expression show. In either case, the conversation may be avoided because of the lack of power one partner may feel by being connected only by a keyboard.

Technological Ambiguity

Another way ambiguity plays out in a relationship is with regard to the knowledge base of electronically based communication. Emoticons and abbreviations have certain meanings that are generally understood by users of these technologies to have particular meanings. It is also the case, however, many users might not be clear on what symbols, emoticons, or abbreviations stand for what. This ambiguity creates interesting scenarios for couple relationships as well. When I (K. H.) began sending instant messages, I began using this emoticon: ": x." I was under the impression that it was someone making a sick face, meaning "yuk." I used this fairly often in my communication with others online, men and women both, when something being discussed was not pleasant, such as a poor work schedule, difficulties within relationships, or other routine complaints. After about 1 1/2 years, my husband texted me using that emoticon. Because we were not discussing anything unpleasant at the time, his "yuk" face seemed out of context. I asked him why he inserted a "yuk" face. He replied, "That's not a yuk face. That means a kiss." I was shocked. I confessed I had been using it as a "yuk" face for nearly 2 years with my texting companions, with both men and women. He laughed and said, "Well, now you know." While my husband was very calm and trusted that I was genuine in my lack of information about usage of symbols, there are many couples for whom the ambiguity around the use of symbols is dismissed as one partner clearly wanting to start up relationships with other people or can even count as evidence of cheating. In these cases, the couple has to rely on the trust that has already been built in the relationship as a way to determine whether there is a need for further exploration or whether the lack of clarity in using symbols is just one more example of one's lack of commitment to the relationship.

Technological ambiguity may also be characterized by lack of knowledge about the capabilities of technology and new media. For example, there may be software or phone applications used by one person to discreetly conceal one's activities. One's partner may be less familiar with such applications and therefore not be able to appropriately appraise a situation as problematic.

Table 5.2 outlines potential benefits and challenges for each of the ecological elements within relationships. While not exhaustive, the main

Table 5.2 Ecological Elements Contribution to Relationships

Ecological element	*Benefits to relationship*	*Challenges to relationship*
Acceptability	• Acceptable way to meet and maintain a relationship	• The acceptable nature of communicating with others online introduces more risk
Anonymity	• Test the waters prior to becoming vulnerable in the early stages of relationship development • Can monitor and edit own reactions prior to reacting in ways that might be hurtful	• Greater potential to hide behind the computer and edit one's authentic self • May lengthen the time that it takes to feel vulnerable with partner
Accessibility	• Routine access to partner • More opportunities to develop greater levels of intimacy	• Increased ability and potentially interest to monitor partner
Affordability	• Long distance relationships can thrive	• May be easier to develop relationships with others that are virtually undetectable to the primary partner
Approximation	• Real time information about emotions, thoughts etc. • May be able to provide some element of sexual gratification remotely that cannot be experienced any other way	• Other elements or people can be attractive to someone because of their realism
Accommodation	• Provides a space for people to experience their real self when they feel otherwise constrained in their day to day lives	• Discrepancies in real versus ought self between partner can create a mismatch in expression, experience of closeness, and ability to be vulnerable with one another
Ambiguity	• Provides an opportunity for couples to periodically revisit their relationship contract, thus increasing intimacy	• Creates complications with regard to the interpretation of the relationship contract and expectations

idea is that interactive communicative technologies both introduce vulnerabilities as well as helpful things into couple relationships.

References

Adams, W. L. (2008). *UK couple to divorce over affair on Second Life.* Retrieved from http://www.time.com/time/world/article/0,8599,1859231,00.html

Atwater, L. (1979). Getting involved: Women's first transition to extramarital sex. *Alternative Lifestyles, 2,* 33–68.

Bacigalupe, G., & Lambe, S. (2011). Virtual intimacy: Information communication technologies and transnational families in therapy. *Family Process, 50*(1) 12–26. doi:10.1111/j.1545-5300.2010.01343.1.0

Badhwar, N. K. (2009). The Milgram experiments, learned helplessness, and character traits. 2.0 *The Journal of Ethics: An International Philosophical Review, 13,* 257–289. doi:10.1007/s10892-009-9052-4

Ben-Ze'ev, A. (2004). *Love online: Emotions on the Internet.* New York: Cambridge University Press.

Birchler, G. R., Doumas, D. M., & Fals-Stewart, W. S. (1999). The seven Cs: A behavioral systems framework for evaluating marital distress. *The Family Journal, 7,* 253–264. doi:10.1177/1066480799073009

Brown, E. M. (1991). *Patterns of infidelity and their treatment.* New York: Brunner/Mazel.

Buunk, B. (1980). Extramarital sex in the Netherlands: Motivation in social and marital context. *Alternative Lifestyles, 3,* 11–39.

Campbell, S. W., & Ling, R. (2009). Effects of mobile communication. In J. Bryant & M. B Oliver (Eds.), *Media effects: Advances in theory and research* (3rd ed., pp. 592–606). New York: Taylor and Francis.

Cooper, A. (2002). *Sex and the Internet: A guidebook for clinicians.* New York: Brunner-Routledge.

Cooper, A., Delmonico, D. L., & Burg, R. (2000). Cybersex users, abusers, and compulsives: New findings and implications. *Sexual Addiction & Compulsivity, 7*(1–2), 5–29. doi:10.1080/10720160008400205

Cooper, A., Galbreath, N., & Becker, M. A. (2004). Sex on the Internet: Furthering our understanding of men with online sexual problems. *Psychology of Addictive Behaviors, 18*(3), 223–230. doi:10.1037/0893-164X.18.3.223

Daneback, K., Cooper, A., & Månsson, S. (2005). An Internet study of cybersex participants. *Archives of Sexual Behavior, 34*(3), 321–328. doi:10.1007/s10508-005-3120-z

Delmonico, D. L. (1997). Cybersex: High tech sex addiction. *Sexual Addiction & Compulsivity, 4*(2), 159–167. doi:10.1080/10720169708400139

Drigotas, S. M., Safstrom, C. A., & Gentilia, T. (1999). An investment model prediction of dating infidelity. *Journal of Personality and Social Psychology, 77*(3), 509–524.

Hertlein, K. M., & Sendak, S. K. (2007, March). *Love "bytes": Internet infidelity and the meaning of intimacy in computer-mediated relationships.* Paper presented at the annual conference of Persons, Intimacy, and Love, Salzburg, Austria.

Hertlein, K. M., & Stevenson, A. (2010). The seven "as" contributing to Internet-related intimacy problems: A literature review. *Cyberpsychology: Journal of Psychosocial Research on Cyberspace, 4*(1). Retrieved from http://cyberpsychology.eu/view.php?cisloclanku = 2010050202&article = 1

Higgins, E. (1987). Self-discrepancy: A theory relating self and affect. *Psychological Review, 94*(3), 319–340. doi:10.1037/0033-295X.94.3.319

Madden, M., & Lenhart, A. (2006). *Online dating*. Retrieved from http://pewinternet.org/Reports/2006/Online-Dating.aspx

McCown, J., Fischer, D., Page, R., & Homant, M. (2001). Internet relationships: People who meet people. *Cyberpsychology & Behavior: The Impact of the Internet, Multimedia and Virtual Reality on Behavior and Society, 4*(5), 593–596. doi:10.1089/109493101753235188

McKenna, K. Y., Green, A., & Gleason, M. (2002). Relationship formation on the Internet: What's the big attraction? *Journal of Social Issues, 58,* 9–31. doi:10.1234/12345678

Mileham, B. L. (2007). Online infidelity in Internet chat rooms: An ethnographic exploration. *Computers in Human Behavior, 23*(1), 11–31. doi:10.4103/0019-5545.5829

Ross, M. W. (2005). Typing, doing and being: Sexuality and the Internet. *Journal of Sex Research, 42,* 342–352. doi:10.1080/00224490509552290

Ross, M. W., & Kauth, M. R. (2002). Men who have sex with men, and the Internet: Emerging clinical issues and their management. In A. Cooper (Ed.), *Sex and the Internet: A guidebook for clinicians* (pp. 47–69). New York: Brunner-Routledge.

Sager, C. (1976). *Marriage contacts and couple therapy.* New York: Brunner/Mazel.

Stephure, R., Boon, S., MacKinnon, S., & Deveau, V. (2009). Internet initiated relationships: Associations between age and involvement in online dating. *Journal of Computer- Mediated Communication, 14*(3), 658–681. doi:10.1111/j.1083-6101.2009.01457.x

Tikkanen, R., & Ross, M. (2003). Technological tearoom trade: Characteristics of Swedish men visiting gay Internet chat rooms. *AIDS Education & Prevention, 15*(2), 122-132. doi:10.1521/aeap.15.3.122.23833

Thompson, A. P. (1984). Emotional and sexual components of extramarital relations. *Journal of Marriage and Family, 46*(1), 35–42.

Treas, J., & Giesen, D. (2000). Sexual infidelity among married and cohabiting Americans. *Journal of Marriage and Family, 62*(1), 48–60. doi: 10.1111/j.1741-3737.2000.00048.x

Whitty, M. T. (2005). The realness of cybercheating: Men's and women's representations of unfaithful Internet relationships. *Social Science Computer Review, 23*(1), 57–67. doi:10.1177/0894439304271536

6 The Interactional Nature of Structure and Function

Computing is not about computers any more. It is about living.
—Nicholas Negroponte

The structural-functionalist perspective is a framework describing the social organization under investigation (in this case, the family or couple) as it is situated within its environment (Johnson, 1971). In other words, the structure of the couple and/or family influences its functions, and its functions feed back into either maintaining or changing the structure. Stability in structure (roles in a system) and function is a primary way in which social organizations such as families survive over time (Kingsbury & Scanzoni, 1993). Structural roles have to be organized in such as ways to promote protection and growth. For example, there has to be enough structure in the system to provide for food and shelter, but not too much so as to interfere with autonomy. Children in chaotic families may, without structure, have little sense of boundaries and rules. Once the family structure is identified, the members of the family can then determine who will perform which functions.

A lack of clarity with regard to understanding the structure can have significant implications for processes in couple relationships. In one case, Phil and Brenda came to treatment to discussion their dissatisfaction with their 30-year marriage. The couple both indicated their relationship was going well until nearly 2 years ago when Brenda suffered an accident in the workplace. The result of the accident left her with a pronounced limp, difficulty walking without a cane, and nerve damage to various parts of her body. Her physical condition had obvious and immediate implications for the couple's sexual relationship and after some time, Phil realized he deeply missed their sexual relationship they had previously found so enjoyable. Subsequently, he became increasingly angry and resentful toward Brenda for not providing for his sexual needs. Phil's anger was rooted partially in his belief that Brenda was dismissing him on purpose. His lack of understanding about Brenda's pronounced medical issues were not considered;

thus he believed Brenda was distancing from him. As a result of Phil's anger, Brenda felt hurt and rejected. She did not understand why he could not accept the prognosis right in front of him. It was not until Phil received clarification of his wife's condition that he was willing to move from a position of blaming his wife to joining her in mourning the loss of some sexual function. Once Phil and Brenda joined together to face the illness, they were able to steadily improve their relationship.

The same issue emerges with technology insofar as technology enables partners to have broader definitions of their relational roles. McMillan and Morrison (2006) highlight one reason cited by young people for using the Internet: They are seeking to clarify their role and identity within family structures. Problems exist when couples are unable to make a shift in their relationship roles and acknowledge the reality of their context. For example, Ted's new job took him on the road much more frequently than his former position. The couple had to recognize this would change the dynamics of their interaction and their relationship. Thus, Ted and Alice would rely on the accessibility of a computer to communicate more frequently. This was a perfect fit for Alice who, like many women, felt more comfortable initiating interactions via computer-mediated communication. Ted, however, believed text messaging and e-mails would suffice as a way to maintain communication during his absences. Ted and Alice had to work together to identify the new structure of how communication would be achieved in their relationship during periods of distance.

One of the clearest ways to conceptualize how the structure of relationships and technology emerge in couple and family relationships is through the lens of functional family therapy. The functional family therapy perspective posits that each behavior provides a separating/distancing function, a merging/closeness function, or midpointing function (neither distancing or merging) (Barton & Alexander, 1981). It emphasizes context by acknowledging the contribution each person makes in creating and responding to the world around them and, in so doing, creating more meaning (Barton & Alexander, 1981). In other words, the environment plays a significant part in shaping subsequent interactions and the meaning ascribed to them. Functional family therapy views development as the result of merging an individual's capacities and environment (Sexton & Alexander, 2003). In the case of technology and new media, the way in which one has a familiarity with online technology and processes (that is to say, their capacities) and their environment (whether they have the ability to access these capacities) has implications for the couple's relationship. For Marcus and Kaydee, the environment conspired against them spending time together because they worked directly opposite schedules. When the couple tried to use a webcam to connect with one another, the capacity of the webcamera was limited because of the age of Marcus's computer. In this way, capacity and environment contributed to their difficulties in spending time together.

Wetchler (1985) describes the process in functional family therapy as it applies to the family life cycle:

> When family members move to a new life cycle stage, they begin to change their way of communicating with other family members. They, in effect, redefine their relationship. If the family can accept this redefinition in relationship and everyone's functions can be met, the family has successfully negotiated the life cycle stage and will continue to develop. . . . Relationship crises occur when there is nonmutuality of relationship definition (Morton et al., 1976). Family members' disagreement as to how the relationship will be defined causes a developmental crisis. Disagreement may be about the form of the relationship or how the process will be used to define the relationship. (p. 43)

In its application to technology, the trajectory followed by couples and families is similar. Technology and new media create new meanings and redefine relationships. Individuals can either choose to accept and function in accordance with the new definition or reject it. Problems emerge when people have different ideas about the roles, rules, and function of technology in their lives. For example, one couple sought premarital therapy. During the course of the conversation about relational strengths and weaknesses, the therapist asked about the couple's definition of infidelity. The couple appeared confused and the female partner responded for the both of them, stating it was "obviously physical intimacy with another person." The therapist asked about the role technology and the Internet factored into their definition of infidelity. The couple looked at one another and the male partner responded, "I guess we never really thought about it." The couple's assignment for the week was to discuss and come to agreement on how technology was to be used inside and outside of their relationship.

The determination as to whether technology and new media provides distance or closeness is best expressed as a function of (a) the type of activity (whether it is physical, psychological, or both), and (b) the target of the behavior (i.e., is it another person or an object). For example, the accessibility of technology may result in more opportunities for closeness or merging; however, if accessibility is used to connect with someone outside of the relationship, then it provides both a closeness function to the outsider and a distancing or separating function from the partner. Table 6.1 highlights specific behaviors that contribute to separating, merging, or both. Though not an exhaustive list, it serves as a baseline for identifying the types of behaviors contributing to the development of closeness or distance in couples.

Table 6.1 Behaviors Promoting Closeness or Distance

Behavior classification	*Behaviors/technology elements that promote closeness*	*Behaviors/technology elements that promote distance*
Psychological *Ambiguity* *Accommodation* *Anonymity* *Acceptability* *Approximation*	• Communicating with partners on a more regular basis (more frequently) • Viewing erotic material online together	• Using technology in instrumental ways • Making self-disclosures to other people outside of your relationship • Viewing erotic material independent of your partner
Physical *Affordability* *Accessibility*	• Communicating with partners on a more regular basis (more frequently)	• Use of headphones or earbuds • Cell phone usage (put it up to the ear to have people stop talking to you) • Sound of a ringer on a cell phone or notification for something • Tendency to use shorter statements

Physical Structure of Technology Versus Psychological Structure

The ecological elements discussed in Chapter 5 may influence whether particular psychological and/or physical behaviors promote closeness, midpointing, or distancing in relationships. Concepts such as ambiguity, anonymity, approximation, accommodation, and anonymity, for example, may alter one's psychological landscape, resulting in potential difficulties with regard to the structure and processes of relationships. For example, Will's knowledge he could alter his reactions to suit a particular situation online.

Affordability and accessibility, on the other hand, tend to be those ecological elements more consistently resulting in physical effects on the relationship, with the potential to translate into psychological implications. For example, the placement of a computer in a home, the accompaniment of laptops, tablets, PCs, and the ability for each person to be on a cellular or smartphone introduces both positive and negative factors into a couple's roles and boundaries. In Bakardjieva's (2005) terms, the Internet has become "the gate in the living room" (p. 149). In some cases, the gate is between family members, prohibiting communication and conversation that otherwise would have taken place (Bakardjieva, 2005). Partners in a relationship may be sitting in the same proximal space, but be separated by their intellectual activities on separate technologies. For example, Hector and Sandy came to treatment to move past Hector's engagement in a series of extramarital relationships. Part of what distressed Sandy was that Hector orchestrated his participation in these relationships when he was sitting next to her on the sofa in their living room or while they were driving somewhere together. In other cases, the 'gate in the living room' serves as a barrier (and sometimes an insulator) between the family and the outside world. Paulo and Mackenzie often found they engaged in parallel Internet activities—participating in online gaming together and were able to identify specific ways in which it drew them closer together.

Another example of the ecological element of accessibility with psychological implications is the increasingly diffuse line between work life and family life (Campbell & Ling, 2009). The work–family conflict (Bellavia & Frone, 2004) manifests in several ways, including cell phones used by our workplace counterparts to communicate with us, e-mail about work that we can receive on a daily basis, and the notion that we can "quickly" complete something since technology is purportedly designed to make our lives easier but instead puts more work squarely on our shoulders. In the case of e-mail, it is relatively easy to compose as a means of reminding employees about certain tasks that need to be managed in the upcoming week. From the employees end, however, e-mails sent outside of business hours might create a sense of obligation to respond, thus generating negative feelings toward the work environment or one's employer. For example, Jackie and Steven were in a standstill over the role of Steven's cell phone usage after business hours. Jackie felt that Steven could be reached at virtually any time was problematic. This issue was ongoing, as Jackie had made repeated requests for Steven to curb his cell phone usage in the evenings. Steven argued this was impossible given the nature of his job. Jackie, however, viewed his decision to answer the phone during off hours as valuing his job over their relationship.

This scenario is not uncommon with regard to couple relationships. As many as one-third of American adults admitted they feel compelled to answer a cell phone, even if a call comes in when they are meeting with someone or having a meal (Pew Internet and American Life Project, 2006). For many, the structure of their environment dictates whether they will be accessible via cell phone. Humphreys (2005) found what governs one's decision to answer a ringing cell phone is due to who is around, who is on the other end of the phone, and other contextual factors. In other words, "the structure of the environment and the timing of the call affect one's response" (Hertlein, 2012, p. 379).

Another example of a physical structure promoting changes to relationship function involves the emergence of headphones and earbuds to accommodate users of technology and new media. When individuals use headphones or earbuds, a clear message is sent that the individual is in his or her own world and is not receptive to receiving incoming information or messages. In other cases, individuals feign a phone call or listening to music as a way to prevent others from initiating communication with them. Zach, for example, frequently spent his evenings participating in online gaming. The nature of his game required he listen to others within the gaming environment, yet he was also interested in keeping the communication between himself and other gamers private to prevent his young son from being interested in online gaming and to focus instead on age-appropriate activities. Therefore, Zach elected to wear headphones during his game time, which took place approximately three to four nights per week, and once every weekend during the day. This arrangement initially seemed to work until Sarah, Zach's wife, noticed a pronounced feeling of loneliness when Zach was playing his games. Further questioning about her feelings revealed Sarah's discovery that during these game-playing times, Zach was totally disengaged from the family, despite being approximately 10 feet away. Part of the issue was when he was behind headphones, eyes fixated on a screen, Zach was unaware of family activities and unable to hear what was discussed between Sarah and their son. By the time he rejoined the family, the topic of discussion was over. Further, Zach did not support Sarah in disciplining their son, leaving Sarah angry that she was left to do the parenting alone. She lost interest in sharing with Zach the events of the day since she did not believe it was fair that he join the family only when it was convenient for him.

Implications for Roles

Regardless of the classification of the structural elements related to technology and new media in relationships, there are implications for roles, rules, and boundaries. Roles, or how we expect people to behave in given situations, also have to be renegotiated in the context of technology and new media. Research has demonstrated couples share a similar attitude regarding the roles in their marriage have higher levels of global relational satisfaction, satisfaction with conflict resolution, financial roles, and leisure activities (Craddock, 1991). Partners in couple relationships experience dissatisfaction when the role enacted varies from one's cognitions or feelings about the role. Though there is likely to be incongruence with regard to roles, couples should strive to reduce the incongruence when possible to avoid the development of negative feelings (Peplau, 1983).

In some ways the Internet and new media help couples to achieve more equitable role balance and within-couple role congruence in their lives. Marital satisfaction has been empirically tied to role balance (Chen & Li, 2012), and the Internet provides a forum that may provide opportunities for individuals to express feelings with regard to a particular role or alternative ways to go about enacting roles consistent with cognitive and affective reactions to the role. Further, in a sample of White married couples, findings regarding role balancing indicated wives feel less balance if they work on weekends but more balance if their husband also works on weekends (Marks, Huston, Johnson, & MacDermid, 2001).

In other ways, the computer and new media have a confusing and detrimental effect on roles. The accessibility of computers has made technology an equal opportunity destroyer—that is, each member of the couple can be targeted to work on weekends or compelled to respond to work because it is so easy to do so, thus blurring the line between the roles of employee and family member. There may also be conflict in roles with regard to household tasks. In general, American women are more responsible for household duties than their husbands (Lachance-Grzela & Bouchard, 2010). This is further complicated when the wives associate the reasons for a husband's lack of participation in activities in the house with entertainment as opposed to work interference. Research in the areas of online gaming and cybersex indicates couples may not agree on whether the other partner is fulfilling his or her obligations at home. When the reason for not completing household duties is ascribed to something related to the Internet, such as participation in online gaming or cybersex, it can create conflict (Daneback, Cooper, & Månsson, 2005; Klein, Izquierdo, & Bradbury, 2007; van Rooji, van den Eijnden, Spijkerman, Vermulst, & Engels, 2010).

Implications for Relational Rules and Boundaries

One of the more common issues in clinical settings is that the computer and new media influence how people respond to and uphold their relationship rules. A classic example is Internet infidelity. Due to the acceptability of using the Internet to foster relationships with many people in wide-ranging geographic locations and from varied backgrounds, there are more complexities introduced into the already-established relationship rules. Thus far, researchers have identified the presence of several rules specifically regarding cell phone usage. Akin to functional family therapy, Duran, Kelly, and Rotaru (2011) investigated whether the rules of cell phones in relationships were associated with separation or merging. Although many participants indicated the rules for communicating via cell phone were not necessary within their relationships, other participants reported conflict regarding cell phone usage in their relationships. One reason for this conflict was related to a need to be autonomous and, therefore, having to separate themselves from a situation to achieve autonomy through the methods available through the structure of a cell phone (i.e., turning off the phone or ignoring the call). A second source of conflict was a need to merge with one's partner but with no means to access the other. In each case, one partner in the relationship had their own expectations of the rules regarding cell phone usage; conflict emerged when the other partner did not share that expectation.

Shaela and Monte were together for 10 years before they each purchased smartphones. They described their relationship as supportive and loving, until the last few years (after Monte's promotion) where the couple noted significant communication issues and emotional affairs on both of their parts. In discussing the communication aspects of their relationship, it became apparent that one implicit rule in the relationship was that Monte had to respond to Shaela's daily phone calls. Yet once the phones entered the relationship, Shaela reported Monte was now "ignoring her." Further investigation revealed the accessibility now provided by the smartphone created a situation where Monte, knowing he could call Shaela at any time, would put off responding to her calls if she was calling at a difficult time. But since Shaela was aware the phone was accessible to Monte at any time, she felt ignored if he did not respond. Knowing Monte had to notice the call was from her but was choosing to ignore it prompted Shaela to call more often, thus resulting in increased irritation on the part of Monte. This dynamic snowballed to a point where, when Monte did have an opportunity to return Shaela's call, it resulted in either an argument or accusations. In this case, the introduction of technology created a context where each member of the couple changed some element of a rule; yet the rules were not discussed or renegotiated, thus causing conflict.

Relationships function better when implicit rules are made explicit, as it gives the couple a better sense of boundaries and expectations (Petronio, 2002). Miller-Ott, Kelly, and Duran (2012) found couples enact certain cell phone rules experience increased relationship satisfaction. First, there needs to be rules for handling instances when one's partner does not respond to the other partner's texts or phone calls. For example, some couples may have rules around the length of time one waits prior to initiating a second contact. In the case above, Monte clearly had a few personal rules about repetitive contact from Shaela, though he did not explicitly communicate those to her. Specifically, the authors also found those individuals who rated themselves as having higher levels of satisfaction had some rules, but not a specific set of rules governing how to respond to a phone call in a particular way (Miller-Ott et al., 2012). This is also consistent with research on texting and messaging norms, indicating that people believe that there is a norm dictating a response when one receives a message via cell phone (Laursen, 2005). Relationship satisfaction is also higher for couples who have rules for when and in what way to introduce emotionally charged content; in other words, couples fare better when there is a specific rule preventing partners from beginning arguments over the phone. Again, in the case of Shaela and Monte, Shaela took the opportunity when she was able to secure Monte on the phone to begin an argument regarding his inaccessibility. This only escalated the conflict that was already unfolding. Finally, couples experience greater satisfaction with fewer rules monitoring their usage of their cell phone placed upon them by their partner (Miller-Ott et al., 2012).

In addition to the negotiation of frequency and content of general interactions in a couple's relationship, the negotiation of rules in a relationship also occurs specifically with regard to emotional expression (Strzyzewski, Buller, & Aune, 1996). Partners in relationships more deeply developed tend to have worked out idiosyncratic rules in their communication that permit the expression of negative emotions such as hurt and pain whereas individuals in the early stages of a relationship generally rely on cultural rules to determine how to express positive emotions while withholding negative emotions (Strzyzewski et al., 1996). This rule development becomes more confusing with increased usage of computers in one's life. According to Strzyzewski et al. (1996), "Emotion expressions may be considered highly personal information and too risky to share completely with new relational partners. Partners may also avoid positive emotions because they do not feel confident enough of the future relational trajectory" (p. 128). The same holds true for online relationships: The individual keeps negative emotions inside when there is fear that revealing the emotion might somehow jeopardize the relationship (Baker, 2007).

Interactions between people who communicate primarily via the Internet are best described as positive and open when emotions are expressed (Baker, 2007). In fact, partners may reveal more online more quickly than in offline relationships, having negotiated the rules around the expression of emotions early in the relational trajectory. Successful online couples appropriately use self-presentation, timing, setting, and selection of obstacles to resolve issues that would have otherwise prevented them from progressing as a couple (Baker, 2002).

Boundaries about sharing information with outsiders that were previously well established in the relationship may change when there are multiple channels for sharing information (Ward, 2006). In some cases, partners become more overprotective when they believe a boundary has been crossed; in other cases, users may feel smothered by their partner's behavior toward them, even though this may not be the partner's intent. Ken and Grace sought to resolve a power struggle in their relationship that was triggered by an argument about Ken's Facebook account. Grace saw a former girlfriend contact Ken on his wall and although the message was benign, she believed it was inappropriate for Ken to have any kind of relationship with this woman. Ken's perspective was that he could not control who posted on his wall. He stated that he was not looking for another relationship with anyone, including his former girlfriend, and that Grace should not be angry at him for things out of his control.

In brief, problems can emerge in relationships because the Internet and new media introduce both people who are known to you and unknown to you into your relationship. Two types of boundaries have been discussed in the literature with regard to technology and users: self-boundaries and dyadic boundaries (Joinson, Reips, Buchanan, & Schofield, 2010). Self-boundaries refer to those surrounding the individual affected by self-disclosures (Altman, as cited by Joinson, Reips, Buchanan, & Schofield, 2010). Dyadic boundaries have historically related to the boundaries around how information is received by someone outside of the system. Couples who use the Internet need to be aware of and attend to both types of boundaries. When couples are clear on both the self and dyadic boundaries (what information is shared outside of the couple), problems are minimized. When partners only attend to one of the two, however, problems emerge. Mark and Chenee came to premarital therapy and in discussing potential problem areas in their marriage. Mark stated that he was not altogether comfortable with the way in which Chenee disclosed their problems and household decisions to her father. What was most problematic was the manner in which she was sharing this information with her father—she would typically send him short text messages or would speak to him when Mark was not around. Mark felt that Chenee was going behind his back to make decisions for the two of them, and that anything Chenee's father said was written in stone. In this case as well as with many other couples, the dyadic boundary became very diffuse when it was easy to post information to others in a variety of forms whether through phones, e-mail, or social networking sites.

Processes and Technology

Humphreys (2005) stated, "The effects of technologies are not direct, but negotiated through people's construction and use of them" (p. 811). As mentioned above, the ecological influences suggest two types of changes in relationships (see Figure 1): *changes to the structure* of relationships and *changes to the process*. The changes to process are associated with the interaction-constructionist perspective in family science. From this perspective, the emphasis is on the manner in which individuals in families and other social groups use gestures, rituals, and behavior as a way to interact with one another (Berger & Kellner, 1970). Technology and new media shape processes through providing new ways to develop intimacy. It modifies the relationship formation and initiation processes (projection processes), and inspires changes in how relationships are maintained (timing/tempo of relationship, commitment, communication with other family, and leisure activities). Yet some of the relationship processes are dictated, in part, by the relationship stage in which the couple is embedded. Information about technology and new media specific to relationship initiation and termination will be discussed in Chapter 9. The section focuses on relationship satisfaction, intimacy, and the pace of relationships.

Intimacy Development With and Without Technology

One of the overarching issues is the way in which technology and new media contribute to or detract from building intimacy within relationships. There is some evidence to support the notion that computer-mediated relationships may augment the intimacy development process. First, the mere presence of more (and easier) ways to communicate with others may allow for greater levels of intimacy (Bargh & McKenna, 2004; DiMaggio, Hargittai, Neuman, & Robinson, 2001). Cell phones, for example, allow individuals to have more detailed information as to their partner's location and activities (Campbell & Ling, 2009). Nearly 75% of respondents indicated they depended on their cell phones to interact with their partner during the day (Kennedy, Judd, Churchward, Gray, & Krause, 2008). Research also showed that many people who use e-mail and spend time on the computer do not experience a loss of time with family and friends; rather, they may spend even more time with family and friends, despite initially experiencing depression and loneliness at the outset of the computer entering their lives (Bargh & McKenna, 2004; Kraut et al., 2002).

One area of investigation related to technology and relationship has centered around the role of electronic communication on social and familial relationships (Kayany & Yelsma, 2000; Lanigan, Bold, & Chenoweth, 2009; Morrison & Krugman, 2001). Lanigan et al. (2009) conducted a survey study involving 103 participants including parents of children under 12, parents of children 12 and up, post parenting families, and couples without children. Their study explored family adaptability and cohesion, alternative use of technology time, and perceived impact of technology on family relationships. The majority of the participants (n = 79, 89%) reported that technology had impacted their family relationships (Lanigan et al., 2009). Further, just under half (n = 36, 45%) indicated computers had a mostly positive impact on their family life, whereas less than one-quarter (n = 16, 20%), reported a negative impact. The remaining participants indicated the risks had both negative and positive impact (n = 19, 25%).

Yet three studies contradict this finding. First, Nie, Hillygus, and Erbring (2002) conducted a time-diary investigation and reported every e-mail sent resulted in a 1-minute loss of family time per day. The authors assert Internet use is directly and inversely related to the amount of time one spends with one's family. Nie et al. (2002) describe the Internet as competing with time spent with colleagues at work as well as with friends and family at home. Second, Czechowsky (2008) found couples did not spend as much offline time together as they had previously once a Blackberry was introduced into their lives. According to one participant, "The constant distraction of the BlackBerry adversely impacted the relationship. . . . There was either a reluctance to address the issues, i.e. attentiveness, or it was not discussed. The spouse without the BlackBerry would experience resentment" (p. 111). Where Blackberrys are concerned, couples still view the cost to the relationship as greater than making up for the pros of flexibility and accessibility (Czechowsky, 2008). Further discussion of the Lanigan et al. (2009) findings revealed time spent with technology, like computers, generally replaced time that would have been spent alone or involved with other forms of technology, like television, rather than time that would have been spent with family members. Participants who perceived the computer interfered with family time were more likely to classify the rules and roles within the family as being less flexible (Lanigan et al., 2009). Another reason provided for the reduction in family time was the increased permeability of boundaries between the family and the outside world. But for most, the use of computers improved family communication, served as a shared activity, helped members meet a variety of needs like entertainment, information gathering, and household management, and increased efficiency resulting in more free family time (Lanigan et al., 2009).

Considering the contradictions in the findings, these results seem to demonstrate it is not necessarily the inclusion of technology in children's and their parents' lives creating problems, but rather how the technology is attended to that makes the difference. For instance, when parents and children collaborate on technological activities together it can actually improve their communication (Kiesler et al., 2000; Orleans & Laney, 2000). In addition, parents who are in need of support, assistance finding extracurricular activities, and childcare providers can find these services much more readily using online access (Mesch & Levanon, 2003). With the rise of new media and home computers more parents have been able to work from home, meaning there is often more time for them to spend at home with children (Watt & White, 1999). Finally, for parents who work outside of the home, the use of new media like smartphones has provided a more consistent bridge through which to stay in contact and monitor one's child(ren) who are often home before their parents (Watt & White, 1999).

Additionally, those who participate in social networking sites experience a pronounced sense of connection and can successfully use the Internet to maintain relationships (Xie, 2007). Research on the use of instant messaging among friendships indicated the frequency of using instant messaging was significantly associated with verbal intimacy, perceived affective intimacy, and social intimacy. Further, the increase in instant messaging is related to a greater desire for friends to meet offline (Hu, Wood, Smith, & Westbrook, 2004) and shapes offline experiences and interactions (Xie, 2007). For example, in an experiment conducted by McKenna, Green, and Gleason (2002), a sample of 31 male undergraduate students and 31 female undergraduate students were assigned to one of three conditions. One condition was where one person initially met another of the opposite sex face-to-face; the second condition was were the initial meeting was online and the partners knew that they would be meeting in person; the third condition was where the participants knew that there was a meeting online and a meeting in person, but were not aware that it was the same person that they were meeting in person as they met online (though it was). Those who met their partner online rated themselves as liking their partner more than those who met with their partner offline. This was even true for the third condition, when the partners did not know that they were meeting the same person offline that they met online (McKenna et al., 2002). Both McKenna (2008) and Rabby and Walther (2002) noted that online relationships might endure over time longer than offline relationships. In research related to romantic relationships, the more opportunity for communication, the greater the likelihood intimacy will develop (Cooper & Sportolari, 1997; Henline & Harris, 2006).

Given the somewhat varied nature of the effect of Internet usage on relationships, therapists need to assess the degree and manner in which the Internet and new media are contributing to or detracting from a couple's life together. This means developing a comprehensive understanding of each person's usage of a computer, Internet, and new media independently as well as within the relationship. For example, if one partner spent a few hours every week surfing the Internet, the reaction from the other partner may be far different than if the time spent surfing the web was specifically for finding ways to improve the relationship.

The Role of Self-Disclosure in Online Relating

Many will agree that talking to others online is a welcome change in their lives, in part because of the ease and increased frequency of communication with partners. Unless conducted by video camera, however, the receiver has to interpret the sender's emotions, meaning, and motivation without observing any nonverbal cues accompanying the message. In relationships initiated offline, partners develop intimacy with one another through self-disclosure (sharing details of their lives and their personality) paired with observations in real world (and unobtrusive) settings (Tidwell & Walther, 2000) where in computer-mediated relationships, intimacy is fostered through reliance on self-disclosure (Henderson & Gilding, 2004; McKenna et al., 2002; Whitty, 2008).

Self-disclosure in relationships often follows a process where partners trust one another (Chaikin, as cited by McKenna et al., 2002). The quantity and quality of self-disclosure in a relationship carries significant implications for the health of the relationship. More frequent disclosures are associated with greater emotional involvement in dating and greater levels of marital satisfaction (Hansen & Schuldt, 1984; Rubin, Hill, Peplau, & Dunkel-Shetter, as cited by Yum & Hara, 2006). Research shows relationships headed toward termination by one or both parties are characterized by fewer instances of self-disclosure. Further, when self-disclosure in relationships headed toward termination does occur, it is generally about superficial topics rather than topics related to emotions and relational content (Baxter, 1979).

Demographics affect how one conceptualizes the norms surrounding online and offline disclosing. For example, there is no difference between men and women with regard to likelihood of posting personal information online. On the other hand, men are more likely than women to believe that posting information about one's offline life is an acceptable practice. Girls are also more likely than boys to post photos and videos online. Specifically, girls are more likely to allow access to photos online than boys where boys are more likely to allow access to videos online (Mesch & Beker, 2010). Age is also another factor influencing how people view the norms of self-disclosure online –for example, the older the adolescent, the more likely they would approve the posting of an email address or other personal online information than younger adolescents (Mesch & Beker, 2010). It is not known, however, at what age (if any) these differences disappear.

Some have discovered that higher levels of self-disclosure to another online are associated with increased liking of that person along with matching communication styles and higher levels of commitment (Lin, 2009; Pornsakulvanich, Haridakis, & Rubin, 2008; Valkenburg & Peter, 2009; Yum & Hara, 2006). There are also qualities about self-disclosure that can affect one's perception of the quality of the relationship. Specifically, the greater the depth of the self-disclosure and the more emotional the disclosures (i.e., the usage of stronger emotional words as opposed to weaker emotional words), the more positive one rates an online counterpart (Rosen, Cheever, Felt, & Cummings, 2008). Self-disclosure in relationships, however, can be a double-edged sword. As much as it can draw people together, it can also pull them apart. According to Schwab, Scalise, Ginter, and Whipple (1998),

> while self-disclosure inherently provides an opportunity to achieve intimacy, it is not free of risks because disclosure also carries with it the possibility of one's being manipulated, embarrassed, exploited, or rejected. And, since lonely individuals frequently suffer from a lack of social skills, the possibility of such adverse outcomes is genuine (Ginter, 1982). (p. 1264)

In a study on loneliness and self-disclosure, people who rated themselves as being lonely were indeed less likely to engage in self-disclosure across many settings, whether with strangers or friends (Schwab et al., 1998). This contradicts some of the conventional wisdom about computer users, which suggests people who use computers do so as a way of interacting with others without taking significant risks or becoming vulnerable in the same ways that might occur in face-to-face interactions.

In relationships mediated by the Internet and new media, self-disclosure may also occur as a means to an end; that is, to determine whether the person on the other end of the keyboard is trustworthy, one engages in a systemic process of self-disclosure. The development of intimacy also depends on what exactly is being disclosed. Intimacy develops more deeply in cases when individuals choose to disclose information of a personal and emotional nature as opposed to limited emotional content (Bargh, McKenna, & Fitzsimons, 2002; Derlega, Winstead, & Greene, 2008; Schnarch, 1997). Much research has shown that computer users tend to engage in more self-disclosing behaviors than those in face-to-face relationships (Joinson, 2001; Parks & Floyd, 1996). Further, it is likely self-disclosure is responsible for the heightened level of commitment experienced by partners in computer-mediated relationships (Eppler & Walker, 2004; Yum & Hara, 2006).

The process of self-disclosure in online relationships is further aided by some of the ecological elements—not the least of which is anonymity (McKenna & Bargh, 2000; McKenna et al., 2002). The fact that the Internet provides anonymity may also contribute to the development of self-disclosure online. Research regarding self-disclosure and gender is generally mixed: Some research contends that men are more likely to participate in self-disclosure than women; other research says that men are less likely to reciprocate high levels of self-disclosure; and finally, some say there is no difference (Klinger-Vartabedian & O'Flaherty, 1989). Despite the contradictions in likelihood of disclosure, there do not appear to be differences between men and women in terms of the depth of the disclosure (Joinson, 2001). Further, the status of individuals engaged in self-disclosing also bears some weight on how self-disclosure is perceived. Men as well as those in higher status positions are provided more latitude with self-disclosure and are viewed more positively. As a consequence, when those in positions of higher power disclose to those of lower status, those in the higher position are viewed as more attractive by those in lower positions because the disclosure is "viewed as a 'gift' which is offered to reduce power differentials" (Klinger-Vartabedian & O'Flaherty, 1989, p. 161). This also appears to be the case for disclosure in psychotherapy and clinical supervision (Barnett, 2011; Faber, 2006; Maroda, 2003). In other cases, however, the timing of self-disclosure may impede a relationship. In investigating physician self-disclosure, for example, McDaniel et al. (2007) found that at times where physicians disclosed too early in the relationship, there was no evidence of a positive effect and, in some cases, the disclosure appeared disruptive. For example, personal ads placed online tend to be longer than ads placed in a newspaper, presumably because of the reduced cost per word (Hatala, Milewski, & Baack, 1999). In fact, there is a negative correlation between one's level of self-disclosure on Facebook and their age, with younger individuals disclosing more than older ones (Nosko, Wood, & Molema, 2010). With the Internet, the anonymity of the person with whom one is communicating may provide an equalizing function for the nature of self-disclosure. In other words, one's social status and, in some cases, gender, may be unobserved and unable to be assessed by the individual with whom one is communicating, thus creating an equal playing field where people initially meet. It is only after they are already invested in the relationship that they learn about each other's status.

Empirical evidence demonstrates the anonymity via the computer can be beneficial to the development of trust and intimacy, even when theory suggests otherwise. Sztompka (as cited in Henderson & Gilding, 2004) contends three elements contribute to trust building in a relationship: accountability of the person with whom one is interacting, precommitment (a surrendering of one's own freedom as a demonstration of commitment), and the environment or situation in which the interaction occurs. Though the Internet can provide a setting through which one can feel connected, there are few channels through which the Internet provides an appropriate amount of accountability or precommitment. Because interactions may be anonymous, there is no way of accounting for the veracity of statements offered by individuals online, particularly as they relate to current emotional states, thus inhibiting accountability. Further, the structure of the Internet and new media create a context where individuals can interact and build relationships with more than one person at a time, thus interfering with the emergence of precommitment in trust building. The findings of Henderson and Gilding's (2004) investigation did reveal that accountability seemed to be one barrier in developing trust, but there was also evidence that computer users had found other ways to assess precommitment and their respective willingness to take risks in their relationships. One way that the computer can improve accountability is through the very nature of the Internet: Online one can find searchable, detailed information about other people, whether it is information specific to the individual or information about how that person behaves in a group (McKenna, 2008).

Another element of online self-disclosure is that there is a difference between directed and nondirected disclosures. Nondirected self-disclosure refers to the type of self-disclosure that reveals information of a personal nature, but not to any one person specifically. One example of this can be seen in blogging (Jang & Stefanone, 2011). Nondirected self-disclosures may also occur within the context of social media, such as in Facebook postings and profiles, or media such as Twitter. Although information is not directed at one person specifically in these formats, information of an intimate nature is nonetheless disclosed and can strengthen the ties to the individuals within the user's network. The frequency of the communication and the ability for other users to comment (an opportunity for some level of reciprocation, albeit limited) on a posting further contributes to the development of intimacy online (Jang & Stefanone, 2011).

Reciprocity in relationships is critical to the development of a trusting and intimate relationship, both online and offline, particularly if the reciprocity is in relation to self-disclosure (Laurenceau, Barrett, & Pietromonaco, 1998). The Internet and new media both provide a forum for reciprocity. Equity theory asserts that as individuals in a relationship build trust, the development of that trust is predicated on the notion that each person in the relationship will make an equitable contribution to disclosing personal information in the relationship (Jang & Stefanone, 2011). Because of the accessibility at any time (both synchronous and asynchronous) and in many forums, the Internet provides for many opportunities and greater degrees of reciprocation. This reciprocity, as explained by Yum and Hara (2006), is also evidence of social penetration theory (Altman & Taylor, 1973), briefly discussed in Chapter 1.

Another way in which technology and new media assist in developing intimacy is people have a tendency to be more forthright in online interactions, especially when conducted over a webcam program (Cooper & Sportolari, 1997; Henderson & Gilding, 2004; Joinson, 2001; Valkenburg & Peter, 2009). One likely reason may be that the physical barrier of a digital screen prevents one from having to experience all of the consequences of personal online activities. Examples of this uninhibited behavior can be observed in daily postings and comments to online news stories or other material. This phenomenon is supported by research showing that computer users are more likely to engage in more aggressive and potentially conflict-causing communication than those who rely primarily on face-to-face methods (Dubrovsky, Kiesler, & Sethna, 1991).

Relationship Satisfaction in Online Relationships

Some of the research relates to the role of computers and new media technologies on relationship satisfaction. Women, for example, experience greater relationship satisfaction with online dating than in face-to-face relationships (Gutkin, 2010; McKenna et al., 2002). Satisfaction in relationships is also related to problem-solving strategies used by couples. For example, couples indicate that they can resolve their conflict more effectively if they can utilize asynchronous communication methods such as e-mail because of its flexibility (Czechowsky, 2008). On the other hand, the emergence of Blackberrys in the relationship was associated with decreased marital satisfaction, with the wives' desire for their male counterparts to be more emotionally present (Czechowsky, 2008).

One of the other issues related to relationship satisfaction is the duration of technology-based communication. With such communication options, there are more frequent and often shorter communications (primarily through e-mail) occurring any time of day (Wilding, 2006). This altering of the tempo has to also be negotiated by couples. For example, Jackson and Felise came to treatment to improve their communication. Felise indicated Jackson was not responsive to her during the day. She stated that the times she did call him, he responded abruptly and did not demonstrate that he was interested in speaking to her. Jackson stated there was no reason for long conversations since she was calling him frequently throughout the day. Felise, however, stated if she had longer conversations with him, she would not feel the need to call repeatedly.

The advent of technology in relationships also carries implications for sexual satisfaction. Research demonstrates that those who engage in compulsive online sexual behavior run the risk of experiencing a reduction in their sex drive and desirability, have less sex, and subsequently feel less satisfaction than those who do not compulsively participate in online sex (Bergner & Bridges, 2002; Bridges, Bergner, & Hesson-McInnis, 2003). Couples who view online porn together experience increased sexual satisfaction and a greater frequency of sex than couples whose partners watch it independently. Women who watch porn alone develop uncertainty with regard to their own body and tend to compare themselves to what they see in the videos, both physically and in terms of performance (Albright, 2008; Grov, Gillespie, Royce, & Lever, 2011). Men also report that they have sex less frequently when watching porn alone, but they also use it as a way to stimulate arousal (Grov et al., 2011).

References

Albright, J. M. (2008). Sex in America Online: An exploration of sex, marital status, and sexual identity in Internet sex seeking and its impacts. *Journal of Sex Research, 45*(2), 175–186. doi:10.1080/00224490801987481

Altman, I., & Taylor, D. A. (1973). *Social penetration: The development of interpersonal relationships*. Oxford, England: Holt, Rinehart & Winston.

Bakardjieva, M. (2005). *Internet society: The Internet in everyday life*. London: Sage.

Baker, A. (2002). What makes an online relationship successful? Clues from couples who met in cyberspace. *CyberPsychology & Behavior, 5*(1), 364–375. doi:10.1177/0093650205285368

Baker, A. J. (2007). Expressing emotion in text: Email communication of online couples. In M. T. Whitty, A. J. Baker, & J. A. Inman (Eds.), *Online matchmaking* (pp. 97–111). London: Palgrave Macmillan.

Bargh, J. A., & McKenna, K. A. (2004). The Internet and social life. *Annual Review of Psychology, 55*(1), 573–590. doi:10.1146/annurev.psych.55.090902.141922

Bargh, J. A., McKenna, K. Y. A., & Fitzsimons, G. M. (2002). Can you see the real me? Activation and expression of the "true self" on the Internet. *Journal of Social Issues, 58*(1), 33-48.

Barnett, J. E. (2011). Psychotherapist self-disclosure: Ethical and clinical considerations. *Psychotherapy, 48*(4), 315–321. doi:10.1037/a0026056

Barton, C., & Alexander, J. F. (1981). Functional family therapy. In A. S. Gurman & D. P. Kniskern (Eds.), *Handbook of family therapy* (pp. 403–443). New York: Brunner/Mazel.

Baxter, L. A. (1979). Self-disclosure as a relationship disengagement strategy: An exploratory investigation. *Human Communication Research, 5*(3), 215–222.

Bellavia, G., & Frone, M. (2004). Work family conflict. In J. Barling, E. K. Kelloway, & M. R. Frone (Eds.), *Handbook of work stress* (pp. 113–147). Thousand Oaks, CA: Sage.

Berger, P. L., & Kellner, H. (1970). Marriage and the construction of reality. In H. Dreitzel (Ed.), *Recent sociology* (Vol. 2, pp. 50-72). New York: Macmillan.

Bergner, R., & Bridges, A. (2002). The significance of heavy pornography involvement for romantic partners: Research and clinical implications. *Journal of Sex and Marital Therapy, 28,* 198–206.

Bridges, A., Bergner, R., & Hesson-McInnis, M. (2003). Romantic partners' use of pornography: Its significance for women. *Journal of Sex & Marital Therapy, 29*(1), 1–14. doi:10.1080/713847097

Campbell, S. W., & Ling, R. (2009). *The reconstruction of space and time: Mobile communication practices.* New Brunswick, NJ: Transaction.

Chen, L. H., & Li, T. (2012). Role balance and marital satisfaction in Taiwanese couples: An actor-partner interdependence model approach. *Social Indicators Research, 107*(1), 187–199. doi:10.1007/s11205-011-9836-3

Cooper, A., & Sportolari, L. (1997). Romance in cyberspace: Understanding online attraction. *Journal of Sex Education and Therapy, 22*(1), 7–14. doi: 10.1089/cpb.1998.1.11

Craddock, A. E. (1991). Relationships between attitudinal similarity, couple structure, and couple satisfaction within married and de facto couples. *Australian Journal of Psychology, 43*(1), 11–16. doi:10.1080/00049539108259090

Czechowsky, J. D. (2008). *The impact of the Blackberry on couple relationships.* Retrieved from. http://scholars.wlu.ca/etd/1056

Daneback, K., Cooper, A., & Månsson, S. (2005). An Internet study of cybersex participants. *Archives of Sexual Behavior, 34*(3), 321–328. doi:10.1007/s10508-005-3120-z

Derlega, V. J., Winstead, B. A., & Greene, K. (2008). Self-disclosure and starting a close relationship. In S. Sprecher, A. Wenzel, & J. Harvey (Eds.), *Handbook of relationship beginnings* (pp. 153–174). New York: Psychology Press.

DiMaggio, P., Hargittai, E., Neuman, W. R., & Robinson, J. P. (2001). Social implications of the Internet. *Annual Review of Sociology, 27*(1), 307–336. doi:10.1146/annurev.soc.27.1.307

Dubrovsky, V. J., Kiesler, S., & Sethna, B. N. (1991). The equalization phenomenon: Status effects in computer-mediated and face-to-face decision-making groups. *Human Computer Interaction, 6*(1), 119–146. doi:10.1177/104649602237170

Duran, R. L., Kelly, L., & Rotaru, T. (2011). Mobile phones in romantic relationships and the dialectic of autonomy vs. connection. *Communication Quarterly, 59*(1), 19–36. doi:10.1080 = 01463373.2011.541336

Eppler, C., & Walker, E. K. (2004). Electronic ecology: An ecosystemic exploration of sisters communicating via email. *Journal of Feminist Family Therapy, 16*(1), 19-37.

Faber, B. A. (2006). *Self-disclosure in psychotherapy.* New York: Guilford Press.

Ginter, E. J. (1982). *Self-disclosure as a function of the intensity of four affective states associated with loneliness* (Unpublished doctoral dissertation). University of Georgia, Athens.

Grov, C., Gillespie, B. J., Royce, T., & Lever, J. (2011). Perceived consequences of casual online sexual activities on heterosexual relationships: A U.S. online survey. *Archives of Sexual Behavior, 40*(2), 429–439. doi:10.1007/s10508-010-9598-z

Gutkin, M. (2010). *Internet versus face-to-face dating: A study of relationship satisfaction, commitment, and sustainability.* San Francisco, CA: Alliant International University, California School of Professional Psychology.

Hansen, J. E., & Schuldt, W. J. (1984). Marital self-disclosure and marital satisfaction. *Journal of Marriage and Family, 46*(4), 923–926.

Hatala, M. N., Milewski, K., & Baack, D. W. (1999). Downloading love: A content analysis of Internet personal ads placed by college students. *College Student Journal, 33*(1), 124–129.

Henderson, S., & Gilding, M. (2004). "I've never clicked this much with anyone in my life": Trust and hyperpersonal communication in online friendships. *New Media & Society, 6*(1), 487–506. doi:10.1177/146144804044331

Henline, B. H., & Harris, S. M. (2006, October 19–22). *Pros and cons of technology use within close relationships.* Poster presented at the annual conference of the American Association for Marriage and Family Therapy, Austin, TX.

Hertlein, K. M. (2012). Digital dwelling: Technology in couple and family relationships. *Family Relations, 61*(3), 374–387. doi:10.1111/j.1741-3729.2012.00702.x

Hu, Y., Wood, J. F., Smith, V., & Westbrook, N. (2004). Friendships through IM: Examining the relationship between instant messaging and intimacy. *Journal of Computer-Mediated Communication, 10*(1), Article 6. doi:10.1111/j.1083-6101.2004.tb00231.x

Humphreys, L. (2005). Cellphones in public: Social interactions in a wireless era. *New Media & Society, 7*(6), 810–833. doi:10.1177/1461444805058164

Jang, C. Y., & Stefanone, M. A. (2011). Non-directed self-disclosure in the blogosphere. *Information, Communication & Society, 14*(7), 1039-1059.

Johnson, H. (1971). The structural-functional theory of family and kinship. *Journal of Comparative Studies, 2,* 133–144.

Joinson, A. N. (2001). Self-disclosure in computer-mediated communication: The role of self-awareness and visual anonymity. *European Journal of Social Psychology, 31*(2), 177–192. doi:10.1002/ejsp.36

Joinson, A. N., Reips, U. D., Buchanan, T., & Schofield, C. B. P. (2010). Privacy, trust, and self- disclosure online. *Human–Computer Interaction, 25*(1), 1–24. doi:10.1080/07370020903586662

Kayany, J. M., & Yelsma, P. (2000). Displacement effects of online media in the socio-technical contexts of households. *Journal of Broadcasting and Electronic Media, 44*(2), 215–230.

Kennedy, G. E., Judd, T. S., Churchward, A., Gray, K., & Krause, K. (2008). First year students' experiences with technology: Are they really digital natives? *Australasian Journal of Educational Technology, 24*(1), 108–122. doi:1449-5554

Kiesley, S., Lundmark, V., Zdaniuk, B., Kraut, R., Scherlis, W., & Mukhopadhyay, T. (2000). Troubles with the Internet: The dynamics of help at home. *Human-Computer Interaction. 15*(4), 223-352

Kingsbury, N., & Scanzoni, J. (1993). Structural-functionalism. In P. G. Boss, W. J. Doherty, R. LaRossa, W. R. Schumm, & S. K. Steinmetz (Eds.), *Sourcebook of family theories and methods: A contextual approach* (pp. 195–217). New York: Plenum Press.

Klein, W., Izquierdo, C., & Bradbury, T. N. (2007). Working relationships: Communicative patterns and strategies among couples in everyday life. *Qualitative Methods in Psychology, 4*(1), 29–47. doi:10.1080/14780880701473391

Klinger-Vartabedian, L., & O'Flaherty, K. M. (1989). Student perceptions of presenter self-disclosure in the college classroom based on perceived status differentials. *Contemporary Educational Psychology, 14*(2), 153–163. doi:10.1016/0361-476X(89)90033-7

Kraut, R., Kiesler, S., Boneva, B., Cummings, J., Helgeson, V., & Crawford, A. (2002). Internet paradox revisited. *Journal of Social Issues, 58*(1), 49–74. doi/10.1111/1540-4560.00248/pdf

Lachance-Grzela, M., & Bouchard, G. (2010). Why do women do the lion's share of housework? A decade of research. *Sex Roles, 63*(11), 767–780. doi:10.1007/s11199-010-9797-z

Lanigan, J., Bold, M., & Chenoweth, L. (2009). Computers in the family context: Perceived impact on family time and relationships. *Family Science Review, 14*(1), 16–32.

Laurenceau, J., Barrett, L. F., & Pietromonaco, P. R. (1998). Intimacy as an interpersonal process: The importance of self-disclosure, partner disclosure, and perceived partner responsiveness in interpersonal exchanges. *Journal of Personality and Social Psychology, 74*(5), 1238–1251. doi:10.1037/0022-3514.74.5.1238

Laursen, D. (2005). Please reply! The replying norm in adolescent SMS communication. In R. Harper, L. Palen, & A. Taylor (Eds.), *The inside text: Social, cultural and design perspectives on SMS* (pp. 53–73). Norwell, MA: Springer.

Lin, C. A. (2009). Effects of the Internet. In J. Bryant & M. B. Oliver (Eds.), *Media effects: Advances in theory and research* (3rd ed., pp. 567–591). New York: Taylor and Francis.

Marks, S. R., Huston, T. L., Johnson, E. M., & MacDermid, S. M. (2001). Role balance among White married couples. *Journal of Marriage and Family, 63*(4), 1083–1098. doi:10.1111/j.1741-3737.2001.01083.x

Maroda, K. (2003). Self-disclosure and vulnerability: Countertransference in psychoanalytic treatment and supervision. *Psychoanalytic Social Work, 10*(1), 43–52. doi:10.1300/J032v10n02_04

McDaniel, S. H., Beckman, H. B., Morse, D. S., Silberman, J., Seaburn, D. B., & Epstein, R. M. (2007). Physician self-disclosure in primary care visits: Enough about you, what about me? *Archives of Internal Medicine, 167*(12), 1321–1326. doi:10.1001/archinte.167.12.132

McKenna, K. Y. A. (2008). MySpace or your place: Relationship initiation and development in the wired and wireless world. In S. Sprecher, A. Wenzel, & J. Harvey (Eds.), *Handbook of relationship initiation* (pp. 235–247). New York: Psychology Press.

McKenna, K. Y. A., & Bargh, J. A. (2000). Plan 9 from cyberspace: The implications of the Internet for personality and social psychology. *Personality and Social Psychology Review, 4*(1), 57–75. doi:10.1207/S15327957PSPR0401_6

McKenna, K. Y. A., Green, A. S., & Gleason, M. J. (2002). Relationship formation on the Internet: What's the big attraction? *Journal Social Issues, 58*(1), 9–31. doi:10.1111/1540-4560.00246

McMillan, S. J., & Morrison, M. (2006). Coming of age with the Internet: A qualitative exploration of how the Internet has become an integral part of young people's lives. *New Media & Society, 8*(1), 73–95. doi:10.1177/1461444806059871

Mesch, G. S., & Beker, G. (2010). Are norms of disclosure of online and offline personal information associated with the disclosure of personal information online? *Human Communication Research, 36*, 570 – 592.

Mesch, G. S., & Levanon, Y. (2003). Community networking and locally based social ties in two suburban communities. *City and Community, 2*, 335–351.

Miller-Ott, A. E., Kelly, L., & Duran, R. (2012). The effects of cell-phone usage rules on satisfaction in romantic relationships. *Communication Quarterly, 60*(1), 17–34.

Morrison, M., & Krugman, D. M. (2001). A look at mass and computer mediated technologies: Understanding the roles of television and computers in the home. *Journal of Broadcasting and Electronic Media, 45,* 135–161.

Morton, T. L., Alexander, J. F., & Altman, I. (1976). Communication and relationship definition. In G. R. Miller (Ed.), *Explorations in interpersonal communication* (pp. 105–125). Thousand Oaks, CA: Sage.

Nie, N. H., Hillygus, D. S., & Erbing, L. (2002). Internet use, interpersonal relationships, and sociability: A time diary study. In B. Wellman & C. Haythornthwaite (Eds.), *The Internet in everyday life* (pp. 215–244). Oxford, England: Blackwell.

Nosko, A., Wood, E., & Molema, S. (2010). All about me: Disclosure in online social networking profiles: The case of Facebook. *Computers in Human Behavior, 26*(3), 406–418. doi:10.1016/j.chb.2009.11.012

Orleans, M., & Laney, M. C. (2000). Children's computer use in the home: Isolation or sociation? *Social Science Computer Review, 18*(1), 56–72. doi:10.1177/089443930001800104

Parks, M. R., & Floyd, K. (1996). Making friends in cyberspace. *Journal of Communication, 46*(1), 80–97. doi:10.1111/j.1083-6101.1996.tb00176.x

Peplau, L. A. (1983). Roles and gender. In H. H. Kelley, E. Berscheid, A. Christensen, J. H. Harvey, T. L. Huston, G. Levinger, et al. (Eds.), *Close relationships* (pp. 220–264). New York: Feeman.

Petronio, S. (2002). *Boundaries of privacy: Dialectics of disclosure.* New York: State University of New York Press.

Pew Internet and American Life Project. (2006, April). PEW Internet Project data memo: Cell phone use [Press release]. Washington, DC: Author. Retrieved from http://pewinternet.org/~/media//Files/Reports/2008/PIP_Adult_gaming_memo.pdf.pdf

Pornsakulvanich, V., Haridakis, P., & Rubin, A. M. (2008). The influence of dispositions and Internet motivation on online communication satisfaction and relationship closeness. *Computers in Human Behavior, 24*(5), 2292–2310. doi:10.1016/j.chb.2007.11.003

Rabby, M., & Walther, J. B. (2002). Computer-mediated communication impacts on relationship formation and maintenance. In D. Canary & M. Dainton (Eds.), *Maintaining relationships through communication: Relational, contextual, and cultural variations* (pp. 141–162). Mahwah, NJ: Lawrence Erlbaum Associates.

Rosen, L., Cheever, N., Felt, J., & Cummings, C. (2008). The impact of emotionality and self-disclosure on online dating versus traditional dating. *Computers in Human Behavior, 24*(5), 2124–2157. doi:10.1016/j.chb.2007.10.003

Schnarch, D. M. (1997). *Passionate marriage: Keeping love and intimacy alive in committed relationships.* New York: Henry Holt.

Schwab, S. H., Scalise, J. J., Ginter, E. J., & Whipple, G. (1998). Self-disclosure, loneliness, and four interpersonal targets: Friend, group of friends, stranger, and group of strangers. *Psychological Reports, 82*(3c), 1264–1266. doi:10.2466/pr0.1998.82.3c.1264

Sexton, T. L., & Alexander, J. F. (2003). Functional family therapy: A mature clinical model for working with at-risk adolescents and their families. In *Handbook of Family Therapy* (pp. 323-348). New York: Brunner-Routledge.

Strzyzewski, K., Buller, D. B., & Aune, R. K. (1996). Display rule development in romantic relationships: Emotion management and perceived appropriateness of emotions across relationship stages. *Human Communication Research, 23*(1), 115–145. doi:10.1111/j.1468-2958.1996.tb00389.x

Tidwell, L. C., & Walther, J. B. (2000). Getting to know one another a bit at a time: Computer-mediated communication effects on disclosure, impressions, and interpersonal evaluations. *Human Communication Research, 28*(3), 317–348. doi:10.1111/j.1468-2958.2002.tb00811.x

Valkenburg, P. M., & Peter, J. (2009). The effects of instant messaging on the quality of adolescents' existing friendships: A longitudinal study. *Journal of Communication, 59*(1), 79–97. doi:10.1111/j.1460-2466.2008.01405.x

van Rooji, T. J., van den Eijnden, R. J. J. M., Spijkerman, R., Vermulst, A. A., & Engels, R. C. M. E. (2010). Compulsive Internet use among adolescents: Bidirectional parent-child relationships. *Journal of Abnormal Child Psychology, 38*(1), 77–89. doi:10.1007/s10802-009-9347-8

Ward, K. (2006). The bald guy just ate an orange: Domestication, work and home. In T. Berker, M. Hartmann, Y. Punie, & K. Ward (Eds.), *Domestication of media and technology* (pp. 145–164). Berkshire, England: Open University Press.

Watt, D., & White, J. M. (1999). Computers and the family life: A family development perspective. *Journal of Comparative Family Studies, 30*(1), 1–15.

Wetchler, J. L. (1985). Functional family therapy: A life cycle perspective. *American Journal of Family Therapy, 13*(4), 41–48. doi:10.1080/01926188508251275

Whitty, M. T. (2008). Liberating or debilitating? An examination of romantic relationships, sexual relationships and friendships on the net. *Computers in Human Behavior, 24*(5), 1837–1850. doi:10.1016/j.chb.2008.02.009

Wilding, R. (2006). "Virtual" intimacies? Families communicating across transnational contexts. *Global Networks, 6*(2), 125–142. doi:10.1111/j.1471-0374.2006.00137.x

Xie, B. (2007). Using the Internet for offline relationship formation. *Social Science Computer Review, 25*(3), 396–404. doi:10.1177/0894439307297622

Yum, Y. O., & Hara, K. (2006). Computer-mediated relationship development: A cross-cultural comparison. *Journal of Computer-Mediated Communication, 11*(1), 133–152.

7 Assessment in the CFT Framework

The Internet is so big, so powerful and pointless that for some people it is a complete substitute for life.

—*Andrew Brown*

The use of formalized assessment measures helps facilitate the therapeutic process, through proper diagnosis and understanding. There are three main areas of assessment, corresponding with the three elements of the CFT framework: assessment of the ecological, structural, and process elements of relationships. Assessments used in the field of couple and family technology include those that generally apply to the broad field of couple and family therapy, with specific attention to the role of technology within the context of the relationship. Assessments in both categories will be discussed below.

Assessment of Specific Issues Related to Technology in Couple Relationships

For couples actively engaging with technology, one area for assessment is shared time, which is specifically assessed through measures targeting suspicion and jealousy. Additionally, the 24-item Multidimensional Jealousy Scale (MJS) by Wong and Pfeiffer (1989) focuses on jealousy among three dimensions: cognitive, emotional, and behavioral jealousy. The MJS is widely accepted by researchers as an effective, comprehensive, and extremely useful tool because of its multifaceted assessment capability. Other scales to measure jealousy include the Chronic (CJ) and Relationship (RJ) Jealousy Scales (White, 1981), the Interpersonal Jealousy Scale (IJS; Mathes & Severa, 1981), the Interpersonal Relationship Scale (IRS); (Hupka & Rusch, 1979), the Romantic Relationship Scale (RRS; Clanton & Kosins, 1991), the Self-Report Jealousy Scale (SRJS; Bringle, Roach, Andler, & Evenbeck, 1979), the Survey of Interpersonal Reactions (SIR; Rosmarin, Chambless, & LaPointe, 1979), and the Dispositional Envy Scale (DES; Smith, Parrott, Kim, Hoyle, & Diener, 1999).

Another assessment strategy is to evaluate the factors shown to predict Internet usage problems. Some research has found men are more likely to experience problems related to Internet usage (see, e.g., Li & Chung, 2006; Serin, 2011); at the same time, other investigations have found the opposite (see, e.g., Kim, Kim, Namkoong, & Ku, 2008). One researcher has posited that communication strategies between men and women may be at the root of this difference (Serin, 2011). Accordingly, an assessment of communication style may be warranted. An assessment of personality types may further be useful; for example, extraverts and those with neurotic personality traits both use the Internet to communicate with others, but those with neurotic personality traits also use it for entertainment (Wolfradt & Doll, as cited in Serin, 2011). Those with narcissistic personality traits are more likely to be addicted to video games, and possess lower levels of self-control while higher degrees of aggression (Kim et al., 2008).

Finally, assessments of overall life satisfaction may be useful in understanding the context in which Internet usage develops in a couple's life. First, the reverse has been demonstrated to be true; that is, compulsive Internet users generally report a lower score on life satisfaction inventories than those who do not participate in compulsive behavior (see, e.g., Morahan-Martin, 2007, 2008; Serin, 2011). Second, life satisfaction may correlate with other states of one's life (Yen, Yen, Ko, Wu, & Yang, 2007). For example, those who are more likely to use the Internet have rated themselves as more lonely than others (Morahan-Martin & Schumacher, 2003). Not surprisingly, increased computer usage adds to increasing levels of depression (Koç, 2011). Moreover, compulsive Internet usage is associated with individuals who have higher levels of impulsivity (Meerkerk, van den Eijnden, Franken, & Garretsen, 2010) and a lowered social self-efficacy (Iskender & Akin, 2010). Other comorbid diagnoses include: ADHD, anxiety disorders, hypomania, depression (specifically the somatic symptoms of depression; see Hinić, Mihajlović, & Dukić-Dejanović, 2010), certain personality disorders (Bernardi & Pallanti, 2009), and personality dispositions such as sensation seeking (Rahmani & Lavasani, 2011), shyness (Ebeling-Witte, Frank, & Lester, 2007), self-judgment, overidentification, and isolation (Iskender & Akin, 2011).

In adolescents, compulsive Internet use has been associated with physiological challenges (including impaired immunity and lack of physical energy), social problems, and other emotional problems (Cao, Sun, Wan, Hao, & Tao, 2011). Some research has also indicated proneness to boredom is connected to compulsive usage of and dependence on the Internet (Rahmani & Lavasani, 2011; Rotunda, Kass, Sutton, & Leon, 2003). Specifically, depression has been linked to text messaging, Internet dependency, and anxiety (Lu et al., 2011). Therefore, assessments on life satisfaction, loneliness, impulsivity, depression, anxiety, and other related areas might be informative to both the therapist and client in understanding the client's motivation for one's particular Internet use.

Other assessments for Internet addiction could be modeled after Internet addiction (Douglas et al., 2008). Based on an investigation of qualitative research regarding the phenomenon of Internet addiction, this model factors in both push and pull aspects that compel one to use the Internet:

> Internet overuse is mainly defined by the inner needs and motivations of an individual (push factors); however, an individual's predisposition (antecedents and Internet addict profile) is also important . . . the perceived attractive features of the medium (pull factors) moderate the relationship between push factors and the severity of negative effects of Internet overuse. (Douglas et al., 2008, p. 3041)

For example, variables such as loneliness and social isolation could be identified as a push factor, while the ease of the Internet may constitute a pull factor. Another element of the model is the extent to which one employs control strategies (i.e., how well one can control one's computer usage). Therefore, therapists may choose to examine how push and pull factors play a part in a client's life to better assess the extent to which one's Internet usage has become a problem.

Assessment of Problematic Internet Usage in Couples

There are also a number of instruments developed to help therapists determine whether someone's computer/Internet usage borders on problematic. One of the most well-known instruments is the Diagnostic Questionnaire developed by Young (1998a, 1998b). In the original version, positive responses to five of eight questions signified an Internet addiction problem. In its later version, the Diagnostic Questionnaire was renamed the Internet Addiction Test (IAT) and had expanded to include 20 items.

Respondents fall into one of three areas based on their score: those with average computer use, those who used a computer frequently enough to experience problems but not qualify as an addict, and those whose Internet addiction created another set of problems. The IAT has also been shown to measure three dimensions of Internet addiction: withdrawal, time management problems, and substituting the Internet for reality (Chang & Law, 2008).The scale demonstrates high internal reliability and has been used in numerous studies (Widyanto & McMurran, 2004; Yang, 2001; Yang, Choe, Baity, Lee, & Cho, 2005). Young's (1998b) scale also demonstrates an association between Internet addiction and other psychiatric conditions (Yang et al., 2005), and other correlates with Internet addiction (Ferraro, Caci, D'Amico, & Di Blasi, 2007; Li & Chung, 2006).

Another well-known scale is the Problematic Internet Usage Questionnaire (PIUQ; Demetrovics, Szeredi, & R zsa, 2008). This 18-item instrument is composed of three subscales including: (a) obsession related to online activities; (b) neglect of offline activities such as work, household duties, relationships, and even eating; and (c) lack of control in the ability to reduce problematic behavior. The PIUQ generates scores that place respondents in one of four categories: (a) those who score one standard deviation below the mean are classified as the "No Problem" (NP) group; (b) those who score one standard deviation above the mean are classified as the "Average Problem" (AP) group; (c) those who score more than one but less than two standard deviations from the mean are the "Problem Group" (PG); and (d) those who score two standard deviations or above the mean make up the "Significant-problem Group" (SG).

A similarly titled inventory, the Problematic Internet Usage scale, was developed to assess problematic Internet usage among university students (Ceyhan, Ceyhan, & Gürcan, 2007). This 33-item scale produces scores anywhere from 33 to 165. Like the inventories discussed above, this scale consists of three subscales: negative consequences of Internet usage, social benefits, and excessive use. This was used in a study of university students; results indicated those who used the Internet for social and entertainment purposes presented a greater risk for developing problems associated with their computer use than those who used the Internet for information seeking alone (Ceyhan, 2011). This is consistent with research that found those who are more highly educated are less likely to use the Internet (Soule, Shell, & Kleen 2003). The authors are careful to note this scale is not intended to diagnose Internet addiction; rather, it is designed merely to highlight the existence of potential problems with Internet use that may ultimately have negative implications for the respondent's life (Ceyhan et al., 2007). A similar scale that broadly measures one's Internet usage is the Internet Use Survey (IUS) developed by Rotunda et al. (2003). It is a self-report survey composed of 32 items across four subscales: absorption (α = .90), negative consequences (α = .85), sleep (α = .73), and deception (α = .65).

Directed at assessing problematic Internet behavior resulting in procrastination, social consequences, and impulsivity, the Online Cognition Scale (Davis, Flett, & Besser, 2002) was developed. It has 36 items and four subscales: social comfort, diminished impulse control, loneliness, and distraction; a subsequent analysis, however, reduced the subscales to two, distraction and dependency (Jia & Jia, 2009). The scale is internally consistent (α = 0.94 for the total scale and between α = .47 and .81 for the subscale reliabilities); the subscales were confirmed through confirmatory rather than exploratory factor analysis

(Davis et al., 2002). The Online Cognition Scale has been used to identify people's thoughts and perceptions concerning their specific Internet usage in lieu of focusing on behavior and amount of time spent online. Sample questions include: "I can't stop thinking about the Internet"; "I am less lonely when I am online"; and "People accept me for who I am online."

Following a review of these instruments, which indicated a lack of convergence on assessing problematic Internet behavior, led Jia and Jia (2009) to question why these studies differed with regard to factors and subscales. Two reasons were proposed: First, the definition of "problematic" Internet behavior changes depending on how the construct itself is defined (Jia & Jia, 2009). This definition certainly has implications for the questions on the inventory as well as the way in which the items are grouped (Tobacyk, 1995). A Delphi study investigating Internet infidelity behavior yielded the same results: Experts in the field of infidelity could not even agree on a definition of "Internet infidelity" (Nelson, Piercy, & Sprenkle, 2005). Jia and Jia (2009) noted, "There is still a lack of commonly adopted construct definition or theoretical view" (p. 1335), partly due to the descriptive nature of the phenomenon.

Differences in methodology also contribute to this discrepancy among instruments (Jia & Jia, 2009). Because many of these studies used factor analysis, concerns arose over how many of these factors were extracted (Jia & Jia, 2009). Second, the populations used in these studies vary and subsequently create differences in the results. Specifically, those studies that used an undergraduate sample found problematic Internet usage centered on online gaming and visiting adult websites. By contrast, problematic Internet use among working adults focused on instant messaging. Jia and Jia (2009) concluded, "These results suggest problematic use may involve different Internet activities across various user groups" (p. 1341).

Finally, methodological issues also emerge within the interpretation of results. For example, the PG, as operationally defined through an interpretation of standard deviations in the Demetrovics et al. (2008) study, is inconsistent with general interpretations of standard deviations. The basic principle of standard deviation means one expects members of a given population to fall within one standard deviation of the mean, with part of that expectation resting on the fact that people will fall both below and above the mean. Therefore, qualifying those who scored negative within one standard deviation as having no problem, while those who scored positive were classified as having an average problem, does not generally fit with the way in which standard deviation is typically interpreted. It would be more fitting to classify scores within one standard deviation of the mean, either positive or negative, which would then make up one category rather than two separate ones.

One of the attempts to resolve the ambiguity around determining problematic or addictive behavior was provided by Jones and Hertlein (2012). There are four dimensions by which one can begin to distinguish sex addiction facilitated by the Internet, Internet addiction, and Internet infidelity: *the involved parties, the view of the problem, the physical symptoms,* and *the presence or absence of addictive properties.* For example, in the "involved parties" dimension, both Internet addiction and Internet sex addiction primarily involve one person—the Internet user. In Internet infidelity, there are generally two people involved—the Internet user and the person on the other end. Similarly, in Internet infidelity and Internet sex addiction, the content of one's activity proves to be problematic whereas in Internet addiction, the prominent issue is the amount of time spent online.

Assessment of the Ecological Elements

Assessment of the ecological elements can occur both within the use of a structured assessment tool as well as over the course of a semistructured clinical interview. The assessment tool described here is the first inventory to be applied to one's computer usage within the context of a relationship. Further, the inventory does not rely solely on understanding these relationships through a pathological addiction and dependency lens (see Appendix A). The questions posed are designed to provide information to both the couple and therapist in seven areas. For example, in the area of accessibility, questions focus on one's perception of one's accessibility in a variety of Internet contexts, the accessibility of communicative technologies, and one's capacity to use technology to block or restrict access from others.

Assessment of Technology Practices Within Family Systems

The Intersystems Approach

The Intersystems approach to treatment was identified by Weeks (1994) and is an attempt to address the complex nature of problem etiology and subsequent treatment. This approach has been applied to a variety of presenting problems, but primarily to the realm of sexual problems. The Intersystems approach attends to five dimensions of problem development and resolution within couple and family relationships: individual biology, individual psychology, dyadic issues, family-of-origin influences, and sociocultural issues.

As noted by King, Delfabbro, and Griffiths (2009), there are many dimensions to assessing Internet issues. Their approach is specific to online gaming and includes many of the same areas within the Intersystems approach (Weeks, 1994). For example, the therapist asks the client about any health concerns and how such concerns contribute to the client's current Internet problem. With regard to psychology, sample questions center on motivations for Internet usage as well as emotions one experiences when online. The social dimension examines the extent to which one's Internet activities interfere with one's social relationships and leisure activities.

Technological Genogram

In general, conducting genograms can be helpful in working with couples, particularly in terms of both assessment and treatment of some of the common presenting problems. Genograms also foster better understanding of one's relationships, life events, and patterns across generations (Bowen, 1966; McGoldrick & Gerson, 1985). The empirical study of genogram usage has received a moderate amount of attention spanning a variety of clinical and training settings, presenting problems, and cultural groups (Coupland & Serovich, 1999; Daly et al., 1999; Daughhetee, 2001; Foster, Jurkovic, Ferdinand, & Meadows, 2002; Helling & Stovers, 2005; Joyce, Love, & Fordham, 2006; Kenen & Peters, 2001; Lim, 2008; Rempel, Neufeld, & Kushner, 2007; Rohrbaugh, Rogers, & McGoldrick, 1992; Swainson & Tasker, 2005; Watts & Shrader, 1998). The nuts and bolts of constructing of a basic genogram have been extensively outlined, documented, and explained (see Bowen, 1966; McGoldrick, Gerson, & Shellenberger, 1999).

Focused genograms can be particularly useful tools for a more focused exploration and examination of a specific intergenerational topic (DeMaria, Weeks, & Hof, 1999). Some of the topics receiving attention include: money and finances (Duba, 2009; Mumford & Weeks, 2003); culture (Hardy & Laszloffy, 1995; McCullough-Chavis & Waites, 2004); spirituality and religion (Duba, 2009; Frame, 2000); ecological sustainability or a greenogram (Blumer, Hertlein, & Fife, 2012); academia and education (Granello, Hothersall, & Osborne, 2000); occupations, career, and balancing work and family (Kakiuchi & Weeks, 2009); military and service (Brelsford & Friedberg, 2011; Papaj, Blumer, & Robinson, 2011; Weiss, Coll, Gerbauer, Smiley, & Carillo, 2010); intimacy (Sherman, 1993); sexuality (Belous, Timm, Chee, & Whitehead, 2012); trauma, attachment processes, anger, emotions, gender, and love (DeMaria, Weeks, & Hof, 1999).

One of the many benefits of using a focused genogram is it helps elicit more in-depth, qualitative-like information about a specific topic or presenting problem, in contrast to the voluminous, quantitative-like amounts of information about a myriad of topics typically acquired via traditional genograms (Quinn, 2000; Wang, 2000) or other forms of assessment (e.g., scaling queries, questionnaires, surveys). When a focused genogram is used as an assessment tool, the gathering of information deemed immediately relevant to the client's specific concerns occurs early on in treatment, and in an intensive manner (DeMaria et al., 1999; Quinn, 2000; Wang, 2000). A focused genogram can also be less time consuming than other assessment methods. Finally, a focused genogram allows both therapist and client to trace patterns that likely have important implications but were never fully noticed or overly acknowledged.

It is commonly recommended that three or more generations be included when constructing a focused genogram (DeMaria et al., 1999). Yet it was not until the 1970s when the first commercial personal computers were released; the first multimedia computers were not available until 1992 (Freed & Ishida, 1995). Moreover, the birth of the Internet did not occur until the 1960s, but its popularity and ease of accessibility did not emerge until approximately 1996 (Coffman & Odlyzko, 1998). People born after 1996 (the year noted as beginning the rise of the Internet) and later are the first generation who has grown up digital (Heim, Brandtzaeg, Kaare, Endestad, & Torgersen, 2007), making many "digital natives" (Prensky, 2001). Since this time, more and more people have been raised side-by-side with technology and while at one time there was a so-called digital divide separating those who owned some element of technology from those that did not, this has almost entirely disappeared in the United States (Horrigan, 2009; Rushing & Stephens, 2011). The generation of digital natives differs from most of their parents, who are more than likely are either digital immigrants, meaning they were not born into a digital age and thus have not easily adopted the digital language, or they may be digital settlers (Prensky, 2001). Digital settlers grew up in an analog world, but are now bilingual in that they speak both the digital and analog languages to varying degrees (Prensky, 2001). Thus, the use of a technological genogram, or technogram, has not been an option until rather recently, but, given the intergenerational implications, is a clear necessity.

A technological genogram consists of general questions about the couple's intergenerational familial dynamics and patterns (see Bowen, 1966; DeMaria et al., 1999; McGoldrick et al., 1999). Also included is a general exploration of the dynamics and patterns each individual has with technology—as if technology itself were a member of the family (see Chapter 9 for a more detailed description of this concept). As an example, consider the following vignette of the technological genogram (see Figure 7.1). To accompany this genogram, general, technologically focused genogram questions are also included (see Appendix B). Finally, questions attending to the transmitted intergenerational patterns around the components compromising the CFT framework—the ecological, structural, and process elements—are also provided (see Appendix C).

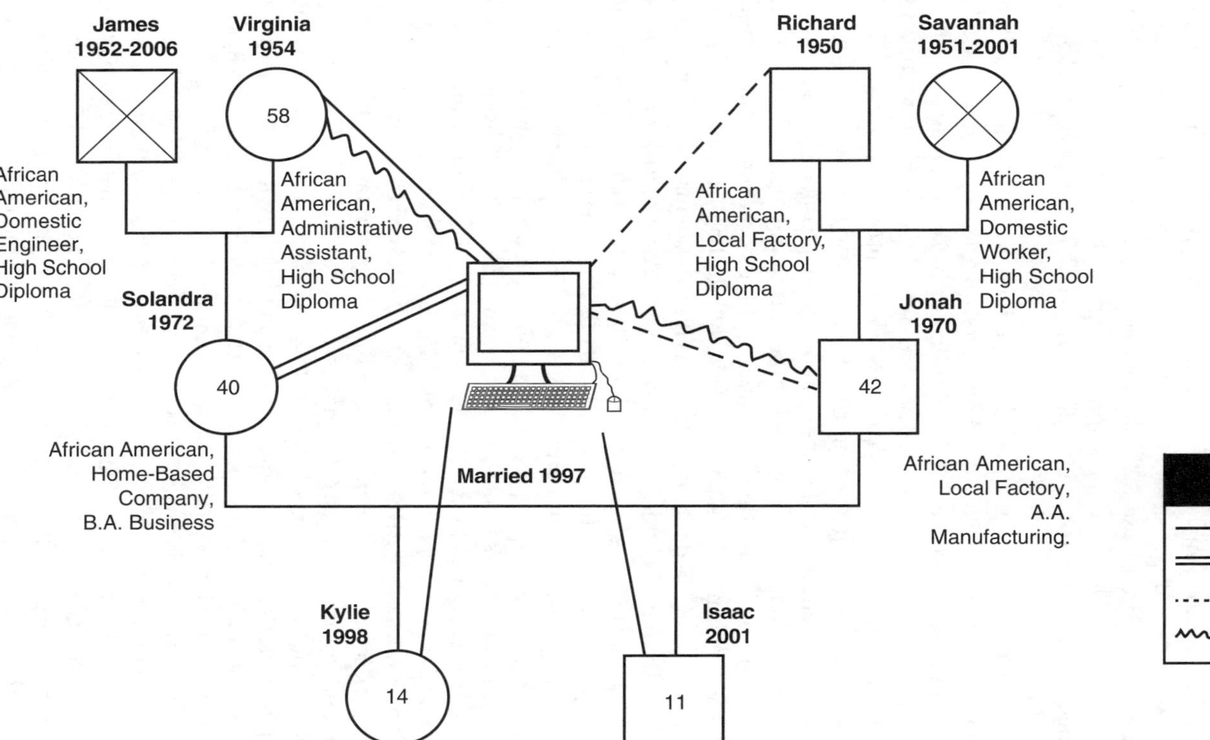

Figure 7.1. Technological genogram.

Technological Genogram Vignette

The Case of Jonah and Solandra[1]

Jonah and Solandra, an African American couple in their early 40s, had been married for 15 years and have two teen children. Solandra worked for a home-based company which required her to be online for most of her workday. Because Jonah worked long shifts at a local factory, he rarely had time to use the computer to accomplish the tasks of his job. Besides checking his e-mail, Jonah otherwise felt unfamiliar with the Internet, in particular, social networking sites like Twitter, Facebook, and LinkedIn.

Up until a few years ago, Solandra ended her workday and logged off the computer when Jonah came home from work. Together, the whole family would enjoy an evening meal, followed by some family time playing board games or watching television. Yet as the children aged, and Solandra's involvement in social networking sites, particularly Twitter, had increased, their evening routine has changed. Recently, Jonah expressed his concerns to Solandra about these changes. He was upset as she seemed constantly to be on her various technological devices (i.e., iPad, iPhone, personal computer) during the day, in the evenings, and sometimes well into the night. He described feeling as if he "lost [his] connection to her" and that it is almost as if she is having an "affair" with all of her "Internet friends." Jonah was particularly sensitive to feelings of abandonment and extramarital affairs, because as a child he "watched [his] mom walk out on [him] and [his] dad for another man."

Jonah was also concerned about his children and their use of technology. From Jonah's perspective, his children's use of technology had exploded in the last year since buying them tablets. Now they accessed computers in school and at home and seemed to have "more technological knowledge" and familiarity than Jonah, and in some cases, even Solandra. Jonah was constantly amazed at all his children can accomplish with technology. Since the children have access to their own tablets, Jonah worried about how they made use of their time, particularly with online gaming and social networking sites. Due to his unfamiliarity with technology, Jonah was uncertain how to approach the children about their technology use. With Solandra spending much of her time on her own technological devices, away from the family, Jonah recognized his children have a lot of unsupervised time online while he was out of the house. Additionally, they currently did not have household rules for the children's computer use.

Jonah decided he and Solandra should talk about the children having supervised Internet use. Solandra was agitated and annoyed by Jonah's presumption that she should have to "take time away" from her own career, and Internet play, to "heavily monitor" the children's use since she did not believe they are engaging in any risky digital behaviors. A few days after this somewhat heated discussion, however, Solandra received a phone call from her mother, Virginia, who told her she saw some photos and wall posts on Kylie's Facebook page concerning her because they appeared overtly sexual. Virginia indicated that "if the kid's grandfather were alive to see those posts he'd surely be dead shortly after looking at them!" Solandra began to think Jonah may have been correct to worry about their children's Internet use. Jonah and Solandra decided it was time to set some clear expectations, rules, and boundaries around family use of technology; they expressed uncertainty, however, as to how these should be constructed.

In the vignette provided, the couple was at first not aware of and then disagreed about their need to renegotiate their relationship with technology. For this couple it was not until the larger system and related feedback from family members, that both members of the couple relationship understood that the rules, roles, and boundaries around technology needed to be renegotiated. It is in these circumstances where conducting an assessment and a technological genogram could be useful in pointing out patterns that could benefit from some intervention.

Assessments in this chapter focused on specific issues related to technology in couple relationships, including: problematic Internet use, the ecological elements related to the CFT framework, and technology practices within family systems. There is value in each one of these assessments in helping couples and clinicians properly assess, diagnosis, understand and ultimately negotiate technology related issues. The later assessment, the technological genogram, is helpful in providing a historical and intergenerational context for couples to trace technological patterns. In tracing these patterns, couples have a larger picture with which to better understand their own usage patterns and to assist them in renegotiating the rules, roles, and boundaries around technology in their relationship and family systems.

Note

1. The case of Jonah and Solandra was developed in part with the assistance of Jaclyn D. Cravens, MS, PhD candidate, visiting lecturer of the University of Nevada, Las Vegas, Marriage and Family Therapy program.

References

Belous, C. K., Timm, T. M., Chee, G., & Whitehead, M. (2012). Revisiting the sexual genogram. *American Journal of Family Therapy, 40*(4), 281–296. doi: 10.1080/01926187.2011.627317

Bernardi, S., & Pallanti, S. (2009). Internet addiction: A descriptive clinical study focusing on comorbidities and dissociative symptoms. *Comprehensive Psychiatry, 50*(6), 510–516. doi:10.1016/j.comppsych.2008.11.011

Blumer, M. L. C., Hertlein, K. M., & Fife, S. T. (2012). It's not easy becoming green: The role of family therapists in an eco-sustainability age. *Contemporary Family Therapy, 34*(1), 1–17. doi:10.1007/s10591-012-9175-9

Bowen, M. (1966). *Family therapy in clinical practice.* Northvale, NJ: Jason Aronson.

Brelsford, G. M., & Friedberg, R. D. (2011). Religious and spiritual issues: Family therapy approaches with military families coping with deployment. *Journal of Contemporary Psychotherapy, 41(4)*, 255–262. doi:10.1007/s10879-011-9174-4

Bringle, R. G., Roach, S., Andler, C., & Evenbeck, S. (1979). Measuring the intensity of jealous reactions. *Catalog of Selected Documents in Psychology, 9*, 23–24.

Cao, H., Sun, Y., Wan, Y., Hao, J., & Tao, F. (2011). Problematic Internet use in Chinese adolescents and its relation to psychosomatic symptoms and life satisfaction. *BMC Public Health, 11*(1), 802–809. doi:10.1186/1471-2458-11-802

Ceyhan, A. A. (2011). University students' problematic Internet use and communication skills according to the Internet use purposes. *Educational Sciences: Theory & Practice, 11*(1), 69–77.

Ceyhan, E., Ceyhan, A. A., & Gürcan, A. (2007). The validity and reliability of the problematic Internet usage scale. *Educational Sciences: Theory and Practice, 7*(1), 411–416.

Chang, M. K., & Law, S. P. (2008). Factor structure for Young's Internet addiction test: A confirmatory study. *Computers in Human Behavior, 24*, 2597–2619. doi:10.1016/j.chb.2008.03.001

Clanton, G., & Kosins, D. J. (1991). Developmental correlates of jealousy. In P. Salovey (Ed.), *The psychology of jealousy and envy* (pp. 132–147). New York: Guilford Press.

Coffman, K. G., & Odlyzko, A. M. (1998). *The size and growth rate of the Internet.* AT&T Labs. Retrieved from http://www.dtc.umn.edu/~odlyzko/doc/internet.size.pdf

Coupland, S. K., & Serovich, J. M. (1999). Effects of couples' perceptions of genogram construction on therapeutic alliance and session impact: A growth curve analysis. *Contemporary Family Therapy, 21*(4), 551–572. doi:10.1023/A:1021683423312

Daly, M., Farmer, J., Harrop-Stein, C., Montgomery, S., Itzen, M., Costalas, J. W., et al. (1999). Exploring family relationships in cancer risk counseling using the genogram. *Cancer Epidemiology, Biomarkers & Prevention, 8*(4 Pt. 2), 393–398.

Daughhetee, C. (2001). Using genograms as a tool for insight in college counseling. *Journal of College Counseling, 4*(1), 73–76. doi:10.1002/j.2161-1882.2001.tb00184.x

Davis, R. A., Flett, G. L., & Besser, A. (2002). Validation of a new scale for measuring problematic Internet use: Implications for pre-employment screening. *Cyberpsychology & Behavior: The Impact of the Internet, Multimedia and Virtual Reality on Behavior and Society, 5*(4), 331–345. doi:10.1089/109493102760275581

DeMaria, R., Weeks, G. & Hof, L. (1999). *Focused genograms: Intergenerational assessment of individuals, couples, and families.* New York: Brunner/Mazel.

Demetrovics, Z., Szeredi, B., & Rózsa, S. (2008). The three-factor model of Internet addiction: The development of the problematic Internet use questionnaire. *Behavior Research Methods, 40*(2), 563–574. doi:10.3758/BRM.40.2.563

Douglas, A. C., Mills, J. E., Niang, M., Stepchenkova, S., Byun, S., Ruffini, C., et al. (2008). Internet addiction: Meta-synthesis of qualitative research for the decade 1996–2006. *Computers in Human Behavior, 24*(6), 3027–3044. doi:10.1016/j.chb.2008.05.009

Duba, J. (2009). Introducing the "basic needs genogram" in reality therapy-based marriage and family counseling. *International Journal of Reality Therapy, 28*(2), 15–26.

Ebeling-Witte, S., Frank, M. L., & Lester, D. (2007). Shyness, Internet use, and personality. *Cyberpsychology & Behavior: The Impact of the Internet, Multimedia and Virtual Reality on Behavior and Society, 10*(5), 713–716. doi:10.1089/cpb.2007.9964

Ferraro, G., Caci, B., D'Amico, A., & Di Blasi, M. (2007). Internet addiction disorder: An Italian study. *Cyberpsychology & Behavior: The Impact of the Internet, Multimedia and Virtual Reality on Behavior and Society, 10*(2), 170–175. doi:10.1089/cpb.2006.9972

Foster, M. A., Jurkovic, G. J., Ferdinand, L. G., & Meadows, L. A. (2002). The impact of the genogram on couples: A manualized approach. *Family Journal, 10*(1), 34–40. doi:10.1177/1066480702101006

Frame, M. W. (2000). The spiritual genogram in family therapy. *Journal of Marital and Family Therapy, 26,* 211–216. doi:10.1111/j.1752-0606.2000.tb00290.x

Freed, L., & Ishida, S. (1995). *History of computers.* Hightstown, NJ: Ziff-Davis.

Granello, D., Hothersall, D., & Osborne, A. L. (2000). The academic genogram: Teaching for the future by learning from the past. *Counselor Education & Supervision, 39*(3), 177-188.

Hardy, K. V., & Laszloffy, T. A. (1995). The cultural genogram: Key to training culturally competent family therapists. *Journal of Marital and Family Therapy, 21*(3), 227–237. doi:10.1111/j.1752 0606.1995.tb00158.x

Heim, J., Brandtzæg, P. B., Kaare, B. H., Endestad, T., & Torgersen, L. (2007). Children's usage of media technologies and psychosocial factors. *New Media & Society, 9*(3), 425–454. doi:10.1177/1461444807076971

Helling, M. K., & Stovers, R. G. (2005). Genogram as a research tool. *Great Plains Sociologist, 17*(1), 78–85.

Hićnić, D., Mihajlović, G., & Dukić-Dejanović, S. (2010). "Internet addiction" in relation to cognitive or somatic depression symptoms. *Journal of Cognitive and Behavioral Psychotherapies, 10*(2), 187–197.

Horrigan, J. (2009). *Home abroad adoption 2009.* Retrieved from http://www.pewinternet.org/Reports/2009/10-Home-Broadband-Adoption-2009.aspx

Hupka, R. B., & Rusch, P. A. (1979). *Interpersonal Relationship Scale.* Unpublished manuscript, California State University, Long Beach.

İskender, M., & Akin, A. (2010). Social self-efficacy, academic locus of control, and Internet addiction. *Computers & Education, 54*(4), 1101–1106. doi:10.1016/j.compedu.2009.10.014

Iskender, M., & Akin, A. (2011). Self-compassion and Internet addiction. *Turkish Online Journal of Educational Technology, 10*(3), 215–221.

Jia, H. H., & Jia, R. (2009). Factorial validity of problematic Internet use scales. *Computers in Human Behavior, 25*(6), 1335–1342. doi:10.1016/j.chb.2009.06.004

Jones, K. E., & Hertlein, K. M. (2012). Four key dimensions for distinguishing Internet infidelity from Internet and sex addiction: Concepts and clinical application. *American Journal of Family Therapy, 40*(2), 115–125. doi:10.1080/01926187.2011.600677

Joyce, J. M., Love, M. M., & Fordham, M. (2006). Discovering gender differences while teaching family genograms. *Medical Education, 40*(5), 459–489. doi:10.1111/j.1365-2929.2006.02452.x

Kakiuchi, K. K. S., & Weeks, G. R. (2009). The occupational transmission genogram: Exploring family scripts affecting roles of work and career in couple and family dynamics. *Journal of Family Psychotherapy, 20*(1), 1–12. doi:10.1080/08975350802716467

Kenen, R., & Peters, J. (2001). The colored, eco-genetic relationship map: A conceptual approach and tool for genetic counseling research. *Journal of Genetic Counseling, 10*(4), 289–309. doi:10.1023/A:1016627426430

Kim, S. J., Kim, E. J., Namkoong, K., & Ku, T. (2008). The relationship between online game addiction and aggression, self-control and narcissistic personality traits. *European Psychiatry, 23*(3), 212–218. doi:10.1016/j.eurpsy.2007.10.010

King, D., Delfabbro, P., & Griffiths, M. (2009). The psychological study of video game players: Methodological challenges and practical advice. *International Journal of Mental Health and Addiction, 7*(4), 555–562. doi:10.1007/s11469-009-9198-0

Koç, M. (2011). Internet addiction and psychopathology. *Turkish Online Journal of Educational Technology, 10*(1), 143–148.

Li, S. M., & Chung, T. M. (2006). Internet function and Internet addictive behavior. *Computers in Human Behavior, 22*(6), 1067–1071. doi:10.1016/j.chb.2004.03.030

Lim, S. L. (2008). Transformative aspects of genogram work: Perceptions and experiences of graduate students in a counseling training program. *Family Journal: Counseling and Therapy for Couples and Families, 16*(1), 35–42. doi:10.1177/1066480707309321

Lu, X., Watanabe, J., Liu, Q., Uji, M., Shono, M., & Kitamura, T. (2011). Internet and mobile phone text-messaging dependency: Factor structure and correlation with dysphoric mood among Japanese adults. *Computers in Human Behavior, 27*(5), 1702–1709. doi:10.1016/j.chb.2011.02.009

Mathes, E. W., & Severa, N. (1981). Jealousy, romantic love, and liking: Theoretical considerations and preliminary scale development. *Psychological Reports, 49*(1), 23–31. doi:10.2466/pr0.1981.49.1.23

McCullough-Chavis, A., & Waites, C. (2004). Genograms with African American families: Considering cultural context. *Journal of Family Social Work, 8*(2), 1–12. doi:10.1300/J039v08n02_01

McGoldrick, M., & Gerson, R. (1985). *Genograms in family assessment*. New York: W. W. Norton.

McGoldrick, M., Gerson, R., & Shellenberger, S. (1999). Developing a genogram to track family patterns. In *Genograms: Assessment and intervention* (2nd ed.). New York: W. W. Norton.

Meerkerk, G., van den Eijnden, R. J. J. M., Franken, I. H. A., & Garretsen, H. F. L. (2010). Is compulsive Internet use related to sensitivity to reward and punishment, and impulsivity? *Computers in Human Behavior, 26*(4), 729–735. doi:10.1016/j.chb.2010.01.009

Morahan-Martin, J. (2007). Internet use and abuse and psychological problems. In J. Joinson, K. McKenna, T. Postmes, & U. Reips (Eds.), *Oxford handbook of Internet psychology* (pp. 331–345). Oxford, England: Oxford University Press.

Morahan-Martin, J. (2008). Internet abuse: Emerging trends and lingering questions. In A. Barak (Ed.), *Psychological aspects of cyberspace: Theory, research and applications* (pp. 32–69). Cambridge, England: Cambridge University Press.

Morahan-Martin, J., & Schumacher, P. (2003). Loneliness and social uses of the Internet. *Computers in Human Behavior, 19*(6), 659–671. doi:10.1016/S0747-5632(03)00040-2

Mumford, D. J., & Weeks, G. R. (2003). The money genogram. *Journal of Family Psychotherapy, 14*(3), 33–44. doi:10.1300/J085v14n03_03

Nelson, T., Piercy, F., & Sprenkle, D. (2005). Internet infidelity: A multi-wave Delphi study. *Journal of Couple and Relationship Therapy, 4*(2/3), 173–194. doi:10.1177/1066480706290508

Papaj, A. K., Blumer, M. L. C., & Robinson, L. D. (2011). The clinical deployment of therapeutic frameworks and genogram questions to serve the servicewoman.

Journal of Feminist Family Therapy, 23(3/4), 263–284. doi:10.1080/08952833.2011.604533

Prensky, M. (2001). Digital natives, digital immigrants Part 2: Do they really think differently? *On the Horizon, 9*(6), 1–6. doi:10.1108/10748120110424843

Quinn, A. (2000). [Book review] Focused genograms: Intergenerational assessment of individuals, couples, and families. *Palliative Medicine, 14*(1), 83. doi:10.1177/026921630001400124

Rahmani, S., & Lavasani, M. G. (2011). The relationship between Internet dependency with sensation seeking and personality. *Procedia—Social and Behavioral Sciences, 30*(1), 272–277. doi:10.1016/j.sbspro.2011.10.054

Rempel, G. R., Neufeld, A., & Kushner, K. E. (2007). Interactive use of genograms and ecomaps in family caregiving research. *Journal of Family Nursing, 13*(1), 403–419. doi:10.1177/1074840707307917

Rohrbaugh, M., Rogers, J. C., & McGoldrick, M. (1992). How do experts read family genograms? *Family Systems Medicine, 10*(1), 79–89. doi:10.1037/h0089325

Rosmarin, D. M., Chambless, D. L., & LaPointe, K. (1979). *The survey of interpersonal reactions: An inventory for the measurement of jealousy.* Unpublished manuscript, Department of Psychology, University of Georgia.

Rotunda, R. J., Kass, S. J., Sutton, M. A., & Leon, D. T. (2003). Internet use and misuse: Preliminary findings from a new assessment instrument. *Behavior Modification, 27*(4), 484–504. doi:10.1177/0145445503255600

Rushing, S. C., & Stephens, D. (2011). Use of media technologies by Native American teens and young adults in the Pacific Northwest: Exploring their utility for designing culturally appropriate technology-based health interventions. *Journal of Primary Prevention, 32,* 135–145. doi:10.1007/s10935-011-0242-z

Serin, B. N. (2011). An examination of predictor variables for problematic Internet use. *Turkish Online Journal of Educational Technology, 10*(3), 54–62.

Sherman, R. (1993). The intimacy genogram. *Family Journal, 1*(1), 91–93. doi:10.1177/106648079300100117

Smith, R. H., Parrott, W. G., Kim, S. H., Hoyle, R. H., & Diener, E. F. (1999). Dispositional envy. *Personality and Social Psychology Bulletin, 25*(11), 1007–1020. doi:10.1177/01461672992511008

Soule, L. C., Shell, L. W., & Kleen, B. A. (2003). Exploring Internet addiction: Demographic characteristics and stereotypes of heavy Internet users. *Journal of Computer Information Systems, 44*(1), 64–73

Swainson, M., & Tasker, F. (2005). Genograms redrawn: Lesbian couples define their families. *Journal of LGBT Family Studies, 1*(2), 3–27.

Tobacyk, J. J. (1995). Final thoughts on issues in the measurement of paranormal beliefs. *Journal of Parapsychology, 59*(1), 141–145.

Wang, T. (2000). [Book review] Focused genograms: Intergenerational assessment of individuals, couples, and families. *Family Relations, 49*(3), 349–350.

Watts, C., & Shrader, E. (1998). How to do (or not to do) . . . the genogram: A new research tool to document patterns of decision-making, conflict, and vulnerability within households. *Health Policy and Planning, 13*(4), 459–464. doi:10.1093/heapol/13.4.459

Weeks, G. (1994). The intersystem model: An integrative approach to treatment. In G. Weeks & L. Hof (Eds.), *The marital-relationship casebook: Theory and application of the intersystem model* (pp. 3–34). New York: Routledge.

Weiss, E. L., Coll, J. E., Gerbauer, J., Smiley, K., & Carillo, E. (2010). The military genogram: A solution-focused approach for resiliency building in service members and their families. *Family Journal, 18*(4), 395–406. doi:10.1177/1066480710378479

White, G. L. (1981). A model of romantic jealousy. *Motivation and Emotion, 5*(4), 295–310. doi:10.1007/BF00992549

Widyanto, L., & McMurran, M. (2004). The psychometric properties of the Internet addiction test. *Cyberpsychology & Behavior: The Impact of the Internet, Multimedia and Virtual Reality on Behavior and Society,* 7(4), 443–450. doi:10.1089/cpb.2004.7.443

Wolfradt, U., & Doll, J. (2001). Motives of adolescents to use the Internet as a function of personality traits, personal and social factors. *Journal of Educational Computing Research, 24*(1), 13–27. doi:10.2190/ANPM-LN97-AUT2-D2EJ

Wong, P. T. P., & Pfeiffer, S. M. (1989). Multidimensional jealousy. *Journal of Social and Personal Relationships, 6*(2), 181–196. doi:10.1177/026540758900600203

Yang, C., Choe, B., Baity, M., Lee, J., & Cho, J. (2005). SCL-90-R and 16PF profiles of senior high school students with excessive Internet use. *Canadian Journal of Psychiatry, 50*(7), 407-414.

Yang, S. C. (2001). Language learning on the World Wide Web: An investigation of EFL learners' attitudes and perceptions. *Educational Computing Research, 24*(1), 155–181.

Yen, C., Yen, J., Ko, C., Wu, H., & Yang, M. (2007). The comorbid psychiatric symptoms of Internet addiction: Attention deficit and hyperactivity disorder (ADHD), depression, social phobia, and hostility. *Journal of Adolescent Health, 41*(1), 93–98. doi:10.1016/j.jadohealth.2007.02.002

Young, K. S. (1998a). *Caught in the net: How to recognize the signs of Internet addiction and a winning strategy for recovery.* Hoboken, NJ: John Wiley.

Young, K. S. (1998b). Young Internet addiction: The emergence of a new clinical disorder. *CyberPsychology and Behavior, 1*(3), 237–244.

8 Treatment of Internet-Based Problems Through the CFT Framework

I think the technology has allowed us to do a much better job of defining where the hazards are, where the strong shaking may be, where the bad ground is.

—*David Schwarz*

Existing Treatment Strategies

Internet Addiction

As with any other disorder, the treatment of Internet addiction is multifaceted. Internet addiction, as with any other addiction, requires a combination of interventions at the biological and psychological levels. For example, combining medication as well as psychotherapy is often a useful strategy (Huang, Li, & Tao, 2010; Murali & Onuba, 2009). One of the key issues for any addiction is to conduct a proper assessment to determine the characteristics contributing to the problem. In addition to providing information about the addiction, therapists should attend to the pattern expressed by the client, per previous literature. Treatment strategies could be focused on the triggers identified in the assessment phase and the exploration of better management strategies. For example, Luke, a client struggling with several years of Internet addictive behavior, realized the times in which he was using the computer in inappropriate ways or as a coping skill were tied to times where his wife was angry with him or where he experienced greater levels of stress at his job. Accordingly, treatment was centered around better management of his work stressors, as well as the referral to couples therapy so Luke and his wife could communicate more effectively. Other strategies for Internet addiction focus on helping the client to emerge from an isolated lifestyle and reconnect with others as a way to experience offline satisfaction (Murali et al., 2009).

With regard to treatment, the primarily modality used is cognitive-behavioral therapy (CBT; Li, Li, Wang et al., 2008; Cao, Su, Gao et al., 2007; Du, Jiang, & Vance, 2010), although in some cases it is paired with motivational interviewing (Orzack, Voluse, Wolf, & Hennen, 2006; Shek, Tang, & Lo, 2009). Employing a CBT framework demonstrates how patterns are developed as a way of coping with difficult thoughts and feelings that are essentially stuck internally, because the client has had ample opportunity to rehearse and reinforce these thoughts and feelings. Therefore, a treatment based on CBT would be one of the most effective approaches (Young, 2011). Some specific techniques and interventions based on CBT include assertiveness training, relaxation training, social skills training, engagement in creative outlets, improvement of family functioning (Yen, Yen, Chen, Chen, & Ko, 2007), limiting online activities, and helping one to develop self-esteem (Murali et al., 2009).

The early phase of treatment for Internet addiction is based on proper diagnosis and identification of triggers, such as one's physiology and psychology, social complications, and motivation (Murali et al., 2009). This phase is also marked by changing behaviors and reducing one's impulsiveness (Hall & Parsons, 2001). Clients may be asked to complete a daily Internet log (Murali et al., 2009; Young, 2011). The tracking of events and behaviors around Internet usage should provide an ability to identify antecedents and set the stage for the next phase of therapy, cognitive restructuring (Young, 2007, 2011). Cognitive restructuring allows the client to develop ways to manage the triggers and develop an understanding of the negative cognitions maintaining the problematic behavior. Triggers may include anxiety, depression, anger, stress, loneliness, and the defenses emerging upon feeling those difficult emotions (Murali et al., 2009). Common problematic cognitions among Internet addicts are generalizing their beliefs about themselves in one incident to apply to many incidents or catastrophizing (Murali et al., 2009). Once the thoughts are articulated, the therapist can challenge them. The third phase of treatment in Young's (2011) model is harm reduction. In this phase, the therapist and client work together to change the context in which the Internet addict resides. This may require some attention to an Internet addict's need to fantasize, addressing dyadic issues contributing to the maintenance of the addiction, or other compulsive behaviors. Other lesser known approaches include reality therapy to treat Internet addiction (Kim, 2008), CBT paired with psychodrama (Zhong, Tao, Zu, Sha, & Yang, 2009), and a Naikan cognitive therapy perspective (Zhao, Mao, & Liu, 2009).

Online Gaming

Zhong (2011) noted, "Whether the effects of MMORPG [massively multiplayer online role-playing game] is anti-social or pro-social depends on how people play the game" (p. 2361). Individuals who play video games with others (such as in MMORPGs) develop their own rules in their interactions with one another. In so doing, they create regulations with regard to problem solving and negotiation. Developed by Boella, Caire, and van de Torre (2009), the agent communication protocol describes the process by which those who participate in online gaming negotiate and solve problems within the game. First, the individual communicates his or her position of power and goals. The individual then advances a solution that the group may or may not accept. Once the group accepts a proposal offered by the individual, there is discussion around how the rules are going to be upheld by the group and thus, norms emerge.

Given the manner in which elements of one's online life can translate into changes in one's offline life (McKenna & Bargh, 2000), it is reasonable to assume the ways in which Internet addicts negotiate norms are going to translate into norms for negotiating offline. Therapists can incorporate this model into treatment where online gaming is an issue as long as it is paired with the couple's other negotiation skills. Tom and Penny, for example, worked to identify the circumstances under which Tom was able and willing to negotiate and solve problems with his online counterparts, and use the insight to inform how those negotiations differed from the less successful negotiations with Penny. After some conversation, it became clear that Tom felt more comfortable being assertive, advancing potential solutions, and solving problems with others online because he was aware they could not see his facial reactions, which, in turn, made him more free in his personal expression.

To date, there is one article addressing the treatment of online gaming in couple relationships. This article outlines treatment of gaming particularly as it relates to the excessive time one may spend in playing online games (King, Delfabbro, & Griffiths, 2012). Rather than providing a detailed treatment strategy, the authors focus on the cognitive-behavioral component to Internet gaming issues. It follows the Davis (2001) model in that it attends to the problematic cognitions preceding the problematic gaming behavior. For example, because the online role in playing games is based less on actual time playing the game and more on the accomplishment of particular tasks within the game, gamers may often leave a game feeing a sense of agitation or anxiety because they have not completed the goal for that particular point in the game (King et al., 2012).

Cybersex and Internet Infidelity Treatment

Like the information related to the treatment of addictive online gaming, the literature with regard to Internet infidelity treatment and cybersex treatment would also benefit from a standard definition. Nelson, Piercy, and Sprenkle (2005) discovered experts did not have a common definition for Internet infidelity; these results were corroborated in Hertlein and Piercy's (2008) findings, where therapists primarily indicated they leave it up to the couple to define it for themselves.

First-Order Change Strategies

First-order change strategies refer to those employed as crisis intervention (Delmonico, Griffin, & Carnes, 2002) and include limiting one's Internet access through physically relocating the computer and reducing the client's accessibility to the Internet. This is a strategy often employed by practicing therapists. In a study regarding practices for treating Internet infidelity, therapists reported the implementation of physical boundaries in an effort to reduce computer accessibility as a first step in treatment. They observed as long as accessibility to the Internet and the person with whom the affair was conducted was the same as prior to treatment, it would be difficult to build safety and trust within the relationship because there would be no changes to the ease of contacting affair partner (Hertlein & Piercy, 2012). Another way to create first-order change is to implement restrictions on specific applications or websites that have played a role in creating and/or maintaining the problem. For example, Jenna and Lou came to treatment because Jenna found Lou communicating with a former girlfriend via Facebook. As a way to manage this threat, Jenna requested Lou give up his Facebook account. Lou was willing to do this and Jenna, as a show of good faith, also elected to give up her account.

Another key task is to assist the client in becoming more aware of his or her Internet behavior (Delmonico et al., 2002). Lack of awareness about specific behaviors may contribute to problematic relationship dynamics in several ways. First, when Ruth was unaware of her own behavior, it put her partner Jesse in the position of monitoring Ruth's actions instead of allowing Ruth to monitor her own behavior. Second, the lack of awareness may also impair one's ability to properly appraise whether behavior is problematic, thus contributing to disagreement between members of couple about what constitutes problematic behavior.

Second-Order Change Strategies

Within the context of Internet addiction, second-order change strategies may take many forms. For example, one may choose to move the computer to another room as a way to manage the behavior and/or activity without addressing potential underlying issues (Delmonico et al., 2002). Other similar interventions include changing passwords, utilizing blocking software on one's computer, and/or keeping the computer in a room used by many people instead of the individual engaging in the problematic behavior. Other possible focuses of treatment include grief, loss, and depression, as they may co-occur with cybersex (Delmonico et al., 2002).

There are also several detailed treatment models developed specifically around Internet infidelity. One of the earliest models is Shaw's (1997), which focuses on understanding the context in which the problem (that is, Internet infidelity) emerges between the couple. Shaw (1997) identifies a few key issues (or vulnerabilities) contributing to the problem, such as relationship issues within the couple (i.e., communication difficulties, problem resolution concerns, and trust issues). Some of the concerns that need to be addressed are more individualized, such as fears around being oneself and emotional maturity, particularly as it manifests in readiness for engagement in an intimate relationship. Part of the way this is addressed in treatment is through increasing the maturity process as well as the level of trust between the partners. The model developed by Young, Griffin-Shelley, Cooper, O'Mara, and Buchanan (2000) is similar in that it, too, prescribes the rebuilding of communication and trust between the partner. It also incorporates second-order change strategies, such as identifying problems in the marriage that arose prior to engaging in Internet infidelity.

Maheu and Subotnik's (2001) framework provides a bridge between some of the interventions deemed appropriate for couples recovering from Internet infidelity. Based on transgenerational theory, their model advocates couples first manage the crisis through exploring their emotions and learning how to cope with them. Once both partners have begun to manage their emotions, they work to develop new skills while acquiring greater understanding of underlying issues in their relationship. At this point, the couple and therapist identify the family-of-origin issues that also might contribute to both the act of Internet infidelity as well as the process of recovery. Couples are taught to listen and respond to one another in empathetic ways. They are then encouraged to begin to experience each other in ways mirroring the beginning of their relationship through a courtship phase, with an emphasis on reducing any codependence. Accountability is also important in this model, as it must be in place for the stages of forgiveness and closure. In this model, couples are also advised there will be setbacks, but the therapist works with the couple to manage them.

In an approach rooted in transgenerational theory and intrapsychic process, Atwood and Schwarz (2002) advise therapists to attend to the concepts of differentiation of both members of the couple (though particular attention is paid to the person who participated in the Internet infidelity), as well how emotions and behaviors are inappropriately projected on the other partner. Consistent with the data suggesting therapists believe that there is a deficit in the couple's relationship that allows Internet infidelity to emerge (Hertlein & Piercy, 2012), Atwood and Schwarz (2002) delineate the importance of addressing intimacy and communication difficulties arising within the couple. These issues are examined within the context of the relationship in which Internet infidelity arose as well as within the context of communication and intimacy problems arising as a result of the Internet infidelity. In this model, it is also important to identify the trigger—whether it is in response to a life stage, the result of an addiction, or something else. As with the other models discussed, Atwood and Schwarz (2002) highlight the importance of a proper evaluation to determine the best treatment plan. This involves recording the type of activities in which the identified patient is involved and the couple's exploration and assessment of their online social networks. Once the therapist has a handle on the extent of the problem and the people involved, he or she provides a safe environment for the couple to process the underlying issues hurting their marriage. The next task is to rebuild trust through rebuilding communication. At this point, the couple can then decide how they want to mark the beginning of a new relationship with one another.

Hertlein and Piercy (2005) provide another transgenerational perspective on treating Internet infidelity, focusing primarily on the role of differentiation in the couple. Predicated on the assumption that infidelity emerges in a relationship as a way to manage anxiety, the therapist and client work to identify the roles differentiation, triangulation, and anxiety play in the face of Internet infidelity. Interventions are designed to detriangulate the system, promote individuation, and develop appropriate communication strategies in the couple. Key elements of this treatment model include genograms, tracking patterns, and teaching the partners to make decisions from a more differentiated stance.

While not a prescriptive article for how Internet infidelity should be treated, Hertlein and Piercy (2012) summarize the strategies by which therapists indicate they currently treat Internet infidelity. Therapists reported they first establish physical boundaries as a way to provide safety from the upcoming treatment process. Once those are in place, psychological boundaries are implemented. These include revisiting relational contracts for the duration of the treatment process and exploring definitions of problematic behavior. Another phase on which therapists embarked is the management of feelings as they emerging within the treatment process, with specific attention to trust and having the person involved in the Internet infidelity demonstrate accountability for his or her behavior. The next phase is to develop awareness around the origin of the problems. This includes an assessment of the motivation for engaging in Internet infidelity as well as determining what, if any, needs remained unmet in the relationship. Based on previous steps, therapists then assess whether the couple is ready for change. This includes having the couple identify their goals and conduct an exploration of their history and context. Once couples appear ready for change, the therapist then conducts an assessment to determine whether there are any unique circumstances needing attention in addition to the infidelity treatment, such as medical conditions or the presence of an addiction. Finally, the therapist works with the couple to develop forgiveness and a plan to move forward (Hertlein & Piercy, 2012).

Critique of Existing Frameworks

The models presented make intuitive sense—identify any vulnerabilities in the relationship, address those gaps, and work to forge a new, stronger union characterized by a higher degree of intimacy and connection than there was prior to the infidelity. This body of literature, however, still suffers from empirical and theoretical gaps (Hertlein & Piercy, 2006; Huang, Li, & Tao, 2010). First, in the treatment protocols for Internet addiction, the published protocols have not described enough detail to allow others to implement it in their own practices. Secondly, the treatment offered tended to be rather brief (no more than 16 sessions) and was not evaluated to determine long-term effectiveness. Third, many of the research articles did not present the validity and reliability of the scales created by the authors. Finally, the operational definition of Internet addiction is not standardized across investigations and limits the potential for comparison across studies (Huang et al., 2010).

There are also shortcomings in the case of Internet infidelity. First, the empirical literature supporting effective treatment for infidelity (see, e.g., Gordon, Baucom, & Snyder, 2005) does not automatically extend to Internet infidelity because it does not attend to the unique features of the Internet and new media (i.e., the ecological elements outlined in Chapter 5). Second, the theoretical approaches published describing how to treat Internet infidelity represent only a small proportion of available frameworks. In the approaches described above, there is a preponderance of approaches based on transgenerational theories (see, e.g., Maheu & Subotnik, 2001). Yet research into the therapist's theoretical orientations with regard to treating Internet infidelity cases yielded a number of approaches, including the development of boundaries, managing feelings, developing awareness, increasing motivation, altering the relationship context, and moving toward forgiveness (Hertlein & Piercy, 2012). There is clearly a need for more variety in treating these types of cases.

Finally, research has also demonstrated therapists commonly use first-order change strategies to manage some of the ecological elements in treatment, such as limiting accessibility to the Internet. Yet when asked about this kind of treatment, therapists often made case conceptualizations rooted in second-order change perspectives, such as noting a deficit in the couple's relationship that led to online infidelity (Hertlein & Piercy, 2008)—a perspective consistent with Shaw's (1997) approach. It seems the most effective treatment modality may be based on incorporating both first- and second-order change strategies in treatment (Hertlein & Piercy, 2012).

The CFT Treatment Framework

Treatment through the CFT framework has several advantages over treatment strategies identified in the literature. First, rather than being a specific theory, it instead serves as an overarching framework through which to view cases involving the Internet in some capacity. Therapists using this framework can continue to employ their preferred theoretical approach. For example, Therapist Shane uses a solution-focused approach with his clients whereas Therapist Layla uses a cognitive-behavioral approach. Both of them can adopt the CFT framework though attention to understanding how technology has affected the structure and process of relationships. Therapist Shane might choose to ask clients about the impact in terms of the positive effects of technology on their relationship, such as assisting the couple in establishing appropriate rules and boundaries. Therapist Layla, on the other hand, may ask clients about the behavior changes that have occurred with the advent of technology in the home, or ask about behaviors specifically associated with problematic computer usage and the concomitant new behaviors with regard to rules and boundaries.

Second, the CFT framework is sensitive to issues of diversity and idiosyncratic characteristics of a couple's relationship. The framework does not offer one way in which a family or couple relationship should be structured; instead, couples and families can use the framework to simply outline their rules, roles, boundaries, and process, and then work with a therapist to determine which ones work for their particular family or couple and which do not. Third, the CFT treatment frame also attends to both first- and second-order changes. The ecological elements are both designed to allow changes to the physical environment (i.e., moving computers to another room as a way to reduce the accessibility) as well as for second-order changes (i.e., the need for anonymity may have to be managed through process conversation and more detailed therapeutic work). The CFT framework is also influenced by similar models attending to structure and intimacy patterns such as the Fundamental Interpersonal Relations Orientation (FIRO) model (Doherty, Colangelo, & Hovander, 1991). Yet the CFT framework is specific to technology problems in that it incorporates factors germane to the Internet, and promotes further understanding as to how these factors affect structure and process.

Two Key Issues in the Treatment of Technology Problems

Evaluate Your Therapeutic Stance on Key Issues

Nelson (2000) conducted research examining how expert therapists conceptualize treatment in Internet infidelity cases. He discovered a therapist's stance on certain key issues affects their decisions in treatment. These issues included the following:

- Should I hold a secret one partner tells me?
- Should I meet with one or both partners?

- What amount and type of information is helpful for the noninvolved partner to know?
- Should I encourage the noninvolved spouse to monitor their partner's activities after the infidelity is discovered or disclosed?
- Should I handle an Internet infidelity case differently than I would a face-to-face affair (i.e., are different theoretical approaches more effective)?

Three of these issues can also be applied to cases beyond Internet infidelity that also involve technology. First, the type of information the therapist believes is important to share might depend, to some degree, on his or her own experiences with technology. If the therapist believes it is important to share passwords for personal electronic accounts, then this might dictate what he or she prescribes to clients with regard to the same issue. Second, the monitoring of activities is also a key issue in which therapists might have particular feelings that would affect treatment. Therapists have to make a decision as to which elements of technology they believe need monitoring, if any, and whether they value the use of monitoring software as a way to achieve this. In cases where there are children, having parents monitor computer usage makes sense; in couples, however, the issue of having one partner monitor the other's activities introduces issues of trust in the relationship. For example, Cara stated that she felt the need to monitor her boyfriend Paul's Internet behavior because she feared he was cheating on her. Paul, however, asserted he felt betrayed because he did not feel his behavior warranted Cara's monitoring and apparent lack of trust. Finally, the therapist has to make a determination about whether he or she believes the couple should be treated differently because of technology than other cases that do not center on technology. The determination of this may vary from case to case, along with the degree of success achieved by the therapist in similar cases involving technology.

Self of the Therapist

Self-of-the-therapist issues also affect one's treatment in Internet infidelity cases and may also ultimately affect treatment for broader technological issues. According to research conducted by Hertlein and Piercy (2008),

> there were times in which therapists' social background characteristics influenced their assessment but not their treatment, influenced their treatment without influencing their assessment, or influenced their treatment and their assessment. This leads one to be curious about the degree to which assessment and treatment are practically linked when a therapist treats Internet infidelity. For example, the gender of the client, the gender of the therapist, and a therapist's age

> all were consistently related to differences in treatment, but not in assessment items. In the case of religiosity and the impact of personal infidelity experience of a therapist, there tended to be more assessment differences, but this did not necessarily translate into treatment. (p. 493)

Specifically, differences between more religious and less religious therapists revealed that more religious therapists rate their clients participating in Internet infidelity as having greater degrees of being sexually addicted, see pornography as more problematic for a relationship than their less religious counterparts, and place more of the treatment focus on environmental and individual issues (Hertlein, 2004). In some cases, therapists may be affected by and respond to their preconceived notions about how people of particular backgrounds should behave with regard to the Internet. Women, for example, are viewed as more pathological than men by marriage and family therapists with regard to their Internet sexual behavior (Hertlein, 2004). These findings accentuate the importance of understanding the variables and belief systems one brings to the table when treating cases with a technological component.

Managing Ecological Elements

Therapists working within the CFT framework need to develop a clear plan of how to assist the couple in better identifying their vulnerabilities as well as the impact of these vulnerabilities on their structure and process, and determine a path to help the couple achieve their relationship goals. This occurs through managing the ecological elements and discussing how these elements add to or detract from a couple's experience with one another. One of the first steps to managing the ecological elements is to understand which elements apply to a particular couple. There are certainly some elements that will make couples more vulnerable to problems, and other elements that need to be retained because they improve the health of the couple's relationship. This can be conducted through both formal and informal methods. The formal method (inventory) was described earlier in this text. The informal method can be ascertained through the in-session interview.

In many cases, the seven ecological elements discussed in previous sections can be managed through a couple's willingness and ability to address several key areas. First, couples can learn to manage accessibility by having conversations regarding the rules around computer usage in the home. Who has access to whose passwords? What are the circumstances under which each partner will use the other's password? If someone logs into your account, is he or she required to tell you? Is it the fact of logging into your account creating the problem or is keeping it secretive that causes the problem? Is it appropriate to use each other's passwords to log into accounts? Therapists can normalize the need for sharing passwords in cases where a betrayal has occurred, but that arrangement may not work for some couples in the long term, because of the potential for a power imbalance, which can threaten the relationship. Such questions include (but are not limited to) the following:

- addressing affordability by inquiring what is the cost of the online behavior to the offline relationship;
- addressing individual needs for anonymity or to adopt different qualities on the computer inconsistent with offline life; specifically may want to ask about the reasons for adopting the varied aspects of the personality;
- addressing the acceptability of particular behaviors related to the computer in the couple's peer and family-of-origin networks;
- assessing things that the computer does which replicate or mimic offline experiences;
- working to understand each person's different definitions of Internet behavior; work toward improving a common language around the definitional issues.

Managing Structural Issues

A second key strategy is the management of boundaries, rules, and roles. As discussed in Chapter 5, ambiguity within the relationship and technology usage can impair a couple's ability to identify one definition of problematic behavior. In addition, when the role of technology in relationships is ambiguous, it creates ambiguity in roles, rules, and boundaries between the partners in a relationship. In relationships where online gaming plays a part in a couple's discord, there may be varying interpretations of one's behavior (Hertlein & Hawkins, in press). For example, one partner may view their game play as not interfering with their offline relationship and the other partner may believe it does, thus creating conflict over what rules around game play should and will win out in the relationship (Cole & Griffiths, 2007).

Boundaries need to be identified and agreed upon within the couple's relationship prior to the emergence of an Internet-related problem as interactive communication technologies emerge and evolve in the couple's lives. Therapists should work with couples to assist them in articulating the boundaries with regard to passwords, personal versus family accounts, posts on social networking sites, and agreement upon when and how to revisit the boundaries. This issue may require some sensitivity on the part of the therapist, as the notion of implementing boundaries may plant the idea that one person is not to be trusted. The therapist and couple should work toward the establishment of equitable and fair boundaries for each partner.

Managing Process Issues

One of the key strategies in treatment is to understand the intimacy needs of each person in the relationship (Hertlein & Hawkins, 2013). In the literature regarding online gaming, for example, the therapist may choose to explore whether differences in the value of online gaming stem from personality differences or a clash in value systems. This would inform the therapist as to how each person in the relationship develops closeness because the person who is gaming may be more inclined toward experiencing social anxieties or other difficulties in relating to people (Hertlein & Hawkins, 2013). Research in the area of online gaming suggests there is a relationship between violent games and aggression, though this relationship is not well understood and differs from individual to individual (Hertlein & Hawkins, 2013).

Another element affecting the process of relationships is the formation occurring with regard to the development of online relationships and friendships. As noted in Chapter 3, meeting online follows a different process than meeting and developing relationships solely in an offline format. Research with regard to online gaming suggests online role-playing gamers exhibit more signs of isolation and identity diffusion (Huang, 2006). This might prompt them to initiate relationships differently than others. Therefore, partners need to be aware that if one individual in the relationship is a gamer, there may be a component of isolation that might ultimately complicate the relationship.

Therapists can also provide ways in which technology can support and enhance relationship maintenance. Couples can use the Internet and other interactive communicative technologies to support and augment their relationship in ways that they were previously unable. Such technologies offer an immediate, direct, and low/no-cost way to interact with one's partner. The ability to instant message one another or communicate through e-mail during the day can create opportunities for sexual or marital enrichment (Hertlein, 2004; Schnarch, 1997). Computers and new technologies can also help maintain the relationship through the ability to share and send pictures and videos through phone or e-mail. In one case, Lydia and Jerome struggled to overcome Jerome's infidelity and used the camera function on Jerome's phone as a way to provide documentation of his immediate whereabouts in the early stages of their recovery. Camera software can also be used to support relationships in lieu of a presenting problem. Couples can send a variety of pictures to one another, from sexually explicit to innocent as a way to share their day with their partner. Electronic greeting cards are also another affordable way to communicate with one's partner or to commemorate a milestone or ritual (Hertlein, Weeks, & Gambescia, 2008).

There are few differences between the ways in which technology is used for long distance or geographically close relationships. In both cases, e-mails exchanged with friends, family, and peers were characterized as open, positive, and educative. With romantic relationships, there was an increased likelihood of providing reassurances (Johnson, Haigh, Becker, Craig, & Wigley, 2008). Further, one study demonstrated as people grow closer, there is an increase in e-mails exchanged, though the nature of those e-mails did not necessarily reflect the intimate nature of the relationship. In short, people are still more likely to rely on telephone communication for intimate conversations (Utz, 2007). The accessibility of cell phones, however, helps to explain this finding.

The computer also affords couples the opportunity to establish relationships in the digital realm and then use those same strategies (computer communication) to maintain these "digital" relationships. Such communication online can actually promote growth and increase the level of intimacy in and commitment to the relationship than those couples who facilitate their relationships primarily offline (Cooper & Sportolari, 1997). This may in part be due to the fact that online relationships initially emphasize emotional connection rather than appearances (Henline & Harris, 2006). This is sometimes accomplished through the incorporation of online games in a couple's life. Couples can also use the Internet and new technologies such as massively multiplayer online role-playing games (MMORPGS) to participate in joint activities. There is even a website that advertises games for couples to play when they are not physically together (http://www.lovingfromadistance.com/multiplayer-games.html). These include word and drawing games, whereby the couple shares their drawings. Freyja and Liam both worked full-time jobs and found it difficult to spend time with one another outside of their busy career schedules and raising of their four children. They found that over the years the only time they really got to spend together as a family was on Sundays: They would attend Mass together, and then come home and have an early supper, followed by participation in family game night. With the advent of new media, however, they were afforded an opportunity to remain connected during the day. Both Freyja's and Liam's jobs required them to work in front of a computer, so they were able to develop an online "date" time during the work week in which they could speak to one another through using instant messenger, and engage in some online word games together.

The Internet may also provide a place for couples to bridge the gap between separate leisure activities. One of the elements contributing to a well-functioning couple is the ability to negotiate how and when to participate in both separate and joint leisure activities. Addressing the impact of disparate leisure activities in the couple's relationship also addresses any perceived neglect experienced by one or both partners, a common source of underlying conflict (Sanford, 2010). For example, couples in which one partner participates in online gaming and the other partner does not may create a feeling of neglect in the nonplaying partner

(Hertlein & Hawkins, in press). Therapists can play a key part in helping couples identify the circumstances in which the sense of neglect is most prominent and subsequently process difficult emotions that emerge.

Another issue prevalent in relationships is the misattribution of one's intentions or motivations with regard to the usage of technology. Attributional theory refers to how people make inferences or provide causal explanations (Kelley, 1967). In other words, it is our explanation of other people's actions and behaviors. Often, clients develop attributions about their own behavior or other family member's behavior that are immutable and believe to be true. They often use these attributions to explain outcomes. These attributions can be (a) accurate or inaccurate, (b) positive or negative, and/or (c) internal or external. In the case of the Internet, problematic misattributions may be negative, inaccurate, and either internal or external. This is, in part, due to the fact that activities involving the Internet or other interactive communication means generally provide a mechanism of communicating that are more private—that is, the screens are typically small enough and designed in such a way (i.e., one keyboard per desktop) that makes it appropriate for couples to communicate via technology. This private way of communicating may create the potential for inappropriate misattributions directed at each other. This is complicated by the fact that the ambiguous nature of the Internet can create further opportunities to make inappropriate attributions to one's behavior (Hertlein & Stevenson, 2010). For example, Nina and Ron spend some of their time in the evenings with their laptops, engaging in independent computer activities while watching television. When the couple began to have issues in their relationship, the games Ron played on the computer became an external, negative, and inaccurate scapegoat for Nina's discontent and observation of Ron's distancing. Trust is also critical in cases of how one attributes intention. In the case of Nina and Ron, the trust had eroded in the relationship to the point where Nina was more comfortable making a misattribution than trusting Ron's behavior and intentions. Another example is in cases of online gaming, where Helsper and Whitty (2010) indicate it is sometimes difficult to trust the online gamer's behavior. Developing trust may call for the therapist to work with the couple to soften feelings, explore each partner's needs in a safe environment, and develop clearer ways for the couple to begin rebuilding trust.

Finally, couples experience challenges when there is little or no spontaneity in their relationship (Sahlstein, 2006). As couples move toward greater usage of technology in their relationships, the reality may be that their lives become more structured and less spontaneous. For example, Martie and Brett came to therapy to address their communication problems. Brett was a software developer who generally worked from home, except for one week a month when he was at his company's headquarters. Martie worked as a manager and small business owner for a local flower shop, which generally required her to stay closer to home, but also involved travel every year for flower shows. As a result of the couple's travel schedule, their opportunities to be spontaneous together became structured and planned via webcam. This was especially evident in their sex life. Despite their interest in maintaining an active sexual relationship, they found it increasingly difficult to get into the right mood at a pre-designated time. Further, there were times when Martie, exhausted from work, nonetheless felt obliged to engage in a webcam session with Brett since they had already arranged it. Part of their treatment, then, involved using the technology present to engage in spontaneous interactions as well as providing time for planned interactions.

The CFT approach spans a broad field and thus allows the therapist to consider the ways in which technology affects the couple or family from a systemic perspective. For example, King et al. (2012), developed a fairly systemic assessment related to online addiction that follows the Intersystems approach (Weeks, 1994) in its attention to the biological, social, and individual psychological areas or problem maintenance. The CFT framework can highlight the aspects of a couple's life that predispose them to being vulnerable to problems stemming from interactive communicative technologies.

Using the CFT Framework: The Case of Jake and Bella

Jake and Bella sought treatment to recover from infidelity. Bella, 34, discovered that her husband Jake, a 35-year-old male who worked in the financial industry, had a year-long affair with a previous girlfriend. Prior to marrying Bella, Jake's relationship with his ex-girlfriend had been conducted offline. But his extramarital affair had been facilitated primarily online, with only a few meetings offline in a hotel in another city where they consummated their relationship. Bella discovered Jake's affair through text messages still on his phone; she confirmed it when she logged into his e-mail account and read their e-mails.

This case as conceptualized within the CFT framework occurred on three levels: an understanding of the ecological elements of the relationship and its effects on both structure and process of the relationship. The therapist began treatment by conducting an assessment of the ways in which the ecological elements influenced the relationship. One of the issues that became readily apparent was the ambiguity around what was considered problematic behavior. Though both agreed that sex outside their relationship clearly violated their established boundaries and rules, when it came to interactions that had been facilitated by the Internet, it was unclear where to draw the line with regard to problematic behavior. This lack of clarity manifested in two ways: lack of clarity around the content of communication with each other and lack of clarity around who was permitted to interact with Jake and with whom Jake communicated. Jake and Bella also had to address how accessible technology and new media were to them. Bella's experience with unwanted e-mails from others attested to the fact that, even though Jake was not actively communicating with his ex-girlfriend, the couple was not immune from interference by outsiders because they, too, were accessible. Further, each time Bella received a message from an anonymous person (another ecological element), it served as a trigger because it reminded her of Jake's infidelity.

In conducting an assessment about the other elements, Bella expressed her particular concern that Jake was acting in a very caring, compassionate, and supportive way in his e-mails to his ex-girlfriend, but Bella did not see or feel those parts of Jake when they directly related with each other. In other words, the computer allowed Jake to accommodate his behavior to match who he wanted to be with his online ex-girlfriend, instead who he felt he *had* to be with Bella in their daily life. Bella struggled with the notion that her husband's online presence differed from his offline persona. She attributed this to her belief that he was not able to be himself with her, which, in turn, reflected negatively on their marriage. Bella interpreted this difference in Jake's personas as evidence that he did not want to be in a relationship with her, and it affirmed a deep-seated and long-lasting fear that she was Jake's "second choice."

The accessibility to communication mechanisms such as Jake's cell phone made it easier for him to communicate with his ex-girlfriend. The accessibility of these devices translated into greater accessibility for both. In fact, his ex-girlfriend's ability to locate him through a social networking site is what enabled them to reconnect. This led to an exchange of contact information and subsequent communications through text messaging, e-mails, and phone calls.

Jake and Bella's problems also altered the structure of their relationship. Their boundaries became more diffuse in that it suddenly expanded outside the family home and invited people into their lives in ways that were not expected nor agreed on. Once the boundaries were disturbed, the rules in the relationship became unclear. Bella had been receiving e-mail communications from who she suspected was Jake's ex-girlfriend and his current paramour. These e-mails were harassing in nature and, unfortunately, were from an external e-mail account that belonged to a fictitious person. Bella found that blocking that particular e-mail account would not stop the problem because the individual who was sending the e-mails would continue to send e-mails from a new account with a new name. Further, because these e-mails could not be directly tied to the ex-girlfriend, Bella experienced an increased level of suspicion toward Jake's outside interactions, and every conversation he had with someone away from her became vulnerable to questions. Bella found that she began placing more rules on the relationship without disclosing them to Jake, who often broke Bella's rules without being aware he was doing so.

The couple also noted there were times when their process was interrupted and altered as a result of the interference of technology in their lives. During one of their sessions, they began to argue about the affair and the lack of trust in the relationship. As they discussed the trust issue, Bella indicated she found it hard to believe she would ever be able to be in a place where she could trust Jake again because of his constant connection to a digital world (and potential to "get in trouble"). In addition to his day job, Jake also participated in restoring cars and selling them on Internet sites such as Craigslist and eBay. This proved to be a constant threat to the trust in their relationship because of the accessibility this work provided to others. There was also the possibility that Jake could use his secondary job as a guise for continuing his affair. In addition, Bella expressed concern that Jake was able to maintain a relationship with his ex-girlfriend through online communication online but was not willing to do the same for his wife. She deeply desired this connection but was not in a place where she felt if Jake provided that to her, it would be because he wanted to be supportive of her and not just because she requested for it.

The first phase of treatment was to establish clarity with regard to expectations and rules over the course of treatment and build a new foundation of trust for their relationship. Bella initially indicated she had not put a restriction on Jake's usage of the computer for selling his restored vehicles, but once ambiguity of his online behavior was identified and discussed, the couple agreed it would be easier if Jake were to suspend his side business for a few months so Bella would not experience constant triggers throughout the treatment process. The couple also was assigned to come to some agreement on the explicit definition of problematic Internet behavior as a way to ensure that they were both clear about their expectations as treatment progressed. The development of trust via managing accessibility was addressed concretely first, and then emotionally. Jake shared the passwords for his accounts and was open to leaving his phone unattended in the event that Bella's suspicions were heightened. The therapist explained this practice was appropriate for some couples in the early stages of healing, but at some point they would maybe want to resume more equal roles rather than having one partner feel he or she had to answer to the other partner. Therefore, the goal of treatment was to work with Jake and Bella so their accessibility to each other's personal information was indicative of a trusting relationship rather than a punitive one.

Treatment also focused to some degree on the content of the e-mails to the ex-girlfriend. Jake had made certain personal disclosures to this woman, which caught Bella off guard. She stated this was a side of Jake she did not see and wondered if they were meant to be together since he obviously felt more comfortable disclosing personal matters to his ex-girlfriend instead of her. Both Jake and Bella acknowledged Jake had made such disclosures to Bella in the early stages of their relationship (within the first few months) but it had been many years since they were able to have that kind of conversation. The therapist worked with them to identify reasons preventing Jake from disclosing personal things and Bella from being responsive to them. Jake indicated it was easier for him to make those disclosures online because otherwise he felt a sense of separation and vulnerability. Therefore, the separation of the computer provided some distance and perceived safety in disclosing information. The therapist connected this with the ecological element of anonymity and directed the couple to instead begin an e-mail correspondence with one another, each subsequently building in terms of disclosure and vulnerability over time.

The couple was also directed to use the accessibility of the Internet to increase their supportiveness and responsiveness to one another instead of using it only to access (or block access) to the ex-girlfriend and the unwanted e-mails to Bella. She was able to identify times Jake's affair triggered her and use the access to Jake through technology as a way to make him aware of her mood, and when she was able to have more trust in him, ask him to provide some support to help her move beyond the trigger.

References

Atwood, J. D., & Schwarz, L. (2002). The new affair treatment considerations. *Journal of Couple and Relationship Therapy, 1*(3), 37–56.

Boella, G., Caire, P., & van der Torre, L. (2009). Norm negotiation in online multi-player games. *Knowledge and Information Systems, 18*(2), 137–156.

Cao, F. L., Su, L. Y., & Gao, X. P. (2007). Control study of group psychotherapy on middle school students with Internet overuse. *Chinese Mental Health Journal, 21,* 346–358.

Cole, H., & Griffiths, M. D. (2007). Social interactions in massively multiplayer online role-playing gamers. *CyberPsychology and Behavior, 10,* 575–583.

Cooper, A., & Sportolari, L. (1997). Romance in cyberspace: Understanding online attraction. *Journal of Sex Education and Therapy,* 22, 7–14.

Davis, R. A. (2001). A cognitive-behavioral model of pathological Internet use. *Computers in Human Behavior, 17,* 187–195.

Delmonico, D. L., Griffin, E., & Carnes, P. J. (2002). Treating online compulsive sexual behavior: When cybersex is the drug of choice. In A. Cooper (Ed.), *Sex and the Internet: A guidebook for clinicians* (pp. 147–167). New York: Brunner-Routledge.

Doherty, W. J., Colangelo, N., & Hovander, D. (1991). Priority setting in family change and clinical practice: The family FIRO model. *Family Process, 30,* 227–240.

Du, Y., Jiang, W., & Vance, A. (2010). Longer term effect of randomized, controlled group cognitive behavioural therapy for Internet addiction in adolescent students in Shanghai. *The Australian and New Zealand Journal of Psychiatry, 44*(2), 129–134. doi:10.3109/00048670903282725

Gordon, K. C., Baucom, D. H., & Snyder, D. K. (2005). Treating couples recovering from infidelity: An integrative approach. *Journal of Clinical Psychology, 61*(11), 1393–1405. doi:10.1002/jclp.20189

Hall, A. S., & Parsons, J. (2001). Internet addiction: College student case study using best practices in cognitive behavior therapy. *Journal of Mental Health Counseling, 23*(4), 312-327.

Helsper, E. J., & Whitty, M. T. (2010). Netiquette within married couples: Agreement about acceptable online behavior and surveillance between partners. *Computers in Human Behavior, 26*(5), 916–926. doi:10.1016/j.chb.2010.02.006

Henline, B. H., & Harris, S. M. (2006, October 19–22). *Pros and cons of technology use within close relationships*. Poster presented at the annual conference of the American Association for Marriage and Family Therapy, Austin, TX.

Hertlein, K. M. (2004). *Internet infidelity: An examination of family therapist treatment decisions and gender biases* (Unpublished doctoral dissertation). Virginia Polytechnic Institute and State University, Blacksburg.

Hertlein, K. M., & Hawkins, B. P. (2013). Treatment strategies for online role-playing gaming problems in couples. *Journal of Couple and Relationship Therapy, 12*(2).

Hertlein, K., & Piercy, F. P. (2005). A theoretical framework for defining, understanding, and treating Internet infidelity. *Journal of Couple and Relationship Therapy, 4*(1), 79–91.

Hertlein, K. M., & Piercy, F. P. (2006). Internet infidelity: A critical review of the literature. *The Family Journal, 14*(4), 366–371. doi:10.1177/1066480706290508

Hertlein, K. M., & Piercy, F. P. (2008). Therapists' assessment and treatment of Internet infidelity cases. *Journal of Marital and Family Therapy, 34*(4), 481–497.

Hertlein, K. M., & Piercy, F. P. (2012). Essential elements of Internet infidelity treatment. *Journal of Marital and Family Therapy, 38*, 257–270. doi:10.1111/j.1752-0606.2011.00275.x

Hertlein, K. M., & Stevenson, A. (2010). The seven "As" contributing to Internet-related intimacy problems: A literature review. *Cyberpsychology: Journal of Psychosocial Research on Cyberspace, 4*(1).

Hertlein, K. M., Weeks, G. R., & Gambescia, N. (2008). *Systemic sex therapy.* New York: Routledge.

Huang, X., Li, M., & Tao, R. (2010). Treatment of Internet addiction. *Current Psychiatry Reports, 12*(5), 462–470. doi:10.1007/s11920-010-0147-1

Huang, Y. (2006). Identity and intimacy crises and their relationship to Internet dependence among college students. *Cyberpsychology & Behavior, 9*(5), 571–576.

Johnson, A. J., Haigh, M. M., Becker, J. A. H., Craig, E. A., & Wigley, S. (2008). College students' use of relational management strategies in email in long-distance and geographically close relationships. *Journal of Computer-Mediated Communication, 13*(2), 381–404. doi:10.1111/j.1083-6101.2008.00401.x

Kelley, H. H. (1967). Attribution theory in social psychology. In D. Levine (ed.), *Nebraska Symposium on Motivation* (Volume 15, pp. 192-238). Lincoln: University of Nebraska Press.

Kim, J. (2008). The effect of a R/T group counseling program on the Internet addiction level and self-esteem of Internet addiction university students. *International Journal of Reality Therapy, 27*(2), 4-12.

King, D. L., Delfabbro, P. H., & Griffiths, M. D. (2012). Clinical interventions for technology-based problems: Excessive Internet and video game use. *Journal of Cognitive Psychotherapy, 26*(1), 43-56.

Li, N., Li, G., Wang, & Y. (2008). The therapeutic effect of 48 Internet in patients with addiction. *Journal of Psychiatry, 21*(1), 356–359.

Maheu, M. M., & Subotnik, R. B. (2001). *Infidelity on the Internet.* Naperville, IL: Sourcebooks.

McKenna, K. A., & Bargh, J. A. (2000). Plan 9 from cyberspace: The implications of the Internet for personality and social psychology. *Personality & Social Psychology Review, 4*(1), 57–75.

Murali, V., & Onuba, I. (2009). Management of Internet addiction. *General Practice Update, 2*(5), 32–35.

Nelson, T. S. (2000). *Internet infidelity: A modified Delphi study* (Unpublished doctoral dissertation). Purdue University.

Nelson, T., Piercy, F., & Sprenkle, D. (2005). Internet infidelity: A multi-wave Delphi study. *Journal of Couple and Relationship Therapy, 4*(2/3), 173–194.

Orzack, M. H., Voluse, A. C., Wolf, D., & Hennen, J. (2006). An ongoing study of group treatment for men involved in problematic Internet-enabled sexual behavior. *Cyberpsychology & Behavior, 9*(3), 348–360. doi:10.1089/cpb.2006.9.348

Sahlstein, E. (2006). Making plans: Praxis strategies for negotiating uncertainty–certainty in long-distance relationships. *Western Journal of Communication, 70*(2), 147–165. doi:10.1080/10570310600710042

Sanford, K. (2010). Assessing conflict communication in couples: Comparing the validity of self-report, partner-report, and observer ratings. *Journal of Family Psychology, 24*(2), 165-174

Schnarch, D. (1997). Sex, intimacy, and the Internet. *Journal of Sex Education and Therapy, 22*(1), 15–20.

Shaw, J. (1997). Treatment rationale for Internet infidelity. *Journal of Sex Education and Therapy, 22*(1), 29–34.

Shek, D. T. L., Tang, V. M. Y., & Lo, C. Y. (2009). Evaluation of an Internet addiction treatment program for Chinese adolescents in Hong Kong. *Adolescence, 44*(174), 359-373.

Utz, S. (2007). Media use in long-distance friendships. *Information, Communication & Society, 10*(5), 694–713. doi:10.1080/13691180701658046

Weeks, G. R. (1994). The intersystem model: An integrated approach to treatment. In G. R. Weeks & L. Hof (Eds.), *The marital relationship therapy casebook: Theory and application of the intersystem model* (pp. 3–34). New York: Brunner/Mazel.

Yen, J., Yen, C., Chen, C., Chen, S., & Ko, C. (2007). Family factors of Internet addiction and substance use experience in Taiwanese adolescents. *Cyberpsychology & Behavior: The Impact of the Internet, Multimedia, and Virtual Reality on Behavior and Society, 10*(3), 323–329. doi:10.1089/cpb.2006.9948

Young, K. S. (2007). Cognitive behavior therapy with Internet addicts: Treatment outcomes and implications. *Cyberpsychology & Behavior, 10*(5), 671–679. doi:10.1089/cpb.2007.9971

Young, K. S. (2011). CBT-IA: The first treatment model for Internet addiction. *Journal of Cognitive Psychotherapy, 25*(4), 304-312.

Young, K. S., Griffin-Shelley, E., Cooper, A., O'Mara, J., & Buchanan, J. (2000). Online infidelity: A new dimension in couple relationships with implications for evaluation and treatment. *Sexual Addiction and Compulsivity, 7*, 59–74.

Zhao, P., Mao, F., & Liu, L. (2009). Control study of Naikan-cognitive psychotherapy on medical university students with Internet addiction disorder. *China Journal of Health Psychology, 17*(1), 429–432.

Zhong, X., Tao, R., Zu, S., Sha, S., & Yang, F. C. (2009). Effect of group psychological intervention in adolescents on Internet addiction. *Journal of Capital Medical University, 30*, 494–499.

Zhong, Z. J. (2011). The effects of collective MMORPG (massively multiplayer online roleplaying games) play on gamers' online and offline social capital. *Computers in Human Behavior, 27*(6), 2352–2363.

9 Electronically-Mediated Communication Across a Couple's Developmental Lifespan

All growth depends upon activity. There is no development physically or intellectually without effort, and effort means work.

—*Calvin Coolidge*

The presence of technology in couple and family life is a constant element across the relational life span. Yet the types of technology and forms of new media that are used, as well as the ways in which they are managed across the relational life span, often differs based on a number of factors. Such factors include, but are not limited to the following: the point in development of the couple or family; the individual development of each member of the family; the diverse backgrounds, views, and experiences of the family members; and the larger context in which the couple or family is technologically connected. How technology both changes and is influenced by couples and families has previously been identified in the literature (Haddon, 2006; Silverstone, Hirsch, & Morley, 1992). Yet the impact at specific points in the developmental life span remains considerably less explored both in practice and research. Few couple and family therapists are consistently inquiring about the role of technology in the lives of the couples and families (Hertlein, Blumer, & Smith, 2012). Results from our 2011 Alaska Association for Marriage and Family Therapy grant-funded national survey of the cyber practices of 227 LMFT, AAMFT clinical, student, and approved supervisor members, indicate that the majority either never (n = 30, 17.8%) or rarely (n = 52, 30.68%) inquire about technology when working with couples (Hertlein et al., 2012). Moreover, when working with families 19.5% (n = 33) report never inquiring about technology, and 31.2% (n = 51) report rarely doing so (Hertlein et al., 2012).

There has also been little attention devoted to technology across the life span in research (Adams & Stevenson, 2004; Hughes & Hans, 2001; Morrison & Krugman, 2001; Watt & White, 1999). Despite the limited attention, at least one study has highlighted the value of the interest between technology and varying developmental points. In a study by Morrison and Krugman (2001) with 105 participants, the authors qualitatively explored the influence of in-home media technologies on the social environment of the home with regards to social facilitation, rule-making, attitudes toward technologies, and shifts and expansions around media usage. Their participants broke down into two different types—families using low/moderate technologies (i.e., continuous technologies like television) and those using high level technologies (i.e., discontinuous technologies like computers). The most definitive theme that emerged was that of the valuing of media technologies. Those with higher level technologies tended to place more value on media technologies than those with low/moderate technologies. Variances in the valuing of technology might be related to the evolution of the family over their life cycle. The authors advocated for examination of the way technology grows and changes as the family grows and changes.

The stages across the couple life span we explore in this chapter are in part rooted in the most well-known and widely cited in the family therapy field (Carter & McGoldrick, 2005; McGoldrick, Carter, & Garcia-Preto, 2010) and include (a) couple initiation, (b) childfree couples, (c) couples with children, (d) couples with adolescents, (e) couples with adult children, (f) couples with aging parents, and (g) relationship termination. At each of these points in the couple life span we briefly consider the part technology plays in development as if technology is a part of the couple and family itself. We also describe how participants in relationships at each point in development need to consider the role of technology in the structuring of the relationship and how the various ecological elements both affect and are affected by each point of couple development. In addition, a comprehensive list of questions to consider across the electronic developmental life span is provided (see Appendix D).

Couple Initiation

Couple initiation has changed drastically with the advent of the Internet and new media. It is both common to use technology to assist with initiating and maintaining relationships. In a nationally representative longitudinal survey between 2007 and 2009 of 4,002 English literate male and female adults (3,009 were partnered or married), 22% of heterosexual and 61% of same-sex couples reported having met their partners online (Rosenfeld & Thomas, 2012). Same-sex couples were more likely to have met online than heterosexual couples (70% as opposed to 30%; Rosenfeld & Thomas, 2012). In fact, online meeting may be the most common way same-sex couples meet (Rosenfeld & Thomas, 2012), perhaps because the online environment may be perceived as a safer place to initiate relationships than offline settings. In addition, interracial married heterosexual couples were less likely than their same-sex counterparts to have met online (16% as compared to 19%; Rosenfeld & Thomas, 2012).

This could be attributed to heterosexual individuals who met online via matchmaking websites having a stronger preference for choosing same-race partners, as has been identified previously in the literature (Hitsch, Hortacsu, & Ariely, 2010). In contrast, same-sex couple initiation online tends to occur more frequently and through more diverse avenues (e.g., GPS-enabled networking sites, community specific social networking sites (SNSs) and applications, and friendly chat rooms), which could equate to there being a more diverse pool of people and greater numbers of people available to date (Patterson, 2005). In general, however, regardless of how same-sex couples meet interraciaility tends to be more common (Gates, 2011). For both heterosexual and same-sex couples who identify as interreligious, they were more likely to have met online (22% of couples) than their same-religion couple counterparts (15%; Rosenfeld & Thomas, 2012).

One key difference in online relationship development is that relationship initiation via the Internet occurs without all of the information one might ascertain in a physical world (McKenna, 2008; Walther, 1996). For instance, in the physical world, one can attend specifically to a certain body physique, hair color, or sex; online, however, these factors may not be observed (McKenna, 2008; Watt & White, 1999). Thus, features that would have potentially blocked relationship initiation offline are side-stepped in relationship initiation online. The Internet also allows users to project particular favorable attributes to their online partner (Baker, 2007; Whitty & Carr, 2005, 2006). The ability to both block certain features coupled with the ability to highlight other attributes can create opportunities for relationships based on fantasy rather than reality.

The process by which online relationships are developed may be influenced by age and accessibility to the Internet. The Baby Boomers are now among the fastest growing group of people online, with social networking among users of the Internet aged 50 and older nearly doubling between 2010 and 2011 (Carracher, 2011). Women over the age of 55 are now the largest and most quickly growing group to adopt the popular SNS, Facebook (Sutter, 2009). Once online, older people tend to spend more time than their younger age counterparts developing romantic relationships (Rosenfeld & Thomas, 2012; Stephure, Boon, MacKinnon, & Deveau, 2009). Heterosexual men hit their peaks for partnering in their late 30s, but electronic meeting remains relatively high for the rest of the life span (about 80%). In contrast, the peak for electronic meeting in women occurs in their early 40s, and then tends to parallel that of men's rate until roughly age 50, when their rate steadily declines (Rosenfeld & Thomas, 2012). These findings have been associated with older women having less Internet access in their homes as they age in comparison to their age mate, gender different peers (21% of women in their 70s have Internet access at home whereas 40% of men of the same age have such access; Rosenfeld & Thomas, 2012). This increased access may also contribute to the equalizing of who initiates relationships (Neilsonwire, 2011).

Finally, there are applications dedicated to assist those who identify as lesbian, gay, bisexual, and/or transgender (LGBT) with a means of quickly finding and making new friends within the LGBT communities, potential dating partners, providing updates regarding the latest pride events, and locating friendly bars, clubs, and restaurants nearby. SNSs, cyber community support groups such as Tranny Boyz, and the rise of websites aimed at empowering and mobilizing transgender and lesbian, gay, and bisexual (LGB) identifying persons and activists have helped people to feel more supported, socially connected and satisfied, and have provided opportunities and safe places to explore sexual and gender orientation (Elderton & Jones, 2011; Gauthier & Chaudoir, 2004; Gudelunas, 2012; Shapiro, 2004).

Regardless of the demographics of those involved in online-initiated relationships, the online relationship often follows a developmental trajectory that most similarly corresponds to couples who participate in long distance relationships (Stafford & Reske, 1990) as has been outlined in Chapter 3. First, couples who meet online participate in tasks differently than those who meet offline (Lawson & Leck, 2006). One of their first tasks involves determining the kind, level, and frequency of their interactions. Questions around these tasks that frequently emerge often include the following:

- Do we chat, and if so, when, and how often?
- Do we video call and if so, when and how often?
- Do we give each other our cell numbers and if we do, do we talk or text or both?

Second, the couple negotiates when the relationship moves from solely online to face-to-face contact. After face-to-face contact has been established and goes smoothly, the couple moves into the third stage where they make decisions as to how to manage regular face-to-face contact (Whitty & Carr, 2005, 2006).

Once a couple has solidified their online relationship, further structural and ecological considerations should be considered. These include decisions around what contact will be permitted in the relationship and with whom, and discussion of the manner and frequency with which the couple maintains contact with family and friends. Another major decision point is whether the relationship will be announced on SNSs. One popular concept in today's society is that a relationship is not official until it is publicly disclosed on Facebook. Users of SNSs may employ the term *Facebook Official* (Tucker, 2006) to indicate when a relationship starts, changes, or ends. Yet this disclosure of relationship status can also be more complex than simply declaring whether a couple is dating. The current Facebook site provides the following options under "Basic Info" to describe relational status: single, in a relationship, engaged, married, it's complicated, in an open relationship, widowed, separated, divorced, in a civil partnership, or in a domestic partnership. Alternately, Facebook users can merely state an interest in women, men, both men and women, or neither men nor women.

Complexity in disclosing relationship status emerges when people outside of the dominant gender or sexual orientations want to disclose relationship status. In same-sex couples, the degree of expressed outtness needs to be negotiated early in the relationship lifecycle. Raúl and Lafe are a couple who identify as gay men. Lafe is of Scandinavian descent, in his mid-20s, working on a graduate degree, and works part-time as a music instructor. Raúl is of Latin descent, in his mid-30s, holds a bachelor's level degree, and is the owner of a small business. The couple had been dating approximately 6 months when they presented with issues around *visibility management* or the decision-making process regarding a same-sex couple's public visibility as a couple (Blumer, Ansara, & Watson, 2012; Blumer & Green, 2012; Iwasaki & Ristock, 2007). Ideas about how visible to be as a couple were complex due to each person's own sexual orientation identity development, age, education level, ethnic identity, level of support from others, and the role that technology played in their lives. Lafe had been out as a gay man since adolescence and was met with support from his friends, family, classmates, and coworkers. In contrast, Raúl was only out as a gay man amongst others in the sexual and gender orientation minority communities. This difference in outness created conflict. One of their biggest disagreements upon entering therapy was with regard to personal and relational statuses on Facebook. Lafe identified as a gay male who liked men, and he wanted to share with his friends that he was in a relationship with Raúl via social networking. Raúl identified as a male and nothing more, fearing the ramifications that could come from identifying himself and his relationship beyond this. In addition, Raúl was also worried about people who knew of their relationship offline and were their friends online commenting on the nature of their relationship online. Similarly, Ruth and Zachary, a married couple, are involved in relationships with Pam and Barbara. The Facebook of 2012 provides options in the "Relationship Status" section that are the same as those listed under the "Basic Info" section and thus there may not be an adequate way to designate Ruth and Zachary's relationships with Pam and Barbara other than the "It's complicated" status.

Childfree Couples

The number of childfree heterosexual couples is increasing (Gillespie, 2003) while the number of childfree same-sex couples is decreasing (Gates, 2011). In 1976, only 10% of heterosexual couples were childfree; whereas this percentage had increased to 18% by 2002 (Abma & Martinez, 2006). In same-sex couples, the number of childfree couples in 2000 was 91% and in 2010 80% (Gates, 2011). The reasons for being childfree are complex and tied to a number of factors, including personal choices, fertility-related issues (Pelton & Hertlein, 2011), legal allowance in terms of adopting or fostering children, and for same-sex couples there is often a lack of societal acceptance, as well as a lack of inherent biological privilege in having children together as a couple (Gates, 2011). When being childfree is by choice, new media can play a supportive part at various points in the couple life cycle. Pelton and Hertlein (2011) proposed a voluntary childfree couple life cycle in which the following are often experienced: (a) decision-making processes around children, (b) management of stigma and societal pressure as related to biological privilege, pro-reproduction, and pro-children views held by the majority of society, (c) the establishment of an identity as a childfree couple, and (d) the building of a support system and the task of leaving a legacy. Childfree couples are often navigating these stages alone and can consequently feel isolated. With the growth of new media, however, childfree couples (and childfree singles) now have access to supportive electronic resources and access to other childfree couples. One such example is the group No Kidding![1] or NK for short (the International Social Club for Childfree Couples and Singles). Groups like this can help couples cope with societal stigmas and pressures (Hughes & Hans, 2001). If a childfree couple is to feel empowered to build a solid identity as a family, and leave a legacy, such support systems can be helpful.

Connecting couples with a support system is just one way that new media has played a part in voluntary childfree couple development. New media has also been playing a part in providing childfree couples with leaving a legacy through the development and maintenance of other relationships with nieces, nephews, siblings, godchildren, and the children of adult friends (DeLyser, 2012). While these close connections could be maintained prior to the rise of new media, such connections have been made easier with technology. SNSs, for example, provide even more ways than in the past to have consistent communication and involvement with the next generation. In addition, video conferencing applications like Skype have made it easier to have contact and related influence in the lives of the next generation with which childfree couples are involved.

Couple Development With Children

Couples who elect to have children have a number of issues related to technology to be addressed, not the least of which is physical. Discussed in Chapter 1 was the impact of cell phones and text messaging on shoulder and neck pain. Yet there are also physical implications for those who seek to become pregnant. Male partners in relationships need to be mindful of the potential adverse effects that carrying cell phones in their pocket or hanging from their belt loop may have on fertility. Many researchers have reported significant adverse effects from cell phones on semen, more specifically in terms of seminal motility and morphology (Agarwal, Deepinder, Sharma, Ranga, & Li, 2008; Agarwal et al., 2009; Erogul et al., 2006; Wdowiak, Wdowiak, & Wiktor, 2007). There also appear to be detrimental effects on sperm quality (Gutschi, Mohamad Al-Ali, Shamloul, Pummer, & Trummer, 2011). The recommendations for men with poor sperm count or quality include limiting extensive use of cell phones and being mindful of cell phone storage, particularly when planning for pregnancy (Gutschi et al., 2011).

New media also has a place in the adoption process. Couples interested in adopting children now have access to more helpful agencies and other resources such as "Adoption,"[2] "Adoptive Families,"[3] and "Open Adoptions."[4] This is particularly convenient for those who are interested in adopting internationally. Additionally, various agencies and organizations now use the Internet to match potential adoptive parents to people who are interested in placing children for adoption. One such example is Parent Match, which was launched in 2008 to help adoption professionals connect expectant parents and potential adoptive parents (https://www.parentmatch.com/). More than 90% of the potential adoptive adults under the age of 44 are networking, promoting themselves, and researching adoption online (Dorsey-Straff, 2012). Further, supportive networks for families formed via adoption can be created online, including various support groups and adoption forums that connect adoptive parents with other adoptive parents. Such networks can be helpful in assisting couples who may be coping with misinformation and stigmatization from those less familiar with the adoption process. Finally, adoption histories may be easily searchable and create a unique situation for a couple. For example, Jasmine, now 20, was adopted at the age of 3 through open adoption via the state foster care system, and thus was aware of her birth parents' names.

Children entering families through biological means may experience new media as playing a part in their lives even before their birth. Many expectant parents share pictures as their body changes on SNSs, via e-mail, and through texting. The use of new media and technology in this way is valuable because it allows for easy updating of friends and family who are geographically distant, and provides a digital record documenting a child's life before arrival. This involvement prior to birth and early into a child's life means for themselves that they will most likely never have an identity apart from technology. Their pictures, videos, and stories are told online before they are able to give permission, and consent offline to others in doing this or before they are able to be mindful about what they share themselves.

Once children enter a couple's life, there may be a period of readjustment (Carter & McGoldrick, 2005), including the role technology plays. With infants, parents may use the Internet to gain support, to manage parental stress and to enhance parental satisfaction (Bartholomew, Schoppe-Sullivan, Glassman, Camp Dush, & Sullivan, 2012). In a study involving 154 new mothers and 150 new fathers, Bartholomew et al. (2012) found that not only did new mothers use Facebook more than fathers, they used it more frequently than prior to becoming a new parent. Moreover, when more of the mothers' friends on Facebook were members of their family they reported better parental adjustment. Fathers reported better parental adjustment when they connected with their friends both offline and online. For mothers, however, it seems necessary to strike a balance between connecting with family on Facebook for support and connecting to update content management, as the researchers found that with an increase in visits to their account with the goal of primarily updating content, parental stress actually increased.

As infants grow into children their relationship and the family's relationship with technology grows and changes with them. Parents of children are faced with many decisions regarding the presence and usage of technology. Some of the questions that parents face include (but are not limited to):

- When do I give my child a cell phone or smartphone?
- Should I let my child engage in gaming; online, offline, both?
- To which types of websites will my child have access, if any?
- Which websites do I block?
- Do I let my child have technological devices (e.g., computers, gaming devices, digital viewing devices) in their room or only in common areas?
- How much is too much when it comes to the number of technological devices in my child's life, or the amount of time spent on these devices?
- What are the pros and cons to my child engaging with technology?
- What are the benefits and drawbacks of technology to our parent–child relationship and family relationships?

One of the challenges is that each member of a couple may differ on their responses, thus creating the potential for conflict. One partner, for example, may not necessarily see a problem with a particular website or activities whereas the other partner will express concern. Questions such as these reflect the need for couples to be mindful of the rules, roles, boundaries, and ecological influences of technology on their children's lives and their couple life during this point in family development. Couples need to make decisions together about when and in what way to introduce particular technologies to children and how they will manage and monitor such technologies once they have been introduced.

In the United States, most children quickly become familiar with a variety of technologies and demonstrate interest in technology at an early age

(Watt & White, 1999). Children can acquire a variety of skills via technology usage such as social skills in kindergarten age children (Shimai, Masuda, & Kishimoto, 1990; Villani, Olson, & Jellinek, 2005). Research suggests computers in the home are associated with higher school achievement in the areas of mathematics and reading (Attewell, 2001; Mesch, 2006). The benefits of playing academic games of various kinds (e.g., board games, competitive games, Internet games) in classrooms is associated with a gain in 20 percentage points in overall student achievements across grade levels (Marzano, 2010). In addition, elementary school-aged children who have computers in their homes tend to have an advantage over those that do not when it comes to having knowledge of technology and in terms of enjoying the process of learning itself via technology (Watt & White, 1999).

Roughly 3% of children under the age of 10, 6% of 10 year olds, and 11% of 11-year-olds have cell phones of their own (Lenhart, 2010). Yet children under the age of 5 experience difficulty understanding and communicating remotely via phone, and the challenges of phone usage impair children's motivations for use (Ballagas, Kaye, Ames, Go, & Raffle, 2009). Taken together, the findings suggest some children may be receiving cell phones before they have the capabilities to successfully negotiate their use or are motivated to use them apart from their parents.

Parents need to make decisions about how they are going to play a part in their children's technological activities. For instance, when parents are a part of the calling process, many of the barriers that exist for telephony by young children are diminished (Ballagas et al., 2009). Parents might consider the use of videoconferencing as a way to increase their children's comfort with telephony. Parents, however, might also be uncomfortable with their children's usage of technology (Adams & Stevenson, 2004). Unmonitored online experiences raise many concerns ranging from cyber bullying, to interactions with cyber predators (discussed further in Chapter 10), to privacy issues (Adams & Stevenson, 2004), to concern over what kids might see and hear that may not be age appropriate (Mesch, 2006), to fear of identity theft of one's child (Smardon, 2012), to concern for children not getting enough exercise, leading a sedentary lifestyle, and not getting enough sleep (Van den Bulck, 2004).

Couples also express concern over the role that the Internet can play in negatively affecting parent–child relationships such as increases in intergenerational conflicts, the weakening of family cohesion (Lenhart, Rainie, & Lewis, 2001; Mesch, 2006; Mesch & Levanon, 2003; Watt & White, 1999), difficulty with competition over technological resources within the family as many households are limited to only one or a few technological devices (Holloway & Valentine, 2002; Lenhart et al., 2001; Mesch, 2006), and decreased time spent between parents and children because their time is taken up by being online instead of with each other (Kraut et al., 1998; Katz & Rice, 2002; Mesch, 2006). This is becoming a growing problem; so much so that there is even a name for children who are receiving less attention by parents due to technological usage, "Technology Orphans" (Teitell, 2012). Responsible adults and parents in children's lives need to be mindful of the roles they play as the gatekeepers of a child's web print, and help children learn how to manage their own web prints as they grow into adolescence and future adulthood.

Couple Development With Adolescents

As a couple's child moves into adolescence, boundaries, roles, and rules within the family system need be renegotiated (Carter & McGoldrick, 2005), including those around the adoption of technology and new media. Frequently, developmental tasks couples should consider in adolescence revolve around the negotiating of an adolescent's amount of privacy, autonomy, and independence versus the degree to which one retains parental and familial control. These same tasks are often central issues of teen–technology and parent–technology interactions (Bacigalupe, 2011; Murphy, Lancey, & Hertlein, in press).

Part of what creates a challenge in determining the degree to which parents allow autonomy for their teens is that motivation around teen technology use is not well understood (Hundley & Shyles, 2010), nor is a teen's pattern of technology usage (Jordan, Trentacoste, Henderson, Manganello, & Fishbein, 2007). Texting is the digital activity in which teens engage more than any other, with 63% reporting they text every day, and older girls tending to text more daily than teens of other ages and genders (Lenhart, 2012). While adolescent girls might be doing more texting, teen boys are engaging in more gaming (Koivusilta, Lintonen, & Rimpela, 2007; Rushing & Stephens, 2011). Teen boys average 41 minutes of gaming per day, while girls average 8 minutes per day. It is important to note, however, that a significantly high proportion of teens play video games—approximately 97% (Rainie, 2009)—with an average of 25 minutes per day engaging in gaming.

One challenge in successfully negotiating roles, rules, and boundaries is that adolescents typically hold a higher degree of technological literacy than individuals at other points in the life span (DiMaggio, Hargittai, Neuman, & Robinson, 2001). Many adolescents are and have always been digital natives—in other words, they are native speakers of the language of technology because they have been raised in a world where technology has always been present (Prensky, 2001). Differences in terms of digital discourse and other areas of digital competency between parents and adolescents can make the negotiating of this developmental period difficult for couples with adolescents. Management of technology usage requires technological understanding that many adolescents acquire before their parents, yet a parent's perception that their child is a computer expert may contribute to conflict between a parent and teen

(Mesch, 2006). Therefore, the establishment of roles, rules and boundaries with adolescents becomes more complicated as adolescents often become those in the household with the most technological knowledge and highest degree of digital literacy (Aarsand, 2007; Mesch, 2006).

This is also the stage of family life where conflicts emerge when parents express concern over the negative consequences of technological usage (Mesch, 2006). Many couples worry about the effects of gaming on their kids ranging from isolationism to exposure to explicit sexual and violent aggression (Villani, Olson, & Jellinek, 2005). This concern comes from seemingly good reasons. Researchers conducting a survey of 15 to 17-year-olds found that 72% believe that such content influences their sexual behaviors to varying degrees ranging from "somewhat" to "a lot" (Kaiser Family Foundation, 2005). There is also a correlational link between exposure to game violence with greater aggression and desensitization to violence in real life and reduced aggression offline associated with digitally violent gaming (Villani et al., 2005). Villiani et al. (2005) indicated that a myriad of individual, cultural, developmental, familial, and parental differences account for outcomes in these various research studies. Since research remains inconclusive, it is essential that parents be available to monitor technological (including gaming) content, interactions, and timing.

Parents also need to find ways to attend to their adolescents having more than one device—they have to quickly learn to understand what devices and applications are used, make decisions about the appropriateness of usage, and communicate these decisions to their adolescents. Simultaneously, 70% to 80% of teens may be updating their social networking pages, texting a friend, streaming a television show, and listening to music (Hundley & Shyles, 2010; Pan, 2004). As a result of the multitasking, the time spent online averages roughly up to 7 hours per day with 11 hours of content (Rideout, Foehr, & Roberts, 2010).

Further, many parents with children in this age range worry about the risks associated with online interactions, particularly with regard to potential victimization by online sexual predators and/or cyber bullies (Crooks & Baur, 2011; Philaretou, 2005). Online sexual predators visit chat rooms and SNSs seeking out unsuspecting, attention-needing children to confuse with notions of sexuality and then lure them into meeting so they can sexually molest them (Crooks & Baur, 2011; Philaretou, 2005). Although companies such as CompuServe and America Online (AOL) have created monitoring devices to protect youth online (Crooks & Baur, 2011), Mesch (2006) noted that increased surveillance of an adolescent's online activities can also create arguments over their growing need for autonomy, potentially compromising development (Rushing & Stephens, 2011). When parents do not or cannot monitor their teens' technological use, they should still identify the manner in which to manage their vulnerability to online perpetrators both known and unknown to them (Landau, 2008). This can include (a) providing media-free zones in the house such as the bedroom, (b) encouraging comprehensive, informational, and positive media education in the home and school environments, (c) supporting other forms of socializing and activities (e.g., athletics, reading, hobbies, traveling, writing, painting, playing musical instruments), and (d) modeling appropriate online behaviors and communications (Villani et al., 2005).

The concerns of parents also include risks related to their adolescent individual mental and physical health. Like adults, adolescents struggle with Internet addiction (Hur, 2006; Ko, Yen, Chen, Chen, & Yen, 2005) and online gaming addiction (Hur, 2006). Associations also exist between pathological Internet use and problem drinking (Ko et al., 2008), depression, relationship problems, aggressive behaviors, ill health (Lam, Peng, Mai, & Jing, 2009), and obesity (American Academy of Pediatrics, 2004). Cell phone use has even been correlated, albeit weakly, with increased body mass index (BMI) levels in adolescents aged 11 to 17 (Lajunen et al., 2007).

Couples with adolescents need to remember that rules, roles and boundaries concerning new media will need to be reestablished. The manner in which this is accomplished should be consistent with what parents are already doing to encourage autonomy across other areas in the lives of adolescents (Villani et al., 2005). Villani et al. (2005) offered some recommendations for families as they negotiate this transitory developmental period from childhood to adulthood. It is recommended that they first assess their children's readiness, strengths, and weaknesses (Villani et al., 2005). Much like couples can benefit from assessing their own technology practices, parents should conduct a similar assessment regarding their teen's usage (see Chapter 7 regarding assessments). With what specific types of technology and new media would their children be ready and how would the parents know? Next, parents need to determine the risks associated with adolescence, focus on preparing and providing guidance for children, set rules and boundaries, and manage ways to cope with their own anxiety (Villani et al., 2005). Parents can advise youth about the potential challenges with media and generate safety plans to implement in the family. Further, parents need to be willing to learn about the different ways in which technology can be used as a way to manage their own anxiety about potentially problematic behavior.

As a way to minimize the conflict when discussing technology usage with their teens, parents need to identify ways to express their concerns with regard to teen technology practices in a way that is more likely to lead to a productive conversation and promotion of healthy practices in both present and future developmental stages. Such dialogues can be weighted more toward the positive consequences of technology in their teens' lives, and with some conversation regarding how they are to successfully negotiate the potential negative consequences, including the ways in which parents may act as allies rather than enemies in managing these concerns (Lanigan et al., 2009; Rushing & Stephens, 2011).

One of the ways that parents may be able to talk with their adolescents about potential problematic use of technology is to encourage the use of technology and new media in positive ways. For adolescents, the Internet serves as a resource for coping, emotion regulation (Ko, Yen, Yen, Chen, Weng, & Chen, 2008; Lam et al., 2009), the gaining of a sense of control, an outlet for negative energy, and stress reduction (Grüsser, Thalemann, & Griffiths, 2007). Similar with the literature with young children, the ability to have access to computers has been associated with higher test scores in school, and may play a major part in future success in higher education (Koivusilta, Lintonen, & Rimpela, 2007). Finally, technology-based interventions like the accessing of health websites (e.g., WebMD.com), the use of smartphones and applications aimed at promoting well-being, and video games that encourage health practices has been shown to inform and change health-related behaviors in Native American adolescents (Rushing & Stephens, 2011).

Couple Development With Adult Children

A couple's experience of having adult children is often characterized by exits and entrances of multiple people in the family's life. For example, the couple's adult children often launch from the home, attend higher education and/or additional training, establish careers, partner, have children of their own, the couple's aging parents become more dependent upon them, and the couple often becomes grandparents themselves (Carter & McGoldrick, 2005). Some common electronic experiences in this developmental stage include dating (Parks & Roberts, 1996), gaming (Entertainment Software Association, 2011), the building of friendships (Adams & Stevenson, 2004), professional networking, working, household management (Lanigan et al., 2009), and community engagement. Another of the more common experiences is engagement in online social contact with friends and family (Henline & Harris, 2006). In the post-parenting stage when adult children leave home, computers can help facilitate family communication (Mesch, 2006; Watt & White, 1999). Intergenerational intimate connections, particularly in newly launched adult children, are being maintained using a variety of technological devices and mechanisms like via phone, e-mail, Skype, and Facebook. Further, there seems to be a difference in the relationship quality between college-aged students and their parents depending on the mechanism for communication. College-aged adults who have more frequent phone conversations with their parent(s) also report having more intimate, satisfying, and supportive parental relationships. Those students who use SNSs to communicate with parents, however, reported more anxious attachment, and higher levels of conflict and loneliness (Gentzler, Oberhauser, Westerman, & Nadorff, 2011).

Though it does not appear there are the same nurturing effects between parents and their newly launched adult children when using SNSs to communicate (Gentzler et al., 2011), this does not change the fact that participation in SNSs (e.g., MySpace, Facebook, LinkedIn) is prominent at this life stage. Through the use of SNSs, smartphone applications, specific websites, community groups and bulletins, some adults are finding support and ways of coping with sexuality, relational, physical, cultural, and/or psychological concerns (Griffiths, 2000; Gudelunas, 2012). For instance, when I (M.L.C.B.) teach human sexuality, I highlight several smartphone applications to support sexual, physical, relational and personal health, such those offered by The Gottman Relationship Institute, including the following iPhone Apps: Give Appreciation, Fun and Play, Expression Needs, I Feel, Open-Ended Questions, and Affection and Lovemaking.[5] Other applications aimed at improving sexual relations and communications include Kamasutra for Android[6] and Safe Sex for the iPhone.[7] Applications attending to fertility and ovulation include the My Days Period and Ovulation Android application.[8]

Couple Development With Aging Parents

The relationship between couples and their aging parents is characterized by high levels of affection, frequent contact, and mutual help (Papalia, Olds, & Feldman, 2009). Yet as the average life expectancy increases (for most people in the United States, this means living over the age of 80), many of the people aging into what is known as the category of the "oldest-old" are turning to their adult children and their partner(s)/spouse(s) for assistance with their daily living skills (Mann, 2005; Papalia et al., 2009). Acting as care providers or powers of attorney for one's parent(s) can prove quite challenging for adult individuals, partners and family members (Papalia et al., 2009). To successfully negotiate this stage, couples need to balance the need for caring for them with their own autonomy and their lives, maintain their careers, and care for their own children and/or grandchildren while minimizing the feeling of burnout (Papalia et al., 2009).

The intersection between this developmental stage and technology has received less attention than any of the other stages discussed in this chapter (Adams & Stevenson, 2004; Watt & White, 1999). This may be because people in the later years of the life span have historically not been viewed as consumers of technology and may experience more physical barriers to technological use (Adams & Stevenson, 2004). The reality is that older adults are experiencing a technological and new media boom. Those in this age group are among the fastest growing demographic group online (Carracher, 2011), with the use of SNSs by those aged 50 to 65 doubling between 2009 to 2011, and a 150% increase occurring during the same time period for those ages 65 and up (Madden & Zickuhr, 2011).

Perhaps the biggest motivator for engaging in new media for older adults is that of connecting with friends and family (Mesch, 2006), particularly grandchildren (Watt & White, 1999). For many families, grandparents live away from their family. Video conferencing software affords grandchildren and grandparents an opportunity to interact with one another despite geographic location in meaningful ways (Harley & Fitzpatrick, 2009). When my (M.L.C.B.) young son was interacting with my mother via a videoconference function, I watched him flatten the laptop on his bed, place the screen portion on his pillow, and lay his head down on the pillow beside the computer. When I asked what he was doing, he simply replied, "Taking a nap with Grandmamma"—as if my question was the silliest one that had ever been asked.

Certain questions that need to be negotiated and considered in this stage revolve around how various technologies can be used as a means of staying in touch and connecting the generations. Couples need to make decisions on the ways in which new media can be used to connect with aging parents, how the potential barriers will be managed (e.g., video calling malfunctions, time zones differences), and the decisions around which events require in-person attendance versus electronic presences.

Relationship Termination

Relationship dissolution can occur in a variety of ways—through death, divorce, physical and/or psychological separation. How these various endings are impacted by new media varies. As new media has emerged in couple life, the spread of more divorces associated with infidelity and other Internet-related issues has been reported more frequently (Kendall, 2011). Yet the increased incidence of opportunities to connect with others outside of one's relationship does not necessarily translate into an actual increase in the number of couple endings themselves. In married households with Internet access compared to those without access, there is little to no evidence that the rise of the Internet has significantly raised the divorce rate above what it would be without such technologies (Kendall, 2011; Rosenfeld & Thomas, 2012). In fact, at the 1-year breakup point, couples who met online had a slightly less likely average (though not significant) rate of being broken up when compared to couples who met in other ways (i.e., through friends, family, work, etc.) Finally, there are no significant differences in terms of relationship quality or fragility between those couples who met online and those that met offline (Rosenfeld & Thomas, 2012).

Although cheating or affairs occurred before the advent of the Internet, the way they are negotiated and managed has changed, and the role of technology in affairs has become more prominent. One study reported that 28% of married Internet users admitted to engaging in cyber affairs (Avila-Mileham, 2003). Further, 42% of matrimonial attorney divorce cases in the early 2000s reportedly involved one party meeting a new romantic or love interest over the Internet (Dedmon, 2002). One's SNS can also be a key player in the dissolution of the relationship. There are even resources aimed at extrarelational engagements like chat rooms such as "Married and Flirting,"[9] classified ad sites on Craigslist,[10] and multiple websites that advertise connecting would-be unfaithful spouses with other partners.

In addition to more opportunities for engagement with others (both inside of one's relationship and outside of it), the disclosing of one's relationship status now takes place publicly. Users of SNSs can change their online relational status to divorced, separated, or single on Facebook. Social media also introduces a decision point—when relationships end, the individuals involved (either separately or conjointly) need to make decisions around how to manage the peripheral relationships that came with/come with the primary relationship. For example, Libby and Alison terminated their 8-month relationship due to high conflict. Libby expressed confusion about whether it would be appropriate for her to send short messages from time to time to a friend of Alison, Kelley, with whom she enjoyed a pleasant relationship. Her confusion stemmed from the fact that, had it been a time when the computer was not so predominant in daily life, she knew that to call Kelley on the phone would be deemed inappropriate. But the ability for Libby to send Kelley a short message periodically afforded by new technology without the requirement of a response by Kelley introduced an area of grey into her decision making.

Some key questions that need to be managed at this stage include the following:

- Who do you keep as an online friend?
- With whom do you maintain contact?
- Who do you unfriend (if anyone)?
- Under what circumstances does one comment on someone's relationship change?

Another element of relationship termination facilitated through technology and new media is the ease in ending relationships through instant messaging, texting, and/or e-mailing. Ending a relationship via technology may be as "simple as logging off the computer or not replying to electronic messages" (Merkle & Richardson, 2004, p. 189). In cases where new media is used to communicate the relationship termination, computer mediated dissolutions tend to be more direct (Starks, 2007).

New media also provides opportunities for survivors to electronically disseminate information when their partner has died. Death of an extended family member, friend, or acquaintance can be discovered via

Facebook or through an Internet search through various obituaries and newspapers. Virtual memorials and/or gravestones can serve as a source of comfort and connectivity among survivors (Jones, 2007).[11] Virtual memorials also exist on SNSs for people who once had their own profiles or accounts, which, after death, transition into memorial pages, cannot be destroyed over time or from weather, and can be visited virtually anywhere and any time.

In addition, there are online support groups for the bereaved. For instance, on Facebook there exist several support groups targeted toward various people experiencing bereavement, groups like Death of a Sibling,[12] Surviving the Death of a Spouse,[13] Death of a Child—Surviving the Loss,[14] to name just a few. The participation in online support groups for spouses of those loved ones who are dying, or have died, has demonstrated positive effects on the quality of the dying and grieving experience (Curtis, Patrick, Engelberg, Norris, Asp, & Byock, 2002).

Technology also affords one the opportunity to send messages to loved ones before death to be delivered after death.[15] Some surviving families have shared that receiving these e-mails has brought a sense of unanticipated closeness and closure (Pfeiffer, 2012). As the essence of people can continue online long after their physical realities have ended, discussing the implications of what this means for oneself, one's partner, and one's family members may be an essential conversation. Finally, there are also websites available such as the Digital Beyond[16] dedicated to exploring death in the context of technology, which can be a useful adjunct in assisting couples.

Notes

1. http://www.nokidding.net/.
2. http://www.adoption.com/.
3. http://www.adoptivefamilies.com/.
4. http://www.openadoptions.com/.
5. http://www.gottman.com/60846/Phone-Apps.html.
6. https://play.google.com/store/apps/details?id=com.kamasutra&hl=en.
7. https://itunes.apple.com/us/app/safwe-sex/id374937863?mt=8.
8. https://play.google.com/store/apps/details?id=com.chris.mydays&hl=en.
9. http://www.marriedandflirtingchat.com/.
10. http://www.craigslist.org/about/sites/.
11. Some of the most popular and respected of such sites include Virtual-Memorials and Gonetoosoon.
12. https://www.facebook.com/#!/groups/58694237476/?fref = ts.
13. https://www.facebook.com/#!/groups/survivingdeathofspousesupport/?fref = ts.
14. https://www.facebook.com/#!/groups/193392497359774/?fref = ts.
15. This service is available via the site Dead Man's Switch.
16. http://www.thedigitalbeyond.com/.

References

Aarsand, P. A. (2007). Computer and video games in family life: The digital divide as a resource in intergenerational interactions. *Childhood*, *14*(2), 235–256. doi:10.1177/0907568207078330

Abma, J. C., & Martinez, G. M. (2006). Childlessness among older women in the United States: Trends and profiles. *Journal of Marriage and Family*, *68*(4), 1045–1056. doi:10.1111/j.1741-3737.2006.00312.x

Adams, R., & Stevenson, M. (2004). A lifetime of relationships mediated by technology. In F. Lang & K. Fingerman (Eds.), *Growing together: Personal relationships across the lifespan* (pp. 368–393). New York: Cambridge University Press.

Agarwal, A., Deepinder, F., Sharma, R. K., Ranga, G., & Li, J. (2008). Effect of cell phone usage on semen analysis in men attending infertility clinic: An observational study. *Fertility and Sterility*, *89*(1), 124–128. doi:10.1016/j.fertnstert.2007.01.166

Agarwal, A., Desai, N. R., Makker, K., Varghese, A., Mouradi, R., Sabanegh, E., et al. (2009). Effects of radiofrequency electromagnetic waves (RF-EMW) from cellular phones on human ejaculated semen: An in vitro pilot study. *Fertility and Sterility*, *92*(4), 1318–1325. doi:10.1016/j.fertnstert.2008.08.022

American Academy of Pediatrics. (2004, September 30). *American Academy of Pediatrics supports Institute of Medicine's childhood obesity recommendation* [Press release]. Retrieved from http://pediatrics.aappublications.org/content/120/Supplement_4/S229.full

Attewell, P. (2001). Comment: The first and second digital divides. *Sociology of Education, 74*(3), 252–259.

Avila-Mileham, B. (2003). *Online infidelity in Internet chat rooms: An ethnographic exploration* (Unpublished doctoral dissertation). University of Florida, Gainesville.

Bacigalupe, G. (2011). Families, emergent technologies, and adolescence. *Family Psychologist, 27*(2), 11–13.

Baker, A. J. (2007). Expressing emotion in text: Email communication of online couples. In M. T. Whitty, A. J. Baker, & J. A. Inman (Eds.), *Online matchmaking* (pp. 97–111). London, England: Palgrave Macmillan.

Ballagas, R., Kaye, J., Ames, M., Go, J., & Raffle, H. (2009). Family communication: Phone conversations with children. IDC 2009 Workshop on Children and Mobile Technology: Interface Development for Mobile Touch Devices. 321–324. doi:10.1145/1551788.1551874

Bartholomew, M. K., Schoppe-Sullivan, S. J., Glassman, M., Kamp Dush, C. M., & Sullivan, J. M. (2012). New parents' Facebook use at the transition to parenthood. *Family Relations, 61*(3), 455–469. doi:10.1111/j.1741-3729.2012.00708.x

Blumer, M. L. C., Ansara, Y. G., & Watson, C. M. (2012). *Cisgenderism in family therapy: How everyday practices delegitimize people's gender self-designations.* Unpublished manuscript.

Blumer, M. L. C., & Green, M. S. (2012, January). *The role of same-sex couple development in clinical practice.* Paper presented at the Nationally Broadcast Professional Continuing Education Workshop, American Association of Marriage and Family Therapy, Alexandria, VA.

Carracher, J. (2011). *How baby boomers are embracing digital media.* Retrieved from http://mashable.com/2011/04/06/baby-boomers-digital-media/

Carter, B., & McGoldrick, M. (2005). *The expanded family cycle: Individual, family and social perspectives* (3rd ed.). Needham Heights, MA: Allyn & Bacon.

Crooks, R., & Baur, K. (2011). *Our sexuality* (11th ed.). Belmont, CA: Thomson Wadsworth.

Curtis, J. R., Patrick, D. L., Engelberg, R. A., Norris, K., Asp, C., & Byock, I. (2002). A measure of the quality of dying and death: Initial validation using after-death interviews with family members. *Journal of Pain and Symptom Management, 24*(1), 17–31.

Dedmon, J. (2002, November). *Is the Internet bad for your marriage? Online affairs, pornographic sites playing greater role in divorces* [Press release]. New York: Dilenschneider Group.

DeLyser, G. (2012). At midlife, intentionally childfree women and their experiences of regret. *Clinical Social Work Journal, 40*(1), 66–74. doi:10.1007/s10615-011-0337-2

DiMaggio, P., Hargittai, E., Neuman, W. R., & Robinson, J. P. (2001). Social implications of the Internet. *Annual Review of Sociology, 27*(1), 307–336. doi:10.1146/annurev.soc.27.1.307

Dorsey-Straff, N. (2012). *Adoptive parents embracing technology to build families*. Retrieved from http://www.parents.com/blogs/adoption-diaries/2012/01/23/must-read/adoptive-parents-embracing-technology-to-build-families/

Elderton, A., & Jones, C. (2011). Finding a safe place to explore sexual identity. *Learning Disability Practice, 14*(5), 14-17.

Entertainment Software Association. (2011). *Essential facts about the computer and video game industry*. Retrieved from http://www.theesa.com/facts/pdfs/ESA_EF_2011.pdf

Erogul, O., Oztas, E., Yildirim, I., Kir, T., Aydur, E., Komesli, G., et al. (2006). Effects of electromagnetic radiation from a cellular phone on human sperm motility: An in vitro study. *Archives of Medical Research, 37*(7), 840–843. doi:10.1016/j.arcmed.2006.05.003

Gates, G. J. (2011). *Family formation and raising children among same-sex couples* (Report No. FF51, F2-F4). National Council on Family Relations. Retrieved from http://williamsinstitute.law.ucla.edu/wp-content/uploads/Gates-Badgett-NCFR-LGBT-Families-December-2011.pdf

Gauthier, D. K., & Chaudoir, N. K. (2004). Tranny boyz: Cyber community support in negotiating sex and gender mobility among female to male transsexuals. *Deviant Behavior, 25*(4), 375–398. doi:10.1080/01639620490441272

Gentzler, A. L., Oberhauser, A. M., Westerman, D., & Nadorff, D. K. (2011). College students' use of electronic communication with parents: Links to loneliness, attachment, and relationship quality. *Cyberpsychology, Behavior and Social Networking, 14*(1–2), 71–74. doi:10.1089/cyber.2009.0409

Gillespie, R. (2003). Childfree and feminine: Understanding the gender identity of voluntary childless women. *Gender & Society, 17*(1), 122–136. doi:10.1177/0891243202238982

Griffiths, M. (2000). Internet addiction—time to be taken seriously? *Addiction Research & Theory, 8*(5), 413–418. doi:10.3109/16066350009005587

Grüsser, S. M., Thalemann, R., & Griffiths, M. D. (2007). Excessive computer game playing: Evidence for addiction and aggression? *Cyberpsychology & Behavior: The Impact of the Internet, Multimedia and Virtual Reality on Behavior and Society, 10*(2), 290–292. doi:10.1089/cpb.2006.9956

Gudelunas, D. (2012). There's an app for that: The uses and gratifications of online social networks for gay men. *Sexuality & Culture, 16*(4), 347–365. doi:10.1007/s12119-012-9127-4

Gutschi, T., Mohamad Al-Ali, B., Shamloul, R., Pummer, K., & Trummer, H. (2011). Impact of cell phone use on men's semen parameters. *Andrologia, 43*(5), 312–316. doi: 10.1111/j.1439-0272.2011.01075.x

Haddon, L. (2006). The contribution of domestication research to in-home computing and media consumption. *The Information Society, 22*, 195–203.

Harley, D., & Fitzpatrick, G. (2009). YouTube and intergenerational communication: The case of Geriatric1927. *Universal Access in the Information Society, 8*(1), 5–20. doi:10.1007/s10209-008-0127-y

Henline, B. H., & Harris, S. M. (2006, October 19–22). *Pros and cons of technology use within close relationships*. Poster presented at the annual conference of the American Association for Marriage and Family Therapy, Austin, TX.

Hertlein, K. M., Blumer, M. L. C., & Smith, J. M. (2012). *Couple and family therapists' use of web-based technologies in clinical practice*. Unpublished manuscript.

Hitsch, G. J., Hortacsu, A., & Ariely, D. (2010). Matching and sorting in online dating. *American Economic Review, 100*(1), 130–163. doi:10.1257/aer.100.1.130

Holloway, S., & Valentine, G. (2002). *Cyberkids*. New York: Routledge-Falmer.

Hughes, R., & Hans, J. D. (2001). Computers, the Internet, and families: A review of the role new technology plays in family life. *Journal of Family Issues, 22*(6), 776–790. doi:10.1177/019251301022006006

Hundley, H. L., & Shyles, L. (2010). US teenagers' perceptions and awareness of digital technology: A focus group approach. *New Media & Society, 12*(3), 417–433. doi:10.1177/1461444809342558

Hur, M. H. (2006). Demographic, habitual, and socioeconomic determinants of Internet addiction disorder: An empirical study of Korean teenagers. *Cyberpsychology & Behavior: The Impact of the Internet, Multimedia and Virtual Reality on Behavior and Society, 9*(5), 514–525. doi:10.1089/cpb.2006.9.514

Iwasaki, Y., & Ristock, J. L. (2007). The nature of stress experienced by lesbians and gay men. *Anxiety, Stress & Coping, 20*(3), 299–319. doi:10.1080/10615800701303264

Jones, L. (2007). *Carving virtual gravestones*. Retrieved from http://www.guardian.co.uk/technology/2007/aug/23/guardianweeklytechnologysection.myspace

Jordan, A. N., Trentacoste, V., Henderson, J., Manganello, J., & Fishbein, M. (2007). Measuring the time teens spend with media: Challenges and opportunities. *Media Psychology, 9*(1), 19–41. doi:10.1080/15213260709336801

Kaiser Family Foundation. (2005). *Survey snapshot: Teens, sex and TV*. Available from http://www.kff.org/

Katz, J. E., & Rice, R. E. (2002). *Social consequences of Internet use: Access, involvement, and interaction*. Cambridge, MA: MIT Press.

Kendall, T. D. (2011). The relationship between Internet access and divorce rate. *Journal of Family and Economic Issues, 32*(3), 449–460. doi:10.1007/s10834-010-9222-3

Ko, C., Yen, J., Chen, C., Chen, S., & Yen, C. (2005). Proposed diagnostic criteria of Internet addiction for adolescents. *Journal of Nervous and Mental Disease, 193*(11), 728–733. doi:10.1097/01.nmd.0000185891.13719.54

Ko, C., Yen, J., Yen, C., Chen, C., Weng, C., & Chen, C. (2008). The association between Internet addiction and problematic alcohol use in adolescents: The problem behavior model. *Cyberpsychology & Behavior, 11*(5), 571–576. doi:10.1089/cpb.2007.0199

Koivusilta, L., Lintonen, T., & Rimpela, A. (2007). Orientations in adolescent use of information and communication technology: A digital divide by sociodemographic background, educational career, and health. *Scandinavian Journal of Public Health, 35*(1), 95–103 doi:10.1080/14034940600868721

Kraut, R., Patterson, M., Lundmark, V., Kiesler, S., Mukopadhyay, T., & Scherlis, W. (1998). Internet paradox: A social technology that reduces social involvement and psychological well-being? *American Psychologist, 53*(9), 1017–1031. doi:10.1037/0003-066X.53.9.1017

Lajunen, H., Keski-Rahkonen, A., Pulkkinen, L., Rose, R. J., Rissanen, A., & Kaprio, J. (2007). Are computer and cell phone use associated with body mass index and overweight? A population study among twin adolescents. *BMC Public Health, 7*(1), 24–32. doi:10.1186/1471-2458-7-24

Lam, L. T., Peng, Z. W., Mai, J. C., & Jing, J. (2009). Factors associated with Internet addiction among adolescents. *Cyberpsychology & Behavior: The Impact of the Internet, Multimedia and Virtual Reality on Behavior and Society, 12*(5), 551–555. doi:10.1089/cpb.2009.0036

Landau, S. (2008). Privacy and security: A multidimensional problem. *Communications of the ACM, 51*(11), 25–26. doi:10.1145/1400214.1400223

Lanigan, J. D., Bold, M., & Chenoweth, L. (2009). Computers in the family context: Perceived impact on family time and relationships. *Family Science Review, 14*(1), 16–32.

Lawson, H. M., & Leck, K. (2006). Dynamics of Internet dating. *Social Science Computer Review, 24*(2), 189–208. doi:10.1177/0894439305283402

Lenhart, A. (2010, December 1). *Is the age at which kids get cell phones getting younger?* Retrieved from http://pewinternet.org/Commentary/2010/December/Is-the-age-at-which-kids-get-cell-phones-getting-younger.aspx

Lenhart, A. (2012). *Teens, smartphones, and texting*. Washington, DC: Pew Internet and American Life Project.

Lenhart, A., Rainie, L., & Lewis, O. (2001). *Teenage life online: The rise of the instant-message generation and the Internet's impact on friendships and family relationships*. Retrieved from http://www.pewinternet.org/reports/pdfs/PIP_Teens_Report.pdf

Madden, M., & Zickuhr, Z. (2011). *65% of online adults use social networking sites: Women maintain their foothold on SNS use and older Americans are still coming aboard*. Retrieved from http://pewinternet.org/~/media//Files/Reports/2011/PIP-SNS-Update-2011.pdf

Mann, W. C. (Ed.). (2005). *Smart technology for aging, disability, and independence: The state of the science*. Hoboken, NJ: John Wiley.

Marzano, R. J. (2010). Using games to enhance student achievement. *Educational Leadership, 67*(5), 71–72.

McGoldrick, M., Carter, B., & Garcia-Preto, N. (Eds.). (2010). *The expanded family cycle: Individual, family and social perspectives* (4th ed.). Needham Heights, MA: Allyn & Bacon.

McKenna, K. Y. A. (2008). MySpace or your place: Relationship initiation and development in the wired and wireless world. In *Handbook of relationship initiation* (pp. 235–247). New York: Psychology Press.

Merkle, E. R., & Richardson, R. A. (2004). Digital dating and virtual relating: Conceptualizing computer mediated romantic relationships. *Family Relations, 49*(2), 187–192. doi:10.1111/j.1741-3729.2000.00187.x

Mesch, G. S. (2006). Family relations and the Internet: Exploring a family boundaries approach. *Journal of Family Communication, 6*(2), 119–138. doi:10.1207/s15327698jfc0602_2

Mesch, G. S., & Levanon, Y. (2003). Community networking and locally based social ties in two suburban communities. *City and Community, 2*, 335–351.

Morrison, M., & Krugman, D. M. (2001). A look at mass and computer mediated technologies: Understanding the roles of television and computers in the home. *Journal of Broadcasting & Electronic Media, 45*(1), 135–161. doi:10.1207/s15506878jobem4501_

Murphy, L., Lancey, K., & Hertlein, K. M. (2013). Attending to social network usage in teen and family treatment: A structural-developmental perspective. *Journal of Family Psychotherapy.*

Neilsonwire. (2011). *Who is winning the U.S. smartphone battle?* Retrieved from http://blog.nielsen.com/nielsenwire/online_mobile/who-is-winning-the-u-s-smartphone-battle/

Pan, G. (2004, March 24). *Seventy percent of media consumers use multiple forms of media at the same time, according to a study for the media center at API*. Retrieved from http://www.americanpressinstitute.org/pages/apinews/api_news_releases/seventy_percent_of_media_consu/

Papalia, D. E., Olds, S. W., & Feldman, R. D. (2009). *Human development* (11th ed.). Boston, MA: McGraw-Hill.

Parks, M. R., & Roberts, L. D. (1996). 'Making MOOsic': The development of personal relationships on line and a comparison to their off-line counterparts. *Journal of Social and Personal Relationships, 15*(4), 517-537.

Patterson, D. G. (2005). Gay male couples: Challenges and possibilities. *Family Therapy Magazine, 6*, 16–19.

Pelton, S. L., & Hertlein, K. M. (2011). A proposed life cycle for voluntary childfree couples. *Journal of Feminist Family Therapy: An International Forum, 23*(1), 39–53. doi:10.1080/08952833.2011.548703

Pfeiffer, E. (2012). *Emails from dead man's account helping family and friends find closure*. Retrieved from http://news.yahoo.com/blogs/sideshow/emails-dead-man-account-helping-family-friends-closure-193306965.html

Philaretou, A. G. (2005). Sexuality and the Internet. *Journal of Sex Research, 42*(2), 180–181.

Prensky, M. (2001). Digital natives, digital immigrants Part 2: Do they really think differently? *On the Horizon, 9*(6), 1–6.

Rainie, L. (2009). *Teens in the digital age*. Retrieved from http://www.nationaltechcenter.org/documents/conf09/back_to_the_future_rainie.pdf

Rideout, V. J., Foehr, U. G., & Roberts, D. F. (2010). *Generation M^2: Media in the lives of 8- to 18-year-olds.*Menlo Park, CA: Kaiser Family Foundation. Retrieved from http://www.kff.org/entmedia/8010.cfm

Rosenfeld, M. J., & Thomas, R. J. (2012). Searching for a mate: The rise of the Internet as a social intermediary. *American Sociological Review, 77*(4), 523–547. doi:10.1177/0003122412448050

Rushing, S. C., & Stephens, D. (2011). Use of media technologies by Native American teens and young adults in the Pacific Northwest: Exploring their utility for designing culturally appropriate technology-based health interventions. *Journal of Primary Prevention, 32*, 135–145. doi:10.1007/s10935-011-0242-z

Shapiro, E. (2004). "Trans"cending barriers: Transgender organizing on the Internet. *Journal of Gay and Lesbian Social Services, 16*(3/4), 165–179. doi:10.1300/J041v16n03_11

Shimai, S., Masuda, K., & Kishimoto, Y. (1990). Influences of TV games on physical and psychological development of Japanese kindergarten children. *Perceptual and Motor Skills, 70*(3), 771–776. doi:10.2466/pms.1990.70.3.771

Silverstone, R., Hirsch, E., & Morley, D. (1992). Information and communication technologies and the moral economy of the household. In R. Silverstone & E. Hirsch (Eds.), *Consuming technologies* (pp. 15–31). London: Routledge.

Smardon, A. (2012). *Identity theft: "Kids don't know they're victims."* Retrieved from http://m.npr.org/story/153030774

Stafford, L., & Reske, J. R. (1990). Idealization and communication in long-distance premarital relationships. *Family Relations, 39*(3), 274–279.

Starks, K. (2007). Bye bye love: Computer-medicated communication and relational dissolution. *Texas Speech Communication Journal, 32*(1), 11–20.

Stephure, R. J., Boon, S. D., MacKinnon, S. L., & Deveau, V. L. (2009). Internet initiated relationships: Associations between age and involvement in online dating. *Journal of Computer-Mediated Communication, 14*(3), 658–681. doi:10.1111/j.1083-6101.2009.01457.x

Sutter, J. D. (2009). *All in the Facebook family: Older generations join social networks*. Retrieved from http://articles.cnn.com/2009-04-13/tech/social.network.older_1_facebook-today-social-networks-social-media?_s=PM:TECH

Teitell, B. (2012, March 8). *Dad, can you put away the laptop?* Retrieved from http://www.boston.com/lifestyle/articles/2012/03/08/in_reversal_kids_now_nag_parents_to_step_away_from_their_phones_tablets_and_laptops/

Tucker, A. (2006, August 6). Baby, your profile still says "single"; It's a sticky sitch: At what point during the dating game do you change your online status? *Seattle Times*, p. L6.

Van den Bulck, J. (2004). Television viewing, computer game playing, and Internet use and self-reported time to bed and time out of bed in secondary-school children. *Sleep, 27*(1), 101–104.

Villani, V. S., Olson, C. K., & Jellinek, M. S. (2005). Media literacy for clinicians and parents. *Child and Adolescent Psychiatric Clinics of North America, 14*(3), 523–553. doi:10.1016/j.chc.2005.03.001

Walther, J. B. (1996). Computer-mediated communication impersonal, interpersonal, and hyperpersonal interaction. *Communication Research, 23*(1), 3–43. doi:10.1177/009365096023001001

Watt, D., & White, J. M. (1999). Computers and the family life: A family development perspective. *Journal of Comparative Family Studies, 30*(1), 1–15.

Wdowiak, A., Wdowiak, L., & Wiktor, H. (2007). Evaluation of the effect of using mobile phones on male fertility. *Annals of Agricultural and Environmental Medicine, 14*(1), 169–172.

Whitty, M. T., & Carr, A. N. (2005). Taking the good with the bad: Applying Klein's work to further our understandings of cyber-cheating. *Journal of Couple & Relationship Therapy, 4*(2–3), 103–115. doi:10.1300/J398v04n02_10

Whitty, M. T., & Carr, A. N. (2006). New rules in the workplace: Applying object-relations theory to explain problem Internet and email behaviour in the workplace. *Computers in Human Behavior*, 22(2), 235–250. doi:10.16/j.chb.2004.06.005

10 Technology, Risks, and Relationships

My favorite thing about the Internet is that you get to go into the private world of real creeps without having to smell them.

—Penn Jillett

Common Risks to Relationships Associated With Technology and New Media

Aggression taking place in relationships is nothing new; however, with the advent of new media there are now different venues and mechanisms through which it occurs. A brief revisiting of the ecological influences on the couple system (see Chapter 5) makes it easier to better understand the context of technology-based aggressive actions. Consider the ecological influences of acceptability and ambiguity for example. Researchers have found that those who use the Internet often participate in greater levels of conflict, increased aggression with regard to online interactions, and inappropriately self-disclose online more frequently (Yum & Hara, 2006). It may be the case that behaviors like online conflict and inappropriate online self-disclosures may not be perceived as real (an example of ambiguity); in comparison to similar behaviors occurring offline, they may have a higher likelihood of being tolerated or even accepted (an example of acceptability). Further, various forms of online aggression can occur via parties who are both known *and* unknown to the person on the receiving end (Landau, 2008), in part due to the anonymous nature of the medium (Lea & Spears, 1991).

Cyberbullying

Some forms of aggression presenting serious risks to relationships include online predators, online sexual predators, cyberhaters, cyberbullying, cyberstalking, and electronic intimate partner violence. Incidences of cyberbullying are on the rise and as technology develops and cyber knowledge grows it is likely to continue to increase (Ryan, Kariuki, &

Yilmaz, 2011). Tokunaga (2010) defined cyberbullying as "any behavior performed through electronic or digital media by individuals or groups that repeatedly communicates hostile or aggressive messages intended to inflict harm or discomfort on others" (p. 278). Cyberbullies may be known or unknown to the cybervictim(s), and can perpetrate from any location (e.g., school, home; Tokunaga, 2010). The effects of being cyberbullied range from psychosocial issues, declines in academic or work performance, troubles with family and peers, and in severe cases, self-harm (Tokunaga, 2010).

Cyberbullying is a widespread problem. Although the experiencing of cyberbullying is more likely to occur in childhood and/or adolescence, with approximately 20%–40% encountering some form, it is the ages of 12 to 14 when people are most susceptible to cyber victimization (Tokunaga, 2010). There do not appear to be any gender differences for either the cyberbully or the cybervictim (Mishna, Khoury-Kassabri, Gadalla, & Daciuk, 2012; Tokunaga, 2010). But, when comparing studies of bullying in general versus cyberbullying, it does appear women are more likely to be both the cyberbully and/or the cybervictim (Mishna et al., 2012). Further, students who were involved in cyberbullying were also more likely to perpetrate violence toward peers, have higher daily rates of computer usage, and share their technological passwords with friends.

Cyberbullying transcends age, culture, and physical abilities (Blumenfeld & Cooper, 2010; Finn, 2004; Lindsay & Krysik, 2012; Mishna et al., 2012; Tokunaga, 2010). It is also not uncommon for young adults in college to experience cyberbullying (Finn, 2004; Lindsay & Krysik, 2012). Cyberbullying also appears to be experienced across people of varied cultural backgrounds (Huang & Chou, 2010); Western culture views it with more seriousness while the Taiwanese culture, for example, views cyberbullying with relative indifference. Cyberbullies also tend to target a wider range of victims (e.g., those with physical inferiorities, those with psychosocial inadequacies) than their offline counterparts (Mishna et al., 2012; Tokunaga, 2010). For instance, one adult woman commented on an "X-Factor" contestant's Facebook wall and became the target of harassment by a group of other users. Using the victim's name and pictures, these bullies created a fake Facebook page, and made it seem as though she was trolling the social networking sites for young girls, drugs and sex. Facebook staff members took the page down and were court-ordered to identify the cyberbullies (Choney, 2012). Finally, cyberbullying is also often experienced differently based on one's sexual and gender orientations. For those who happen to identify as members of the sexual and gender orientation minority communities, or as lesbian, gay, bisexual, and/or transgender (LGBT; Blumenfeld & Cooper, 2010), the rates of cyberbullying across the schooling experience (e.g., middle, high school, and college) tends to be higher than their sexual orientation majority, or heterosexual, counterparts (Finn, 2004).

For couples, strategies need to be developed to minimize the risk of cyberbullying with their children. This means incorporating information related to developmental stage and creating a safe space for sharing as a family about online interactions, including ones of a more aggressive nature. This is imperative as cybervictims (and likely bullies) do not often report being bullied (or bullying; Huang & Chou, 2010; Tokunaga, 2010). Researchers report 1% to 9% of child cybervictims report the bullying to their parent(s) (Aricak et al., 2008; Dehue, Bolman, & Völlink, 2008; Slonie & Smith, 2008). LGBT youth, however, are less likely than their heterosexual counterparts to report cyberbullying (Blumenfeld & Cooper, 2010) because they believe it will be ignored or tolerated (Casey-Cannon, Hayward, & Gowen, 2001; Peterson & Skiba, 2001). One of the biggest barriers to children and teens reporting cyberbullying is that of fear that they will lose their computer, Internet, or phone privileges (Blumenfeld & Cooper, 2010; Tokunaga, 2010).

For couples, another key piece is to know that adolescents seem to have a good grasp on who online can be trusted. To manage these risks, adolescents employ particular strategies including altering or omitting sensitive information, friending people they only know in their actual offline social world, routinely blocking those people who are unknown to them offline, taking necessary precautions to help ensure safety from hackers, and just starting over online (i.e., building a new profile page or creating a new gaming world) if they get bothered or hacked (Hundley & Shyles, 2010). In addition, many victims seek support and feedback on how to manage the bullying from friends (Segrin, 2003). This includes developing a plan for assessment, management, and consequences of cyberbullying (for additional resources, see Appendix E).

Cyberstalking

Cyberstalking is a term that emerged in the mid-1990s (Southworth, Dawson, Fraser, & Tucker, 2005) and includes repeated online threats and/or harassment, that is perceived as unwelcome and intrusive, and which would make most people fearful or concerned for their safety. Research on cyberstalking is scant with prevalence difficult to determine (Brewster, 2003; Finn, 2004; Fisher, Cullen, & Turner, 2000). At best, it is estimated that 20% of the more than one million people who are stalked annually in the United States are cyberstalked (Finn & Atkinson, 2009; Tjaden & Thoenes, 1998; U.S. Department of Justice, 1999), with reports on the rise (Stephenson & Walter, 2011). Little information exists on how to assess for cyberstalking, and/or a way of typologically categorizing cyberstalkers (Stephenson & Walter, 2011). Keppel and Walter (1999) identified four subtypes of stalkers: (a) power assertive (PA), (b) power reassurance (PR), (c) anger retaliatory (AR), and (d) anger excitation (AE). The PA cyberstalker is focused on controlling the victim(s) using power and aggression (Stephenson & Walter, 2011). With this stalker, online control may not be enough. It may escalate to offline encounters that result in violence toward the victim(s) (Stephenson & Walter, 2011). PR cyberstalkers engage the victim(s) through their magical thinking and fantasy-focused reality, becoming increasingly aggressive over time (Stephenson & Walter, 2011). As the online interaction grows less satisfying, this subtype of stalker may try to go from online to offline engagement (Stephenson & Walter, 2011). PR stalkers tend to be unorganized and may leave more clues online, making the stalker easier to detect and capture (Stephenson & Walter, 2011). Viewing the PA and PR stalking behaviors in the context of ecological influences (see Chapter 5), practicing online control may be enough of an approximation and accommodation of their desire for control offline, eventually the ability for these ecological influences to satiate their offline violent needs wanes.

The AR cyberstalker is believed to be less common online than the PA or PR subtypes (Stephenson & Walter, 2011). This type is hostility ridden and rage filled, typically toward a specific source (e.g., symbolic target, real person(s) or organization; Stephenson & Walter, 2011). These cyberstalkers rarely meet victim(s) offline (Stephenson & Walter, 2011). It may be that the reality offered online is enough to approximate and accommodate offline needs. AE cyberstalkers are believed to be the rarest subtype occurring online (Stephenson & Walter, 2011). They primarily focus on terrorizing their victim(s) until the target of their terror is destroyed (Stephenson & Walter, 2011).

In one case, Darla and Jon were coming to treatment to improve their communication. During the course of a session, Darla indicated that she was being stalked by a former coworker via a social networking site. Darla and Jon had tried everything they could think of to manage the threat—set privacy settings to the strictest possible, filed a half a dozen stalking reports with the police, contacted the staff of Facebook—all to no avail. Jon became concerned for her safety and urged her to quit her Facebook page altogether. Darla was adamant that she wanted to maintain her page in spite of the stalker, thus creating a conflict for the couple. The individual stalking her was able to get to her profile page via those of some of her friends as their privacy settings were set to allow the public to see theirs' and their friends' pages, pictures, wall post comments, and so on. In other words, the less strict privacy settings made her information more public. Darla's solution was to get a new Facebook page that was really her, but under a pseudonym. Rather than delete her old account as many often do, Darla chose to keep it, but post misleading information. In this way, she hoped her cyberstalker would believe they were still stalking her when in reality they were stalking nothing more than a cyber figment.

This example typifies one of the biggest fears that people have about being online—being vulnerable to risks like predators and cyberstalkers due to a lack of privacy. For instance, researchers have found that over 80% of consistent Internet users are somewhat concerned to very concerned about issues related to privacy (Ackerman, Cranor, & Reagle, 1999). Women generally tend to be more concerned than persons of other gender backgrounds (Sheehan, 1999). This gender difference makes sense given that more women appear to be cyberstalked more frequently (Violence Against Women Online Resources, 2010).

Options exist for assessing, preparing and dealing with online stalking. As with the options for attending to cyberbullying, these options include utilizing technological, Couple and Family Technology, and/or developmental life span strategies. Regardless of the strategy employed to assess and manage cyberstalking it is imperative that it be done. From the little research and case study data that exists with regard to cyber stalking, assessing for safety risks, the extent of the stalking, and the prevalence of the stalking in one's life and relationships is urgent (Southworth et al., 2005). There are a number of cyberstalking assessments that have been developed. One of the most reputable is the Stalking Assessment Screen (SAS) developed by McEwan, Strand, and Mackenzie (2011). The SAS was designed as a decision-making tool for people dealing with stalking situations. It is a 12-item checklist that lets the user identify the level of the threat of a given stalking situation, and prioritize resources needed for addressing the various risks to the victim. Also included are a few questions designed to identify false victims of stalking. Although the SAS is not a comprehensive risk assessment tool, it can serve as a quick and easy to use assessment of cyberstalking until assessment of a more comprehensive nature can be conducted. The SAS is currently undergoing validation trials in Australia and Sweden. In addition, to assist individuals, couples and families plan, assess, and/or respond to issues related to cyberstalking and there are reputable apps that can be accessed (see Appendix E).

Intimate Partner Violence

Perhaps one of the most frightening realities for couples is that there appears to be a strong link between cyberstalking and intimate partner violence (Southworth et al., 2005). According to Finn and Atkinson (2009) "intimate partner violence often involves a pattern of behavior that functions to limit a victim's access to the outside world" (p. 53). Where technology intersects with partner violence it is often called "intimate partner technology stalking" (Southworth et al., 2005). Here the pattern of control extends to technologies that would otherwise promote greater communication with the world outside of the relationship (Finn & Atkinson, 2009). The abuser seeks control over the social space of their victim(s) to increase dependency on them as the abuser (Finn &

Atkinson, 2009). Through technology, a gateway to emotional, physical, relational, and psychological control via constant monitoring of one's partner is easily and readily accessible (Burke, Wallen, Vail-Smith, & Knox, 2011).

For victims of intimate partner violence fostered by technology and new media, it is almost as if the victim is kept on an invisible leash. With the advent of technology, the abuser has the potential to exert control and encourage dependence on a more subtle level due to the ease with which a person can, unbeknownst to their partner, access their significant other's digital devices and related information. Abusers can do this through keystroke logging hardware, where they can keep track of every key on a computer keyboard that their partner strikes. They can check the browser history of their partner's Internet use to determine what sites they are going to and when. In this way, the abuser has the power to monitor all computer communications, with the victim often unaware until the situation escalates.

Katrina, who ethnically identified as Russian American, and Luis, whose ethnic identity was French Canadian, were a couple in their late 40s, and had been partnered for almost 25 years. They had two grown children who were both in their second year of university studies out of state. The couple was coming to treatment for "trust issues" in their relationship. Katrina reported that since the kids went to college she felt like Luis was "not interested in spending time with [her], but was able to make time for friends and business colleagues." Luis stated he was interested in spending time with Katrina, until she started accusing him of being interested in others more than her. He shared she even went so far as to accuse him of "having an affair with a guy on the side," which he denied. Katrina reported that even if he was not having a physical affair with this guy, she had "caught" him having an "online affair." Katrina stated that she "caught" him by "virtually stalking [his] online behavior." She implemented keystroke logging hardware, constantly checked the Internet browser history, looked at his call records, and checked his texting history to "catch him." Luis reported that it felt like he was being "put in a cage by all her online monitoring." Katrina thought Luis's explanation of her behavior was "ridiculous" and just his "attempt to distract from the real problem—his never ending flirtations that had now lead to a relationship online and maybe offline with this guy." Luis disagreed, stating that Katrina had "always been one to think [he] was having an affair, even though her suspicions and accusations were never proven to be true, but with the rise of more technology her paranoia and monitoring had just grown worse."

In the case above, intimate partner aggression is one that is not all that uncommon; with the exception of the gender of the person driving the aggressive acts. Typically, in an intimate partner violence situation facilitated by technology, the perpetrator is a man and the victim is a woman—much like in cases of offline intimate partner violence (Southworth et al., 2005). "By conservative estimates, at least 1 in 12 women versus 1 in 45 men [are] stalked at some point in the lives" (Southworth et al., 2005, p. 2). In an estimated 62% of stalking cases toward women, the perpetrators are their husbands, partners, or boyfriends (U.S. Department of Justice, 2001). Of those women stalked, the consequences can be severe; with roughly 81% being physically assaulted and 31% being sexually assaulted (U.S. Department of Justice, 2001). The prevalence and outcomes of e-intimate partner violence remain virtually unknown, as little research has been conducted (Finn & Atkinson, 2009).

While it is not necessarily that intimate partner violence has increased with technological developments, it is that with technology such violence is occurring via ecological influences (see Chapter 5) that make it seem to occur or be perceived as occurring differently. For instance, social networking sites provide a source for current and/or past partner(s) to monitor partners or former partners by providing anonymity at a distance, but also with practically constant accessibility (Lyndon, Bonds-Raacke, & Cratty, 2011). In their study of 804 university undergraduates, Burke, Wallen, Vail-Smith, and Knox (2011) found that 50% (n = 402) reported being either the initiator or victim of online personal intrusions and excessive e-monitoring (e.g., checking partner's e-mails, social networking sites, texting histories) involving their partners. In addition, almost one third (31%, n = 250) of respondents viewed such behaviors as acceptable (Burke et al., 2011). There was a gender difference, with women more likely than their gender counterpart peers to view such behaviors toward their partners as acceptable (25% versus 6%; Burke et al., 2011). These research findings point to at least three of the seven ecological influences—anonymity, accessibility, and acceptability—as being a significant part of intimate partner violence.

The ability to easily access one's partner through technology is particularly evident through resources that can be used to help people monitor others. FlexiSPY[1] is one of the most popular monitoring applications that can easily be installed to someone's smartphone or cell phone. Once installed one has the ability to read all e-mail and text messaging on the device, view the entire call history, retrieve the address book, use global tracking software to locate the device, send text messages from the device, call into the device and listen in real time to situations of the person and to active phone calls, and all of these features can be accessed remotely, even without the device turned on. In addition, FlexiSPY is undetectable, so one might not even know it is on their phone.

As much as technology can be used by perpetrators of intimate partner violence, it can also be used in ways to assist and empower the victims or survivors of intimate partner violence (Finn & Atkinson, 2009). Through various organizations that exist online and offline, survivors have means of getting help via professionals, and social support networks composed of other survivors (Finn & Atkinson, 2009). One such organization is Working to Halt Online Abuse[2] (WHOA), which has existed since 1997. WHOA provides education with regard to cyber abuse, information on cyberstalking laws, and provides links to online self-help groups where victims/survivors can connect with other victims/survivors. An example of an application that can serve as a helpful resource is HopeLine from Verizon,[3] which gives people the option to donate their old cell phones to be recycled and given to survivors of intimate partner violence to serve as a link between them and emergency or support services (see Appendix E).

It is essential to discuss the strategies that can be used to safeguard against e-intimate partner violence before, during and after such occurrences. Online based options for assessing, and creating a safety plan for addressing intimate partner violence, also exist via various reputable apps (see Appendix E). These resources can be used to assist individuals, couples, families, and clinicians plan, assess, and/or respond to issues related to intimate partner violence. Based on the work of the National Network to End Domestic Violence[4] (NNEDV) in 2003, Southworth et al., (2005) have created a technology safety plan for use with intimate partner violence survivors. This plan includes some of the same considerations often reviewed with survivors of offline intimate partner violence like suggesting that the survivor trust themselves and their instincts, have a sustainable plan for safety, and get a private postal mailbox rather than use their home address for mail (Southworth et al., 2005). Yet in this plan additional considerations related to the online nature of the survivors experiencing of partner violence are included. These online related tips include: (a) taking precautions of the techy abuser, (b) using digital devices that are more secure, (c) creating completely new e-mail, social networking accounts, (d) setting cell phone and/smartphones settings to the most secure, (e) changing all passwords and pins on accounts related to daily living (e.g., online banking, voicemails), (f) minimizing the use of cordless phones or baby monitors, (g) utilizing new or donated cell phones or smartphones, (h) requesting that one's records and other data (e.g., court and medical records) be kept private or sealed, and (i) using Internet search engines to search for oneself to see how available you are to your abuser or stalker (NNEDV, 2003; Southworth et al., 2005).

Notes

1. http://www.flexispy.com/.
2. http://www.haltabuse.org/.
3 http://aboutus.verizonwireless.com/communityservice/hopeLine.html.
4. http://www.nnedv.org/.

References

Ackerman, M., Cranor, L., & Reagle, J. (1999). Privacy in e-commerce: Examining user scenarios and privacy preferences. *ACM Conference on Electronic Commerce,* 1–8. Retrieved from dl.acm.org/citation.cfm?id=336995. doi:10.1145/336992.336995

Aricak, T., Siyahhan, S., Uzunhasanoglu, A., Saribeyoglu, S., Ciplak, S., Yilmaz, N., et al. (2008). Cyberbullying among Turkish adolescents. *CyberPsychology and Behavior, 11*(3), 253–261. doi:10.1089/cpb.2007.0016

Blumenfeld, W. J., & Cooper, R. M. (2010). LGBT and allied youth responses to cyberbullying: Policy implications. *International Journal of Critical Pedagogy, 3*(1) 114–133.

Brewster, M. P. (2003). Power and control dynamics in prestalking and stalking situations. *Journal of Family Violence, 18*(4), 207–217. doi:10.1023/A:1024064214054

Burke, S. C., Wallen, M., Vail-Smith, K., & Knox, D. (2011). Using technology to control intimate partners: An exploratory study of college undergraduates. *Computers in Human Behavior, 27*(3), 1162–1167. doi:10.1016/j.chb.2010.12.010

Casey-Cannon, S., Hayward, C., & Gowen, K. (2001). Middle-school girls' reports of peer victimization: Concerns, consequences, and implications. *Professional School Counseling, 5*(2), 138–147.

Choney, S. (2012, June 8). *Facebook ordered to identify cyberbullies who harassed mom.* Retrieved from http://digitallife.today.com/_news/2012/06/08/12125655-facebook-ordered-to-identify-cyberbullies-who-harassed-mom?lite

Dehue, F., Bolman, C., & Völlink, T. (2008). Cyberbullying: Youngsters' experiences and parental perception. *CyberPsychology & Behavior, 11*(2), 217–223.

Finn, J. (2004). A survey of online harassment at a university campus. *Journal of Interpersonal Violence, 19*(4), 468–483. doi:10.1177/0886260503262083

Finn, J., & Atkinson, T. (2009). Promoting the safe and strategic use of technology for victims of intimate partner violence: Evaluation of the technology safety project. *Journal of Family Violence, 24,* 53–59. doi:10.1007/s10896-008-9207-2

Fisher, B. S., Cullen, F. T., & Turner, M. G. (2000). *The sexual victimization of college women.* Washington, DC: National Institute of Justice, Bureau of Justice Statistics.

Huang, Y., & Chou, C. (2010). An analysis of multiple factors of cyberbullying among junior high school students in Taiwan. *Computers in Human Behavior, 26*(6), 1581–1590. doi:10.1016/j.chb.2010.06.005

Hundley, H. L., & Shyles, L. (2010). US teenagers' perceptions and awareness of digital technology: A focus group approach. *New Media & Society, 12*(3), 417–433. doi:10.1177/1461444809342558

Keppel, R. D., & Walter, R. (1999). Profiling killers: A revised classification model for understanding sexual murder. *International Journal of Offender Therapy and Comparative Criminology, 43*(4), 417–437. doi:10.1177/0306624X99434002

Landau, S. (2008). Privacy and security: A multidimensional problem. *Communications of the ACM, 51*(11), 25–26. doi:10.1145/1400214.1400223

Lea, M., & Spears, R. (1991). Computer-mediated communication, de-individuation, and group decision-making. *International Journal of Man-Machine Studies, 34,* 283-301.

Lindsay, M., & Krysik, J. (2012). Online harassment among college students: A replication incorporating new Internet trends. *Information, Communication, and Society, 15*(5), 703–719. doi:10.1080/1369118X.2012.674959

Lyndon, A., Bonds-Raacke, J., & Cratty, A. D. (2011). College students' Facebook stalking of ex-partners. *Cyberpsychology, Behavior, and Social Networking, 14*(12), 711–716. doi:10.1089/cyber.2010.0588

McEwan, T., Strand, S., & Mackenzie, R. (2011). *Stalking assessment screen.* Retrieved from http://www.stalkingriskprofile.com/stalking-risk-profile/stalking-assessment-screen

Mishna, F., Khoury-Kassabri, M., Gadalla, T., & Daciuk, J. (2012). Risk factors for involvement in cyber bullying: Victims, bullies and bully-victims. *Children and Youth Services Review, 34*(1), 63-70. doi:10.1016/j.childyouth.2011.08.032

Patchin, J. W., & Hinduja, S. (2006). Bullies move beyond the schoolyard: A preliminary look at cyberbullying. *Youth Violence and Juvenile Justice, 4,* 148–169. doi:10.1177/1541204006286288

Peterson, R. L., & Skiba, R. (2001). Creating school climates that prevent school violence. *The Clearinghouse: A Journal of Educational Strategies, Issues, and Ideas, 74*(3), 155–163. doi:10.1080/00098650109599183

Ryan, T., Kariuki, M., & Yilmaz, H. (2011). A comparative analysis of cyberbullying perceptions of preservice educators: Canada and Turkey. *Turkish Online Journal of Educational Technology, 10*(3), 1–12.

Segrin, C. (2003). Age moderates the relationship between social support and psychosocial problems. *Human Communication Research, 29,* 317–342. doi:10.1111/j.1468-2958.2003.tb00842.x

Sheehan, K. B. (1999). An investigation of gender differences in on-line privacy concerns and resultant behaviors. *Journal of Interactive Marketing, 13*(4), 24–38. doi:10.1002/(SICI)1520–6653(199923)

Slonie, R., & Smith, P. K. (2008). Cyberbullying: Another main type of bullying? *Scandinavian Journal of Psychology, 49,* 147–154. doi:10.1111/j.1467-9450.2007.00611.x

Southworth, C., Dawson, S., Fraser, C., & Tucker, S. (2005). A high-tech twist on abuse: Technology, intimate partner stalking, and advocacy. *Violence Against Women Online Resources,* pp. 1–15.

Stephenson, P. R., & Walter, R. D. (2011). *Toward cyber crime assessment: Cyberstalking.* Paper presented at the 6th annual Symposium on Information Assurance, June 7-8, 2011, Albany, NY. Retrieved from http://www.albany.edu/iasymposium/proceedings/2011/5-StephensonReview.pdf.

Tjaden, P., & Thoenes, N. (1998). *Stalking in America: Findings from the National Violence Against Women Survey.* Washington, DC: U.S. Department of Justice.

Tokunaga, R. S. (2010). Following you home from school: A critical review and synthesis of research on cyberbullying victimization. *Computers in Human Behavior, 26*(3), 277–287. doi:10.1016/j.chb.2009.11.014

U.S. Department of Justice. (1999). *Cyberstalking: A new challenge for law enforcement and industry.* Retrieved from http://www.usdoj.gov/criminal/cybercrime/cyberstalking.htm

U.S. Department of Justice. (2001). *Stalking and domestic violence: Report to Congress.* Retrieved from http://www.ncj.gov

Violence Against Women Online Resources. (2010). *The facts about stalking.* Retrieved from http://www.vaw.umn.edu/documents/inbriefs/stalking/stalking.html

Yum, Y., & Hara, K. (2006). Computer-mediated relationship development: A cross-cultural comparison. *Journal of Computer-Mediated Communication, 11*(1), 133–152. doi:10.1111/j.1083-6101.2006.tb00307.x

11 Final Thoughts on Technology and Relationships

The Web as I envisaged it, we have not seen it yet. The future is still so much bigger than the past.

—*Tim Berners-Lee*

Technology's Place in the Field of Couple and Family Therapy

Sitting on a plane writing this, I (K.H.) am acutely aware of the place technology has in our lives. I am typing away these final few pages on my laptop; my young son sitting to my left, watching the classic *Milo and Otis* on a portable DVD player; my husband to my right, reading on his e-reader. There is no question that technology has a significant place in our daily life. Yet as this book was being written, my coauthor M.L.C.B. and I noticed that the predominant areas in which we drew and cited research was not to be found in couple and family therapy literature. In fact, most of the scholarly information related to technology and relationships were found in education and computer science journals, as well as in the literature from communication studies. This inattention to technology in the discipline of marriage and family therapy (MFT) is not representative of the true impact technology has on our lives. As we cited in our technological genogram in Chapter 7, we firmly believe that technology and new media—our laptops, portable DVD players, e-readers, smartphones, social networking sites, e-mail, and other technologies—are entities in couple and family life with whom we have both simple and complicated, transient yet enduring, relationships.

This separation between the scholarly literature about technology and literature about couple and family therapy limits the capacity of what we can discover about both technology and couple and family relationships. While this is the first book of its kind to outline a framework through which to assess and evaluate relationships where technology plays a part, M.L.C.B. and I saw ourselves less as the progenitors of this material and more as the translators between couple and family therapy and the other disciplines. The greater extent to which the field of couple and family therapy can bridge the gap through the field of Couple and Family Technology, the more successful practitioners and scholars will be at understanding the impact of particular programs and devices and be informed when moving toward more effective practices. This might include the development of a distinct journal that seeks to bridge the gap, more textbooks, increased training and educational opportunities, or other ways to structure our learning so that we can translate with the most appropriate context.

Promoting a Systems View of Technology and Interpersonal Relationships

Another task accomplished by this book is the application of a systemic perspective to the understanding of couple problems related to technology. In its truest form, the framework presented in this text posits that technology shapes structure and process, two key areas of couples and families. In other words, it is not one person using the technology who is at risk for developing problems in his/her relationships: The focus of treatment is the individual, couple, and family as the assumption is that technology usage is woven into the very fabric of our interactions. Yet in many circumstances such as cases of Internet sex addiction, online gaming, and others, the blame may fall on one person contributing to the problems in a relationship. The Couple and Family Technology framework assists therapists in maintaining a systemic focus in assessing and treating couples where issues of Internet and new media are problematic. Further, while the focus of this particular text is directed at implications for couple relationships, it is our fervent hope that future books will be written detailing more specifically the implications for family members and applications for children, parents, and other family members.

Other ways in which this book contributes to a systemic perspective is its focus on diversity. The reader will note that in this book, we did not identify what the appropriate roles, rules, and boundaries are for a particular family system. It is our belief that appropriate roles, rules, boundaries, intimacy practices, and the timing and tempo of relationships will differ based on a number of contextual factors. These factors include (but are not limited to) family traditions and customs, learning histories, cultural context, ethnic backgrounds, sexual orientations, gender socialization, age, and other factors. For example, couples may have different agreements around who can be friends with whom on various social networking sites: differences that may in part be tied to the unique configuration of how these contextual factors come together in their relationship. One couple may agree that neither person is permitted to be friends or communicate with persons of a gender the same as oneself on Facebook; in other couple relationships, the rule may be that one can communicate with people of a different gender but not former romantic partners. In other relationships, it may be the rule that communication on Facebook with persons of any gender identity is an unregulated practice. In any case, the therapist needs to work with the couple to determine what fits for them based on the culture and relationship contract and then, through understanding of the implications for each action, work with the couple to organize their relationship in a way that fits them, and will promote long-term success.

Filling a Theoretical Gap

The field of Couple and Family Technology was born out of a theoretical gap in existing literature. The knowledge related to technology, new media, and people was published among various disciplines, and the treatment literature that could be found in the couple and family treatment literature was spread among a variety of theoretical approaches. The identification of a distinct field and framework allows for practicing therapists to organize their existing treatment approaches under an umbrella that takes into account the unique aspects of technology into their client's lives. The framework associated with the field of couple and family therapy is not restrictive in the theories that can be applied. For example, one who operates predominately from a behavioral perspective can quite easily implement interventions regarding technology once the therapist has an understanding of the impact on structure and relational processes; at the same time, an emotionally focused therapist could adapt their treatment to discuss the primary and secondary emotions associated with the structure and process experiences of a couple with a technology issue. The possibilities are almost limitless in utilizing this framework with a variety of theoretical approaches. In so doing, it will help to bridge the gap between couple and family treatment, and fields where the information with regard to technology is primarily published, such as communication studies, education, and information systems.

Implications for Research and Training

The implications of the development of the field of Couple and Family Technology overlap in research and training. As mentioned in an earlier section, the separation between the field of couple and family therapy and the fields (e.g., education, computer science, communication studies) in which the information about technology is often housed impairs the ability of members of the family therapy field from being able to develop solid ideas about the ways in which technology interfaces with couple and family life. The Couple and Family Technology field should work to develop its own base of research, potentially through its own journal, even a database that collects information and scholarly literature about couples, families, and technology as a way to strengthen this research base. Further, what is presented in this book as far as assessments and my (M.L.C.B.) development of the technological genogram has been used successfully in clinical practice, but not, as of yet, have empirical evidence associated with it (though there are some projects currently ongoing that are seeking to collect data on the ecological elements). Future research should focus on evaluating the specific ways in which technology contributes to or detracts from relational satisfaction.

Not only is there a need for more information with regard to couples and technology in general, there is also a necessity for more clinical and research-based attention to the relationship that couples of diverse backgrounds (e.g., sexual orientation minority couples, couples involving persons of color, couples of diverse age ranges) have with technology. Scholars within the couple and family therapy field have an opportunity to address the relationship between technology and families of diverse backgrounds to a greater extent than has been provided in the literature across fields to date. Such information would be particularly valuable as we know that while there are many similarities in the prevalence and patterns of technology usage across couples of all demographic backgrounds, there are also differences. For instance, some such differences are discussed in Chapter 9 and highlighted that researchers indicate that individuals and couples whose sexual orientations have been minoritized (e.g., persons identifying as bisexual, lesbian, or gay) tend to meet partners online more frequently, make purchases online more often, and have a much longer history of general Internet usage than their heterosexually identifying counterparts. Information from more diversity inclusivity research aimed at exploring things like differences, similarities and uniqueness of couples across a variety of demographic backgrounds, in terms of interfacing with technology and new media, would be of great benefit. With more research of this kind being conducted, an increase in tailored and culturally sensitive practices can be further developed to attend to the technology-related issues and experiences that may be more specific to couples of diverse backgrounds.

The implications for training are more broad. There are currently no courses to our knowledge within graduate-level couple and family therapy programs that teach about the impact of technology on couples and families. This is surprising since many therapists have reported having cases by which the presenting problem was related to technology (Goldberg, Peterson, Rosen, & Sara, 2008). This book may serve as a first step toward a more formalized and rigorous education for clinicians to prepare them for the cases that will likely face them in their clinical practice.

Before this book, we have not seen another book on the market that attends to the interface of couples and technology before. It is our hope that the introduction of the field of Couple and Family Technology will better organize the scholarly and clinical literature on the impact of technology and new media on couples and families and have contributed to a deeper understanding of these issues. As an introductory text, we are aware that this may be the beginning of the conversation, even if that conversation begins through electronic means. The field of Couple and Family Technology will also undoubtedly experience changes over time. As software and hardware change in ways that we cannot yet imagine, it is imperative that Couple and Family Technology practitioners continue to stay apprised of developments and assist us as we continue to translate to the larger majority.

Reference

Goldberg, P. D., Peterson, B. D., Rosen, K. H., & Sara, M. L. (2008). Cybersex: The impact of a contemporary problem on the practices of marriage and family therapists. *Journal of Marital and Family Therapy, 34*(4), 469–480. doi:10.1111/jmft.2008.34.issue-4

Appendices

Appendix A: Ecological Elements Questionnaire

This inventory was developed with the assistance of our dedicated and talented research team, including Katrina Ancheta, Mackenzie Clark, Jennalyn Eigner, Tamara Marsar, Christine Morehead, Sarah Steelman, and Michael Thomas.

General ICT Usage Within a Relationship

Please indicate how often you:

	Never	*Rarely*	*Sometimes*	*Often*	*Frequently*
Participate in electronic or Internet-based activities for sexual enjoyment	1	2	3	4	5
Participate in physical activities for sexual enjoyment	1	2	3	4	5
Experience sexual arousal when in communication with someone with whom you are not in a committed romantic relationship	1	2	3	4	5
Asked for a date via text	1	2	3	4	5
Been asked for a date via text	1	2	3	4	5
Asked someone for a date via e-mail	1	2	3	4	5
Been asked by someone for a date via e-mail	1	2	3	4	5
Asked someone for a date via e-chat	1	2	3	4	5

(*continued*)

	Never	*Rarely*	*Sometimes*	*Often*	*Frequently*
Been asked by someone for a date via e-chat	1	2	3	4	5
Told someone that you loved them for the first time via text	1	2	3	4	5
Been told by someone that they loved you for the first time via text	1	2	3	4	5
Told someone that you loved them for the first time via e-mail	1	2	3	4	5
Been told by someone that they loved you for the first time via e-mail	1	2	3	4	5
Told someone that you loved them for the first time via e-chat	1	2	3	4	5
Been told someone that you loved them for the first time via e-chat	1	2	3	4	5
Had an argument with your partner via text	1	2	3	4	5
Had an argument with your partner via e-mail	1	2	3	4	5
Had an argument with your partner via e-chat	1	2	3	4	5
Broken up with someone via text	1	2	3	4	5
Been broken up with by someone via text	1	2	3	4	5
Broken up with someone via e-mail	1	2	3	4	5
Been broken up with by someone via e-mail	1	2	3	4	5
Broken up with someone via e-chat	1	2	3	4	5
Been broken up with by someone via e-chat	1	2	3	4	5
Been "caught" using technology for sexual purposes	1	2	3	4	5

(*continued*)

	Never	*Rarely*	*Sometimes*	*Often*	*Frequently*
Engaged in sexting where it lead to an unexpected sexual encounter (i.e., booty call)	1	2	3	4	5
Used your mobile phone to initiate any sexual purpose through phone calls, texts, internet, or apps?	1	2	3	4	5
Been the recipient of this type of request?	1	2	3	4	5
Successful in fulfilling a request for an intimate encounter, sexual relation, or hook-up by using an app on a Smartphone?	1	2	3	4	5
Sent a sexually suggestive nude or nearly nude photo or video of yourself to someone else using your cell phone?	1	2	3	4	5
Been the recipient of nude or nearly nude photo or video of someone on your cell phone?	1	2	3	4	5
Used your mobile phone to exchange text messages, picture messages, video messages, or voice calls to fulfill a sexual purpose with your <u>partner</u>?	1	2	3	4	5
Used your mobile phone to exchange text messages, picture messages, video messages, or voice calls to fulfill a sexual purpose with someone who is <u>not</u> your partner?	1	2	3	4	5
Been sexually harassed over e-mail?	1	2	3	4	5
Been sexually harassed over mobile phone?	1	2	3	4	5
Sent a sexual text to a number of people at one time in order to increase your chances at meeting up with someone for a sexual encounter?	1	2	3	4	5

Affordability

Please indicate how affordable the following are to you:

	Very Affordable	*Affordable*	*Unaffordable*	*Very Unaffordable*
Cell phone	1	2	3	4
Internet service	1	2	3	4
Computer maintenance	1	2	3	4

What technology do you share with another person in your household?

I do not share any

Desktop computer

Laptop computer

Tablet

Phone

Who pays for your phone usage?

Self

Partner

Family member

Parent

Employer

Other

If the bill for your phone usage is not paid for by you, what restrictions have been implemented on the activities in which you participate?

None – the bill is paid by myself

Anonymity (based on Qian & Scott, 2007 Perceived Anonymity Scale)

How many of the people you interact with online are those that you initially knew in the outside world?

1	2	3	4	5	6

What type of visual anonymity do you provide on your…

	No photo	*Obviously fake photos*	*Non-obviously fake photos*	*Partial actual photos*	*Actual photos*	*Revealing actual photos*
Social networking accounts?						
Blogs						
E-mail accounts						

What is the general information that you provide via your….

	No identification information	*Obvious pseudonym*	*Non-obvious pseudonym*	*Partial real name*	*Real name*	*More than real name*
Social networking accounts?						
Blogs						
E-mail accounts						

Accessibility

How accessible do you think you are in the following contexts?

	Not at all accessible	*Not very accessible*	*Pretty accessible*	*Very accessible*
Via e-mail				
Via cell phone				
Via social networking sites				

How accessible are the following technologies to you at home?

	Not at all accessible	*Not very accessible*	*Pretty accessible*	*Very accessible*
Computer	1	2	3	4
Tablet	1	2	3	4
E-mail	1	2	3	4
Cell phone	1	2	3	4
Social networking sites	1	2	3	4

How accessible are the following technologies to you outside of home (i.e., work)

	Not at all accessible	*Not very accessible*	*Pretty accessible*	*Very accessible*
Computer	1	2	3	4
Tablet	1	2	3	4
E-mail	1	2	3	4
Cell phone	1	2	3	4
Social networking sites	1	2	3	4

Please indicate the extent to which you use the following to restrict access from potential and/or previous romantic partners:

	Never	*Rarely*	*Sometimes*	*Often*	*Frequently*
Blocking the contact on your phone	1	2	3	4	5
Ignoring the contact on your phone	1	2	3	4	5
Blocking e-mail address	1	2	3	4	5
Being invisible on chat/instant messaging functions	1	2	3	4	5
Enable password protections	1	2	3	4	5

Accommodation

Please indicate the degree to which you are able to express yourself through:

	Not at all	*Low Degree*	*Somewhat*	*High Degree*
E-mail	1	2	3	4
Instant messaging	1	2	3	4
Text messaging	1	2	3	4
Video games	1	2	3	4

How many avatars (an electronic image that represents and is manipulated by a computer user) do you have? ____

Please indicate to what degree:

	Not at all	*Low Degree*	*Somewhat*	*High Degree*
Is the identity you portray similar to your actual sense of self?	1	2	3	4
Is your partner aware of your other self?	1	2	3	4
Do others know of your other self?	1	2	3	4
Can internet persona be connected/traced back to your real life persona?	1	2	3	4

Approximation

Please indicate the degree to which you agree with the following statements:

	Strongly Disagree	*Disagree*	*Agree*	*Strongly Agree*
Masturbating to content online is no different than having sex offline	1	2	3	4
Viewing pornographic photos online is no different than viewing pornographic photos in magazines	1	2	3	4
Viewing pornographic movies online is no different than viewing pornographic movies in a store	1	2	3	4
People sext as a way to move toward a sexual encounter with someone	1	2	3	4

Acceptability

Please indicate the degree to which you agree with the following statements:

	Strongly Disagree	*Disagree*	*Agree*	*Strongly Agree*
A romantic online relationship with someone other than a romantic partner acceptable	1	2	3	4
Online sex with someone outside of a relationship is emotionally damaging to the relationship	1	2	3	4
Online sex with someone outside of a relationship is physically damaging to the relationship	1	2	3	4
Sexting someone outside of a relationship is emotionally damaging to the relationship	1	2	3	4

How acceptable are the following behaviors?

	Strongly Disagree	*Disagree*	*Agree*	*Strongly Agree*
Interacting online with a person of the same sex acceptable within Your relationship	1	2	3	4
Interacting online with a person of the same sex acceptable within Your peer group	1	2	3	4
Interacting online with a person of the same sex acceptable within Your family	1	2	3	4
Interacting online with a person of the same sex acceptable within your local community	1	2	3	4
Interacting online with a person of the same sex acceptable within your region of the country	1	2	3	4
Interacting online with a person of the same sex acceptable within the United States	1	2	3	4

(*continued*)

	Strongly Disagree	*Disagree*	*Agree*	*Strongly Agree*
Interacting online with a person of the same sex acceptable outside of the United States	1	2	3	4
Is interacting online with a person of the opposite sex acceptable within your relationship	1	2	3	4
Is interacting online with a person of the opposite sex acceptable within your peer group	1	2	3	4
Is interacting online with a person of the opposite sex acceptable within Your family	1	2	3	4
Is interacting online with a person of the opposite sex acceptable within your local community	1	2	3	4
Is interacting online with a person of the opposite sex acceptable within your region of the country	1	2	3	4
Is interacting online with a person of the opposite sex acceptable within the United States	1	2	3	4
Is interacting online with a person of the same sex acceptable outside of the United States	1	2	3	4
Is sexting acceptable within your relationship	1	2	3	4
Is sexting acceptable within your peer group	1	2	3	4
Is sexting acceptable within your family	1	2	3	4
Is sexting acceptable within your local community	1	2	3	4
Is sexting acceptable within your region of the country	1	2	3	4
Is sexting acceptable within the United States	1	2	3	4
Is sexting acceptable outside of the United States	1	2	3	4

(*continued*)

How often you discuss *your* mobile phone sexual activities with:

	Never	*Rarely*	*Sometimes*	*Often*	*Frequently*
Partner(s)	1	2	3	4	5
Best friend(s)	1	2	3	4	5
Sibling(s)	1	2	3	4	5
Parent(s)	1	2	3	4	5
Child/Children	1	2	3	4	5
Grandparent(s)	1	2	3	4	5
Co-worker(s)	1	2	3	4	5
Classmate(s)	1	2	3	4	5
Stranger(s)	1	2	3	4	5

Please indicate the frequency in which you engage in sexting using the following methods:

	Never	*Rarely*	*Sometimes*	*Often*	*Frequently*
Text messaging	1	2	3	4	5
Voice call (phone sex)	1	2	3	4	5
Video chat (Facetime/ Skype/Google Video)	1	2	3	4	5
Picture messages	1	2	3	4	5
E-mail through mobile phone	1	2	3	4	5
Other	1	2	3	4	5

Ambiguity

Please indicate to what degree the following are impacted by rules/standards of the relationship:

	Not at all	*A Little*	*Somewhat*	*A Lot*
What pictures you can post online?	1	2	3	4
The friends you can have on social networking sites?	1	2	3	4
With whom you can communicate online?	1	2	3	4
Your relationship status on your online profile?	1	2	3	4

Appendix B: General Technology-Focused Genogram Questions

General technological focused genogram questions were developed in part with the assistance of our dedicated graduate student, Lauren McCoy, and influenced by the work of McGoldrick, Gerson, and Shellenberger (1999).

- What is the relationship of each family member with technology (e.g., close, distant, conflicted, etc.)?
- Is there a member of the family that uses technology excessively more than other family members?
- How does the relationship with technology influence your relationship with your partner? Children? Friends? Co-workers? Parents?
- How has your relationship with technology made you more successful? Less successful?
- How long during the day does each member engage with technology?
- How do other family members react when they use technology? When they are not able to use technology?
- Does the relationship with technology inhibit family members from helping out when assistance is needed?
- Do family members find their relationship with technology a hindrance in communication? Does this relationship make family members unavailable or not present in communications?
- How does the relationship(s) with technology influence/affect your parents' and siblings' marriages or partnerships?
- Does your relationship with technology make it hard for you to attend to your children?

Appendix C: Couple and Family Technology-Focused Genogram Questions[1]

Ecological Element

- How many generations of your family have been making use of technology?
- At what age did each family member have their first technological experience and what kind of technology was involved (e.g., mobile phones, smart phones, desktop computers, Internet, computer games)?
- What kinds of technology do each of you currently use individually, together as a couple, or as a family? What kinds of technology do your parents, grandparents, children, and/or grandchildren currently

use? How much time is spent with these technologies by various persons and in various configurations (e.g., parent-child, partners)?

- Is the time that is currently spent with technological devices significantly different from the time previous generations spent with earlier forms of technology?
- What role does gender, race, ethnicity, religion, spirituality, sexual orientation, geography, income, bodiedness, and education play in your and your family's technological practices?
- What role does geographical region, setting (e.g., rural, urban, suburban) play in your and your family's technological practices?
- How has technology influenced your parenting or caregiving styles? What about your grandparenting?
- What behaviors, feelings, or thoughts did you experience from others around technology while growing up? What about in the present?
- Have you witnessed other individuals, couples, and families engaging with technology in a similar manner as you? Have you ever discussed these experiences with them?
- Are your relationships with people based on the types of technological "toys" you own? For instance, would your friends still be your friends if you did not have the newest electronic gadget?
- What is the main function of technology for each member (e.g., connect to friends, learn, relay information/plans, get work done)?
- How much does your work, school, or retirement include technology?
- Where did or do members learn about technology?
- Who in the family is considered a "technology expert" or "technology guru"? How does this affect the relationship between family members and technological practices?

Structural Element

- If I were to spend a day in your home what would a typical day with technology look like? What is the daily technological routine of each person in the marriage or family? How would this look similar to or different from your families of origin?
- How has technology affected your partnering relationship with each other? With your children? With your parent(s)? With grandparent(s)? With grandchildren?
- How has technology affected your roles as a partner(s), parent (s), child, grandchild, grandparent? How have these roles been different, better, and/or more challenging post-technological involvement in your lives?
- What are some of the boundaries (e.g., physical, psychological, relational, emotional, temporal) you have established, negotiated, and maintained around technology in your partnership? Parent-child relationship? Grandparent-grandchild relationship? Were these modeled in your families of origin? Are you modeling them for your future family?

- Boundaries may include places, times, mediums, and persons around technology. In light of this, are there certain places (e.g., bedrooms, living rooms, dining room tables, in public) where members can and cannot use technology? Are there certain times (e.g., after dinner, after work, before bedtime) and time limitations (e.g., 30 minutes or 1 hour per session) during which people can and cannot use technology? Are there some people for whom members are not to engage in technological practices and are there some people where exceptions to the "rules of couple and family technology use" can be broken? Are there some forms of technology (e.g., online gaming, video gaming, distance education, social networking) that members can and cannot use?
- What kinds of rules have you established, negotiated, and maintained around technology in your partnership(s)? Parent-child relationship(s)? Grandparent-grandchild relationship(s)? Were these modeled in your families of origin? Are you modeling them for your future family?
- What are the rules around technological interruptions or distractions?
- Who decides the rules around technology?
- How satisfied are each of you with the technological lifestyle each of you has adopted as individuals? As partnership(s)? As family(ies)?
- How have you as partner(s), parent(s), and grandparent(s) managed technological risks (e.g., cyber stalking, cyber bullying, identity theft, privacy invasion, cyber infidelity, cyber pedophilia) and related safety practices around technology? Have these practices been modeled in your families of origin? Are you modeling them for your future family?
- What is the level of trust (e.g., is there monitoring software on technological devices or checking up on each other's cyber practices via technological mechanisms) around technology for each member of the partnership(s) and/or family(ies)?
- Are there certain partner(s) or family(ies) ceremonies, holidays, rituals, special events that are conducted solely online, or in some combination of online and offline? Are some made available online for people who could not be there offline? What are the effects and meanings of participating in these e-vents, especially if only done online?

Process Element

- What kind of motto does the family have with regard to technology (e.g., "A byte a day keeps the boredom away!"; "The family that games together stays together"; "Long live technology!"; "Our home is a technology-free zone"; "What is this technology you speak of?"; "Those who die with the most tech toys wins!"; "We prefer to look out windows, not @ Windows"; "Just call us the 'Borg' = half human, half computer"; "The only thing we have to fear is technology itself"; "Plugged in and dialed up 24/7!"; "Computers are for human use, not consumption"; "The only thing we have to fear is losing technology itself"; "Life is what's happening offline, not online"; "Who needs emotions when you've got emoticons!")?

- What is each person's (e.g., partner(s), parent(s), grandparent(s), child(ren), grandchild(ren)) relationship with technology (e.g., netiquette practices, techno resistant techno phobia, techno savvy)?
- How much time is spent talking face-to-face with members as compared to the amount of time communicating through technology? On a daily basis? On a weekly basis?
- What kind of value is placed on face-to-face interaction? Does contention arise more with face-to-face interaction, or interaction via technology?
- How much time do you spend with or without technology as individuals? Partner(s)? Family(ies)?
- What does it mean to you when a member of your family (e.g., partner(s), parent(s), child(ren), grandparent(s), grandchild(ren)) talks with you about your use of technology?
- What are some of the positive affects you have observed in your partnership(s) and across generations in relation to technological usage? What about some of the negatives or drawbacks?
- When you communicate with your partner(s), child(ren), grandchild(ren), parent(s), and grandparent(s) via technological means, do you feel you are more distant or closer with each other? Do you feel loving, angry, or more avoidant?
- Have there been times where you have felt abandoned or deserted by your partner(s), parent(s), child(ren), grandchild(ren), grandparent(s), in relation to their technological use? Have there been times where you have felt like you have abandoned or deserted family members because of your use of technology? How have you helped each other successfully negotiate through these times? Did or do you see these types of technology related behaviors in the partnered relationships of your parent(s) and/or grandparent(s)? How did or do they successfully negotiate through these times?
- Have there been times where you have felt in conflict in your relationship with partner(s) and/or family member(s) around technological practices? Describe this please.
- When are the times in your relationship where you felt more open and vulnerable with your partner(s) so that you could turn toward them for comfort, love, and support? How was this communicated? What role did technology play (or not play) during these times or communications?
- If you were separated (e.g., lost, stolen, no Internet access, broken) from your phone, computer, or other technological device, for an extended amount of time, how would you feel? What kind of person

would you be without technology? Does your technology define you as a person? Does it define your relationships? With whom and how would you communicate with others?

- If your partner(s), parent(s), child(s), grandparent(s), and/or grandchildren were separated from their technology for a long period of time, how would they feel? What kind of people would they be? How much does technology define each of them? With whom and in what way would they communicate with others?

Appendix D: Electronic Developmental Life Span Questions

Following are some sample questions for consideration by couples and families across the development. Each question is meant to be asked about the various technologies (e.g., smartphones, cellphones, online gaming, video gaming, laptops, tablets, games, music devices, social networking sites, applications, YouTube, digital calling, texting, e-mailing, television streaming) with which person(s) have contact. This is not an exhaustive list but rather is one way to help couples, families, and professionals to begin a conversation regarding the who, what, when, where, why, and how around technologies for them at various points across the developmental life span.

Who?
• Who has permission to use technologies with (and without) supervision? • Who makes the decisions around technological usage? • Who physically shares technologies? • Who engages in technologies together? • Who makes the decisions around attaining technologies? • Who initially purchases technologies? • Who maintains the cost of technologies? • Who can afford their technologies? • Who monitors whose technological usage? • With whom do members share information about their technological use? • Who makes the decisions around technological appropriateness? • Who are members friends, acquaintances, family, dating, etc. apart from technologies and how can these same kinds of relational boundaries, rules and roles apply to technological relationships? • Who in the family, as well as outside of the family, do you interact with online via gaming, social networking, e-mailing, etc.?

What?
• What age(s) are technologies permitted for use in supervised (and unsupervised) formats? • What age(s) are technologies not permitted for use? • What are the needed technologies? • What are the desired technologies? • What factors (e.g., economic, educational, ethnicity, gender, able-bodiedness, sexual orientation, gender orientation, religious or spiritual affiliation, etc.) go into considering technological usage? • What factors (e.g., economic, educational, ethnicity, gender, able-bodiedness, sexual orientation, gender orientation, religious or spiritual affiliation, etc.) go into considering technological purchasing? • What is considered appropriate (and inappropriate) usage of technologies? • What are considered appropriate (and inappropriate) forms of technologies? • What influence do members outside of the couple or family have on the usage of technologies? • What influence do members outside of the couple or family have on the purchasing of technologies? • What barriers are needed (not needed) around technologies? • What regulations are in place by others around technological usage? • What is the normative time to spend daily using technologies? • When is the normative time to start and stop using various technologies? • What are the benefits (and drawbacks) to the technologies for each member and for the couple or family as a whole? • What are the resources that can help with monitoring technological usage? • What are the resources that can be accessed to inform us as to which technologies are rated appropriate for which ages? • What are the consequences of inappropriate technological engagement? • What are members' thoughts, behaviors, and feelings before, during and after technological engagement? • What, if any, kind of technological schedule should there be for members? • What are the rules, roles, and boundaries around various technologies? • What things are private about members and should not be shared via technologies?

- What technologies are more appropriate for some family members, but not others?
- Which information can and cannot be communicated via technologies?
- What are the rules, roles, and boundaries around technologies in other contexts (e.g., work, school, etc.) for various members of the couple or family?
- What are the technologies, if any, that people permitted to share with members outside of the couple or family?
- What are the risks around the usage of certain technologies for members of the family?

When?

- When (time of day, during which activities, etc.) are people permitted (or not) to use technologies?
- When do members share about their technological usage with each other?
- When making decisions around technology usage are some technologies considered more developmentally appropriate than others?

Where?

- Where are people permitted to use technologies?
- Where do members share information about their technological usage?
- Where do the rules, roles, and boundaries around technologies come from?

Why?

- Why are certain technologies permitted (or not)?

How?

- How do mature or adult members of the family model appropriate technological usage to less mature or younger members of the family?
- How do members of the family who hold power model appropriate technological usage to those with less power in the family?
- How is technological usage modeled in the family?
- How do members outside of the couple or family use technologies?

- How are decisions around technological appropriateness made?
- How is the losing or breaking of technologies managed?
- How are technologies used as punishment?
- How are technologies used in rewarding ways?
- How are the risks around the usage of certain technologies managed?
- How do technologies positively (or negatively) influence the physical health of couple or family members?
- How do technologies positively (or negatively) influence the mental health of couple or family members?
- How do technologies positively (or negatively) influence the social and relational health of couple or family members?
- How are decisions about usage of technologies similar to or different from other developmental decisions?
- How does each member of the family view technologies?
- How do the rules, roles and boundaries established for other activities across the lifespan influence the rules, roles and boundaries around technological usage?
- How portable are our rules, roles and boundaries around technologies outside of the family and family home?
- How can technologies be used in a beneficial way as a family before, during, and after engagement?
- How are the family rules, roles and boundaries around technologies communicated to those outside of the family?
- How do people decide when it is time to revisit these questions?

Appendix E: Technology-Based Resources

Cyberbullying Resources

Application/ website	*Developer*	*Cost*	*Description*	*Review*
Bully Shield	Penn Innovations, LLC	$0.99	– Defines and describes – Provides solutions – Can create a personal action plan for how to help the bullied person(s) to share with support network – Victim(s), and family/friend(s) of victim(s) focused	– Moderate amount of information – Provides victim(s) and support network with information for addressing bully(ies) – Hi-tech – Inexpensive
Cyber Bullying	Maple Tree	$0.99	– Defines, describes, and addresses how different from and similar to other forms of bullying – Prevalence provided – Provides signs for identification – Explains affects and outcomes – Reviews legal involvement – Provides solutions – Victim(s), bully(ies), and parent(s) of both focused	– Very thorough – Stresses seriousness of the aggressive e-behavior – Provides parent(s) with information for addressing victim(s) and bully(ies) – Moderate-tech – Inexpensive
Report It Student/ Home Version	ARSS, Inc.	$0.99	– Defines and describes – Provides solutions – Can create an anonymous report of being bullied and identify the bully to share with specific school or program in which occurs – Victim(s) and school focused	– Moderate amount of information – Provides victim(s) with a means of anonymously reporting bullying – Hi-tech – Inexpensive

(*continued*)

Cyberbullying Resources

Application/ website	*Developer*	*Cost*	*Description*	*Review*
Stop Cyber Bullying 101	CIA Solutions	$0.00	– Defines and describes – Provides signs for identification – Explains affects and outcomes – Provides solutions – Parent(s) of victim(s) focused	– Provides very basic information – Stresses seriousness of the aggressive e-behavior – Lo-tech – Free
No Bully Zone	James Martin, Brooklyn Clark, Cindy House, and Kathy Roges, Tennessee Voices for Children	$0.00	– Youth-developed and youth-led campaign implemented in a middle school. – Steps in achieving the powerful assembly that united the students, teachers, and school administration were discussed, as well as approaches used to involve the entire student body. – Workshop highlights how youth voice had a positive impact on both personal and system change	– Very easy to understand – Ready for presentation – Guides educators into how to get students involved
https://www.wiredsafety.org/	WiredSafety.Org	$0.00	– Information on what to do if you're cyberbullied – How to report and links to do so – Information for parents and children/tweens/teens alike	– Easy to understand site – Free – Ways to join "cybersafety expert" groups
http://www.nasponline.org/resources/cyberbullying/index.aspx	National Association of School Psychologists	$0.00	– Resources of free online lessons for educators	– Free – Easy access to different curricula

Intimate Partner Violence Resources

Application/ website	*Developer*	*Cost*	*Description*	*Review*
Choose to Stop	Virtual College Education	$0.00	– Defines and describes – Provides signs for identification – Explains affects and outcomes – Provides solutions – Contacts for help and support provided nationally – Abuser(s) focused	– Unique as abuser focus – Very thorough – Support provided in real-time nationally – Moderate-tech – Free
Domestic Violence Information	Connecting People Software	$0.00	– Defines, describes, and addresses the differences between myths and facts around domestic violence – Provides signs for identification – Explains affects and outcomes – Provides safety plan for victim(s) – Contacts for help and support provided nationally – Victim(s) focused	– Very thorough – Support provided in real-time nationally – Moderate-tech – Free
HopeLine from Verizon	Verizon Wireless IT	$0.00	– Provides a means for people to recycle or receive old cell phones and smartphones – Recycled phones given to survivors or victims of domestic violence to help remain hidden and safe from their abusers – Victim(s) focused	– Provides little information – Provides victim(s) with a means of getting a new or recycled phone to increase their anonymity – Moderate-tech – Free

(*continued*)

Intimate Partner Violence Resources

Application/ website	*Developer*	*Cost*	*Description*	*Review*
Justice for All	D Studios	$0.00	– Defines and describes domestic violence, as well as child abuse, homicide, and justice for adults and juveniles – Provides safety plan for victim(s) – Contacts for help and support provided nationally, and for each state in the United States – Information on volunteering to help – Victim(s) focused	– Moderate amount of information – Support provided in real-time on national and local levels – Moderate-tech – Free
American Institute on Domestic Violence	American Institute on Domestic Violence	Website is free, some of the resources charge	– Ways DV can come into the workplace – Resources on how to train employees – Safe kids and pets ID programs	– Free – Useful tools (ID programs in particular) – Information for employers, employees, and victims
FaithTrust Institute	FaithTrust Institute	$0.00	– Interreligious, educational resource that addresses sexual and domestic violence issues. – Ways to take action against violence	– Free – Easy to navigate – Religious components
National Domestic Violence Hotline	National Domestic Violence Hotline; US Department of Health and Human Services/ Administration for Children and Families	$0.00	– Connects individuals to help in their area by using a nationwide database that includes detailed information about domestic violence shelters, other emergency shelters, legal advocacy and assistance programs, and social service programs.	– Very safe (quick escape button for if you're being monitored) – Deaf services – Ways to tell if you're being abused

Note

1. Couple and family technology-focused genogram questions were developed in part with the assistance of our dedicated graduate students, including Harrison Allen, Katrina Ancheta, Rachel Augustus, Marby Bartone, Stephanie Bixler, James Brittain, Mackenzie Clark, Vicki DeBeauvernet, Caitlin Delaney, Joe Dentice, Katherine Disney-Fairchild, Jennalyn Eigner, Austin Ellis, Sohei Fujita, Vanya Georgieva, Amna Haider, Alicia Hite, Heather Hoshiko, Quintin Hunt, Clai Joiner, Lindsey Lee, YuJung (Celine) Liu, Tamara Marsar, Luisa Martinez-Cruz, Jennifer Mihaloliakos, Christine Morehead, Matthew Nelson, Rebecca Nemecek, Caitlin Olsen, Sheila Osterhuber, Gianna Russo-Mitma, Sarah Schonian, Theresa Scott, Laura Smedley, Jordan Staples, Stephanie Steed, Sarah Steelman, Michael Thomas, Nicole Thomte, Samuel Tielemans, Linda Walker, Preston Walker, Courtney Watson, Amber Young, and Tod Young.

Index